DIARY OF A CORNISH FISHERMAN
NEWQUAY, 1962–1967

by

TREVOR SIMPSON

TMP
Publications

First Published in 2014 by **The Manuscript Publisher**, publishing solutions for the
digital age www.TheManuscriptPublisher.com

ISBN: 978-0-9576729-2-5

A CIP Catalogue record for this book is available from the British Library

Typesetting, page layout and design by DocumentsandManuscripts.com, the print and
digital media specialists

Cover design by Christine Simpson

Photographs and illustrations used are copyright of Trevor Simpson, except where
stated. Maps and cartography used courtesy of Google Maps.

Diary of a Cornish Fisherman
Newquay, 1962-1967

Dedication

To Skipper, Mike Lyne and all of the Newquay fishermen, past and present.

Contents

List of Illustrations and Diagrams

Introduction

I was just sixteen when I joined the Royal Navy as a Boy Seaman, 2nd Class. Surely the lowest form of marine life on the planet! The year was 1947 and, compared to the rations available to civilians in those, immediate post–war days, we got good food. Well, that was the best thing about it anyway.

Nine years later, in 1956, I got my demob. I had risen to the rank of Able Bodied Seaman, which was unavoidable actually. This hardly fitted me to earn my living in

'Civvy Street'. However, there I was, keen to work and I would do just about anything. Anything, that is, except going back to sea, because, as I promised myself, "Me and the sea is finished!"

So, within a few hours of leaving the Royal Navy, I found myself in a trench along with several Irishmen. We were armed with picks and shovels and together we tore into the tough boulder clay. I got quite good at it.

During the next couple of years, I did numerous different jobs but eventually I got lucky. I became Head Lifeguard at the Cornish town of Newquay. This was a life–changing event for me. It was exciting and it was challenging and I was, along with eight other young men, responsible for the safety of the swarms of summer visitors using the Towns' magnificent beaches. Almost in spite of myself, I was back by the sea.

Every day, as I patrolled the beaches, I breathed in the salt air and my ears were full of sound of the surf and so, bit–by–bit, the sea was calling me back. From my vantage point at the Lifeguards' hut, I watched the boats leaving and re–entering Newquay's Harbour.

It seemed natural then, that after a few more adventures in the labour market, I shipped on as crewman on a small lobster boat.

Map and aerial view of Cornwall
(Newquay area)

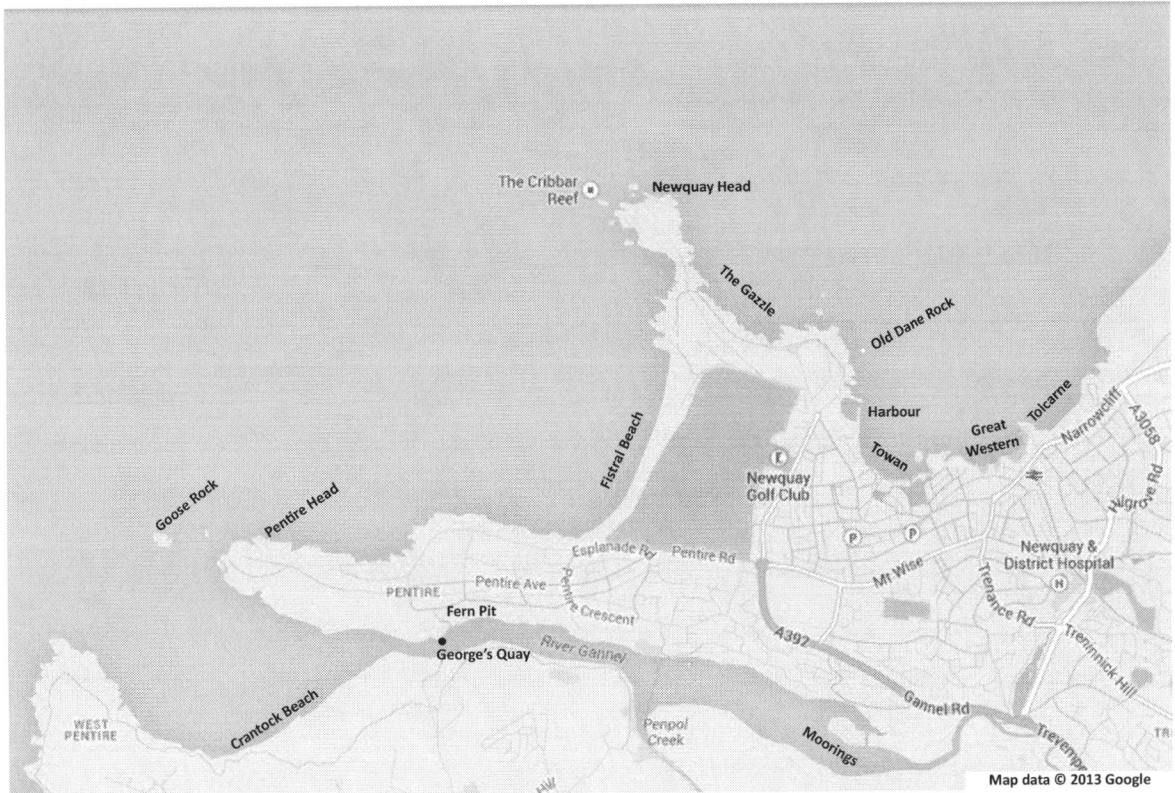

The Cribbar Reef • Newquay Head

The Gazzle

Old Dane Rock

Goose Rock

Pentire Head

Fistral Beach

Harbour

Towan

Great Western

Tolcarne

Narrowcliff

A3058

Pigrove Rd

Newquay Golf Club

Newquay & District Hospital

Esplanade Rd

Pentire Rd

PENTIRE

Pentire Ave

Pentire Crescent

Mt Wise

Trenance Rd

Trenmnick Hill

Fern Pit

•
George's Quay

River Gannel

A4392

Gannel Rd

Trevempe

WEST PENTIRE

Crantock Beach

Penpol Creek

Moorings

TR

Map data © 2013 Google

Newquay Head

The Gazzle

Newquay Bay

Fistral Bay

Fistral Beach

Harbour

South Quay

Great Western

Tolcarne

Narrowcliff

Towan

Imagery © 2013 DigitalGlobe, Getmapping plc, Infoterra Ltd & Bluesky, Landsat. Map data © 2013 Google

Twilight

Just after Christmas, in 1962, I was busy making lobster pots. There was a lovely little 20ft motor boat I was hoping to buy. When I approached my bank manager, he threw me out saying, "I'm not going to lend you money on the colour of your eyes. Go to him next door, he'll lend it to you!"

So, fuming I did just that and marched out of one bank and into another. In between times, someone else had expressed an interest in the 20 footer, so the owners had to abandon me in favour of him. I was stuck. I couldn't see any suitable boat for a single hander like me, who knew very little about fishing anyway, so I continued making pots and pondered what to do next. I then heard that Mike Lyne was without crew. His boat was called *Twilight* and was clinker built of elm on oak ribs. She was 24 feet 6 inches long with a 14hp petrol parraffin Brit engine. It was with some trepidation that I approached Mike's shed down at the harbour. I didn't know him very well and was rather in awe of him. He was an experienced fisherman who had learned his trade with the old–timers, whilst I wasn't even a local anyway.

Mike was working at something on the bench when I stepped inside the shed. He looked up in surprise and said, "Well Old Man, you've just broken my dream! I dreamed last night that you and I were out there fishing together!"

So that broke the ice for me and I told him it would suit me fine if that dream were to come true. We took it from there. We became fishing partners. Mike was the boat owner of course and I would own all the gear. If we parted company, we could make a clean break of it. That was the deal and I could hardly believe my good fortune. I was Crewman on the lovely little crabber, *Twilight*.

I borrowed enough money from the new bank to buy 10 coils of manila rope and some more material for making wire lobster pots and we were in business. I spent every spare moment making pots and Mike worked on his boat. He painted it and put anti–fouling on the bottom. Winter turned to spring and the days lengthened. The weather was still very broken when we started fishing in 1963. Mike had some old pots that we made up into strings of 15 or 20. They didn't fish very well but Mike wouldn't risk putting out my new wire pots.

"We can't afford a smash–up at this stage in the game, it's too early," he said.

Thus began my education. Left to myself, I wouldn't have had the patience to wait for the weather to settle and at that stage, I was not the least bit weather wise. Not far from the entrance to Newquay Harbour is a rock called The Old Dane. At low water, it stands up like a great pyramid but at high water, it is out of sight. Usually then you would only see the swells breaking over it. It is fairly close to the cliff, not too close though. In fact, it is just where you would head off for the open sea! One morning, as we cleared the harbour, Mike stepped out of the wheelhouse and said, "Here, you catch her a minute."

I went in and took the wheel. It was a great feeling and happily, I set a course that would take us roughly in the direction of our lobster pots. Mike busied himself out on deck. Suddenly he looked up at me and asked, "Where is The Old Dane?"

I nearly jumped out of my skin and looked around and about in cold panic.

"It's right underneath you at this very moment," said Mike calmly. It was quite a while before my heartbeat returned to normal. It was high water spring tide and Mike had let me steam right over the Dane. It was a lesson that I will never forget anyway.

As it turned out, conditions were slow to improve and I was glad that Mike had insisted on caution. I had spent the previous summer fishing from St Agnes, a few miles to the westward. That was the year I'd lost very many pots to recurring bouts of ground sea. I didn't want that again.

Mike had a system for everything. We got on just fine and worked well together as a team. I found it heavy going because I had been laid off work with an injured back a few months earlier, and so I was not very fit. However, long days at sea hauling and shooting lobster pots put me right and I was soon back to full strength. Spring became summer but the wind kept shifting into the NW and then backing SW again. It wasn't what you'd call a bad summer because we had plenty of sunshine. We also had rain and squally showers and of course, the northwesters were right in on us.

One morning I opened our front door and a chill wind hit my face. When I reached the top of South Quay hill, I could see that the wind was north–west. Big lumpy uneven waves heaved in towards the shore and broke, flinging white spray up against the cliffs. Mike was already down there when I arrived. He shook his head and said, "Not a hope boy, it's been freshening this last hour."

Together we walked along the South Quay to check on our lobster and crab carves. The sea surging in through quay gap made the floating wooden carves, containing their precious cargo, charge back and forth on their chains. We were satisfied that all was well and we went and looked at the fishing boat, which was tied to the quay. She was the *Mon Rêve*, a fine 36 Ft carvel built boat from Padstow. She had two Lister diesel engines and was fully decked. Her Skipper/owner was David Chapman (Chapper) and he came out on deck to talk to us.

He invited us down into the cabin. It was still only about 7am and Crewman John Brinham (Pablo) was sitting on one of the bunks with a mug of tea in his hand. I sat down on the other bunk opposite Pablo. I wondered how he got his nickname and thought; perhaps it had something to do with his glossy black hair. I had often seen Chapper and his mate Pablo when *Twilight* and *Mon Rêve* passed each other at sea but I had never actually met them. Now here I was in the confined space of the cabin facing Pablo.

I was really concentrating or what our two Skippers were saying and, for the moment, they had my whole attention. They were saying something about us all going off together in the *Mon Rêve*, but meanwhile something was nudging me to look at Pablo, I glanced at him but he looked OK, a fine looking lad really.

Chapper said, "Oh we could handle it alright but all our gear is too far away. By the time we punched our way off there in this weather, it would be time to come back. Where is your gear?"

I glanced at Pablo again. Something was slightly amiss but I just couldn't put my finger on it. Mike said, "We've got three strings near enough to the Headland in around seventeen fathoms and another two strings a bit further off."

My eyes were drawn again to Pablo. Suddenly it hit me. I was staring at Pablo's legs and there was an empty trouser leg staring back at me! There was only one foot, in its thick woollen sock and an empty space where his other foot should be. Indeed his leg, from below the knee, was missing! It made no sense to me at all and I just sat there gawping!

"Well let's go and haul 'em then," Chapper said.

Mike agreed and, like a man in a trance, I followed him up out of the cabin. We walked quickly along the quay to the steps and got into the punt.

"Mike," I said, "Pablo has only got one bloody leg!"

"Yes of course," He said. "Didn't you know that?"

He sculled us over to the *Twilight* to get our oilskins.

"But how can he fish like that?" I persisted.

"I dunno; you've seen him enough times out there fishing haven't you?"

Mike explained that Pablo had lost his leg in a motor cycle crash a couple of years ago.

When we got back to the *Mon Rêve*, Chapper had the two engines running. We jumped aboard and put on our oilskins for what we knew would be a wet trip. Chapper opened the throttles and headed out through the quay gap.

I noted that this boat had tons of power. Immediately our bow drove into a big on–rushing wave with a crash. I was surprised by the sheer force it. *Mon Rêve* ploughed through it and so, up and over and into the next wave. The sea curled over her bow and water rushed back along her decks. So we continued, with Chapper at the wheel and Mike alongside him to show him where our pots were. Meanwhile I sheltered from the spray and clung to the back of the wheelhouse as we hammered into the weather. I was accustomed to the more sedate progress of our little *Twilight*, popping along with her 14 hp Brit, but never in this kind of weather either.

We approached the first dahn and Chapper reduced speed. I let go of the wheelhouse to make my way forward and promptly fell on my hands and knees. The motion of the *Mon Rêve* changed to a heavy unpredictable rolling. I couldn't even stand, never mind walk! I crawled my way forward. Mike was there ahead of me. He had the boathook and caught the dahn and boarded it. I saw that Mike was on his knees too and I was relieved to know that it wasn't just me who was affected.

Chapper stood at the capstan hauling the buoy–rope. Up came the first pot and Mike, still on his knees boarded it and changed the bait. I had placed myself behind him on all fours. He passed the pot back to me. What now? I wondered, but help was at hand because Pablo came marching along the deck. He snatched the pot from me and marched back and stowed it behind the wheelhouse. That's the way we continued, Chapper hauled, Mike boarded and dealt with the pots, I took them from him and Pablo took them from me and stacked them ready for shooting. Nothing could have been simpler, providing your Crewman has his artificial leg of course.

That year we were plagued by sea–boils, from the oilskins chafing our wrists and necks. The cause has something to do with bacteria in the sea and the result was persistent itchy sores.

That was the spring the Burt brothers, John, David and Mickey, bought the *Patsy Anne*, a beautiful 40ft St Ives gig. They fitted her out with the French barrel type pots, which proved to be a great success. They landed crawfish in numbers that no one thought existed in the area. We bought six large withy, inkwell–type Cornish pots. These were crawfish pots made by a fisherman called Bill Heard of Newlyn, and we caught a lot of crawfish in them. The trouble was, we were so involved with the lobsters and it was too late to change over, even if French crawfish pots had been available. We pulled those six withy pots every time we passed them. Always we got something, even after only a couple of hours, we'd get lobsters and crawfish. Mike always placed these pots most carefully and we made sure they had the best of bait.

One guy used to haunt us. When he finished work in the evening, he would come out in his little boat and plonk his pots down on top of ours. It was such a torment having to pick our way out of the fouled up gear. Spider crabs were a problem in those days. We used to catch hundreds and as there was no sale for them, we simply killed them all.

One day, we hauled the withy pots and as usual; they were tangled with our friends gear! We had such a struggle dragging the great bunch of pots on board and then getting them untangled that we decided to teach him a lesson. We stuffed his pots full up to the top with dead spider crabs. Now they were so heavy, it took two of us to lift each pot onto the rail to shoot them away again.

A couple of days went by and a rising gale kept the boats in harbour. We were in the shed working on gear and Mike was hammering on a galvanized pipe. Our friend's father arrived at the door and accused Mike of hauling his son's pots. Mike denied this and countered by accusing his boy of shooting down on top of our pots. Well, they got really hot and heavy about it and Mike flogged the pipe even harder, which because he is a left–hander, caused the glass in his wristwatch to pop out and go spinning across the shed. His accuser broke off the engagement and retreated at that point. Anyway, not surprisingly, the guy shifted away from us and fished elsewhere.

October came in and the part–timers brought all their lobster pots ashore and stacked them up on the pier. This left the whole of the rocky ground close to Newquay Headland, which had been dotted with dahns and buoys all summer long, suddenly deserted. We ran our strings of pots right across it, not really expecting much. To our surprise, there were lobsters all over the place, despite the previous activities of so many other boats all summer long. We fished very well.

By now, our gear was in a very worn out condition, from being hauled twice and three times a day. Several pots were not worth repairing so we just cast them off. The main backropes were worn out too. They were made of a natural fibre, manila and we'd had to tie several knots where the rope had parted or chafed through.

Then the strangest of things happened. The weather settled. We thought it couldn't last but it just went on, really fine, day after day. The wind held steady E to NE force 2–3. Every morning we watched the sun rise like a big red orange only to see it vanish in the haze moments later. The lobsters kept coming up in the pots. It was a pleasure to be on the water. The price of lobsters rose from 4/6 to 6/6 per lb and we were full of optimism and already planning for the next season.

It was Mike's opinion that *Twilight* was no longer adequate. She was too small and hadn't enough power. He said we needed something with more carrying capacity to give us more range. The Burts had done very well with their 40ft *Patsy Anne*, with its two diesel engines and Mike was looking for something similar, though not quite as big. He made enquiries and looked at several boats that were offered for sale. Nothing suitable turned up until Mike spoke to Ronnie Harvey, who bought all our lobsters and crawfish. Ronnie said he would be selling the *Shamrock*. Mike was very excited at this news because the *Shamrock* was a St. Ives gig. She had been built by Tommy Thomas and was of larch on oak. She had a 21hp Lister in the centre and a 16.5hp Petter on the port quarter, both diesel engines. At 34ft 6ins, she was superior in every way to the *Twilight*. Mike wanted to buy *Shamrock* there and then but Ronnie had three men employed, fishing in her. He had bought another St Ives gig, a 37 footer called *Dos Amigos*, so he didn't want to part with *Shamrock* until this boat arrived.

A few days later having gathered up a couple of baskets of lobsters, we put them into Mike's van and drove the 38 miles to Harvey's Fish Merchants in Newlyn. Mike and Ronnie chatted away as our lobsters were being weighed. It seemed to me that Ronnie was playing hard to get, while Mike was trying not to sound too keen. They pussyfooted around, until it appeared that they had come to the understanding, that when the *Dos Amigos* arrived, Mike would have first refusal on the *Shamrock*.

A week later, we trucked our lobsters to Newlyn again. Again, Ronnie and Mike discussed the sale of the boat. No decision was arrived at but it all sounded very encouraging. Our business concluded we stepped out into the street. We met up with Maurice James, a fisherman from Portleven and stopped for a chat. I heard him say, "My boat is up for sale. I'm going to buy Harvey's *Shamrock*."

I was really shocked by this statement but tried not to let my face show it.

"You are?" said Mike quite calmly, "Well, that's a good move! *Shamrock* is a fine boat."

We made our way towards the van and as soon as we were out of earshot, we discussed this sudden bombshell. If what the man said was a done deal, then it would be a terrible blow to us. It was already November and there was no time to look for an alternative.

Before many days had passed, we were heading for Newlyn again. Ronnie weighed up the lobsters and handed Mike the cash. Mike said, "Ronnie, sell me the *Shamrock*."

Ronnie busied himself pushing a broom around the wet concrete floor, sweeping up nothing. "I can't Mike, not until I get the *Dos Amigos* here to replace her."

Mike followed him as he continued his aimless sweeping. "I have the cheque in here," said Mike, patting the top pocket of his overalls.

Ronnie paused, leaning on the broom, "Well, I don't know, the *Dos Amigos* is in Scotland and what if something should happen to her?"

"Don't worry! You'll get her here. Nothing is going to happen to the *Dos Amigos!*"

Ronnie leaned the broom against the wall and ran his fingers through his thinning hair. "OK then!" Ronnie said at last, and they shook hands on it.

I think Ronnie really wanted Mike to have the *Shamrock* but it worried him that his own men might be idle, without a boat to fish.

Out of the store and on the road once more Mike and I discussed the prospect with enthusiasm. A whole new horizon had opened up for us.

Shamrock

One morning early in December, we left Newquay and drove to Newlyn to collect the *Shamrock*. As we drove onto the quay, a man wearing a peaked cap stepped out and halted us. Mike explained that he had bought Harvey's *Shamrock*.

"Well then," said the man, "do your business and then get that van off the quay!"

This show of authority surprised us. We were used to Newquay piers being crowded with the cars of summer visitors and all and sundry. We located the boat and put our oilskins and few bits of gear aboard and Mike moved the van away as instructed. Gerald Harvey, Ronnie's younger brother, arrived and went over last minute engine details with Mike. When everything was ship shape and the two engines were running, Gerald bid us farewell. His last words were, "Now remember, she isn't a lifeboat you know!"

Mike and I were thrilled to get our hands on such a superior boat.

"Don't you worry about us Captain, we'll be alright!" Mike shouted back to Gerald as we waved our goodbyes.

Shamrock's speed picked up, heading for open water. Mike steered, following the shore around to our starboard. The towering mass of Land's End looked wonderfully green and rocky. The sky was clear blue without a hint of cloud and the sea was a calm blue with only the brilliant white foam surging around the rocks. Mike pointed out the various landmarks to me and then the rock called The Shark's Fin and the Longships Lighthouse. We were pleased to have the weather so fine for our first trip through such hazardous waters. The wind held steady E to NE 3–4 and the sun shone out of a clear sky. As we made our way eastward, the wind was in our faces but coming off the shore a bit too. The sea under us was smooth, so I was surprised when Mike pointed out the Runnel Stone buoy. As we passed it, the buoy was being flung upwards and plunged about in a welter of spray. I couldn't understand the cause of this, but Mike explained that it was, 'just the tide.'

We were making good time and reckoned we should be entering Newquay Harbour at about 4pm. We would be steaming home with the powerful flood tide under us. We ploughed on, listening to the reassuring beat of *Shamrock*'s two diesels. The boat felt good and we had every right to be pleased. As Gerald had reminded us, she was not a lifeboat but after what we were used to, she was like a battleship!

We ate our sandwiches and talked about what we would do when we got the boat home to Newquay. As the sun dropped away behind us, the day grew colder. The wind increased to E to NE 5 and white horses appeared everywhere. In no time at all the *Shamrock* was heading into steep short seas and the spray was flying back into her. Without waiting to put on my oilskins, I jumped out of the wheelhouse and started pumping. The hand pump shifted a lot of water, but what I had thought was going to be a quick fix solution, proved otherwise.

The wind was increasing. Still we had some shelter from the land and still it was no more than force 5 to 6, but the *Shamrock* was plunging wildly. Mike struggled to keep her head to sea. I was soon soaked through as great sheets of spray came inboard. The worry was that the water would get back to the engines. She was, after all, an open boat. I stuck to the task. Though something of an antique, the pump was powerful. It was operated by pulling on a T–handle set at an inconvenient height.

Things got worse. Great gouts of solid spray seemed to come at us from all angles. Soon it was quite dark and bitterly cold. I knew it was a losing battle and that the rising water in the bilges would beat us. All I could do was shut my mind to everything else and keep pumping. Suddenly there was a large boat close up to us; it was the 50ft *Castle Wraith*, formerly called *Lamorna*. The Skipper shouted across to us, asking if we were ok. When Mike answered him, he shouted, "Follow me!"

Gratefully we followed him and soon found ourselves safe and sound in Hayle Estuary. We had been caught and battered by the tide race off Godrevy Head. The strong flood tide meeting the strengthening wind had created a maelstrom and we, being strangers to that part of the coast, had sailed right into it.

As soon as the exertion of pumping had ended, I stood beside Mike in the wheelhouse. I felt very, very cold. We got alongside in Hayle and secured the *Shamrock*, then made our way to a nearby pub to phone for a taxi. Mike being a non–drinker never went into a pub and was clearly ill at ease. As we entered the empty bar, Mike removed his cap. The lady of the house appeared behind the bar. Mike enquired about the telephone and said, "I'll just have a glass of milk if I may Ma'am."

"And I'll have a double brandy," I said through chattering teeth. The taxi took us the mere six miles across the Peninsular, back to Newlyn, where we got into Mike's van and drove home to Newquay. Early next morning, we drove to Hayle and boarded the boat. It was still dark when we left the estuary. It dawned another fine clear morning. The wind was a steady; N to NE 3–4 and, with the west–going ebb tide heading in the same direction, the sea was smooth. We made the remaining fifteen miles to Newquay without incident.

When the *Shamrock* slid into her berth, she caused quite a stir. Newquay, like every other port, has a group of people who, because they know everything there is to know about boats and fishing, are happy to comment on such things. In Newquay, the group was always referred to as 'The Critics'. The Critics were a brotherhood. They all had connections with the sea, though in some cases rather slight. They all belonged to the older generation. When the tide dropped and the boats rested on the sand, The Critics' first duty was to come down and inspect *Shamrock*'s under water area. So they came in twos and threes to peer under her bilge, to turn her propeller blades and to take the rudder in their hands and shake it, checking for play in the pintals. As one party trudged off up the beach, so another would arrive.

Some of the comments were rather blunt, but then, what are critics for? Tom Rowse stood a few feet away from *Shamrock*'s stem. He looked back along her length, cocking his head first to the left and then to the right. He suddenly let out a great guffaw, "She looks like she's got a gumboil," he announced, referring to the cladding of one–inch thick oak planks added to her starboard side to protect her hull from the lobster pots.

Of course, the best and most colourful comments would come later when The Critics met at the PSA, or up at Rose Cellars, and it might take several days to filter down to us. Anyway, the general consensus wasn't long arriving. It was that, "Two men will never work she!"

Fair enough really, I suppose. After all *Shamrock* was only five feet shorter than the Burts' *Patsy Anne* and the three Burt brothers worked her. *Shamrock* was much smaller all round than the *Patsy Anne*, but that cut no ice with The Critics.

The weather held fine. We loaded what was left of our battered pots from the jetty into the boat. Then we went out and shot them on the rough ground off Newquay Headland again. *Shamrock* was a dream to work. True the winch was a brute and revved too fast, but as we got more used to her, so we got to like her more every day.

Still the lobsters came up in the battered pots. It was amazing to us that we were catching more lobsters per pot than we had caught in the height of the summer. On 17 December, we had seventeen fine lobsters in one haul of our 45 remaining pots.

Up Gannel

One morning, just before Christmas, Mike steered the *Shamrock* in past The Goose rock and, keeping close to Pentire, we made our way into Crantock Beach's narrow channel and so up to the Gannel estuary. 'Going Gannel' was always a tricky operation, only possible at high tide and there was usually the added hazard of big swells as you approached the beach. All went well however, and we got the boat safely to her prearranged moorings. We had two anchors aft and two anchors forward, all with heavy ropes. Mike was what you might call a 'belt and braces' man.

"You want as good a moorings here as you want in Newquay Harbour," he announced. I couldn't see it myself, because the boat would only come afloat for short spells on the tops of the big tides, and so for most of the time she would be sitting high and dry. She was after all now a long way inland!

Mike had decided to change the boat's name from *Shamrock*. He went through the rather complicated business with the MAFF and the Customs and so, from then on, she would bear the name *Reaper*, which Mike told me was the name of a well–known Newquay boat in the past.

We were now free to launch ourselves into the pot making. I bought a small electric circular saw to cut all the laths to the right length and we had steel formers made so that the pots and their entrances all turned out the right shape and size. We bought 1 cwt. of one and a quarter inch galvanized nails and went into production with a passion. We would be targeting the crawfish. We skinned the bark from the hoops. We sawed and we bent and we nailed, and we dreamed of crawfish and lobsters, and of fishing in fine summer weather.

Gales raged outside the loft. Horizontal rain lashed the windows. Sometimes it froze. Sometimes we got snow. The work kept going and the stack of pots grew bigger until there were 125 of them. All we had to do was breed netting into the ends of each pot and tie the entrances in place. Finally, each pot got two dollops of concrete whacked into the bottom and smoothed down to serve as ballast.

The loft where we worked was quite near the harbour. It was a large space above some garages. Next door, through a wooden partition, was the workshop of Old Bill Brown. Bill was well into his sixties. He was stringy and tough. He hardly ever laughed, or smiled, but he had a keen sense of humour. He had sailed on the trading schooners in his younger days and now spent his summers taking trips around the bay in his boat *Silver Spray*. I loved his stories, whether about the schooners, or about his trips with the visitors.

Bill was a skilled carpenter and his workshop was neat and tidy. His tools were bright and sharp. He demonstrated what a good handsaw should be like by bending the blade around and tucking it into its handle! When he laid his boat up for the winter, he removed the two Stuart Turner engines and serviced them in his workshop. They were beautifully kept. He started one of them to show me how smoothly it ran. He didn't use the starting handle but instead, he just spun the flywheel with his hand. It started and ran as smoothly as a sewing machine.

Sometimes, when things were quiet, we would hear a crash and a string of curses. Bill sure could curse! All it meant was that, whatever Bill was working at had gone wrong and he had hurled his hammer at the partition wall.

Dos Amigos

It was towards the end of February 1964 when we heard of the terrible ordeal experienced by the crew of Ronnie Harvey's *Dos Amigos*. Her Scottish previous owners had delivered her to Milford Haven and, on 19 February, three of Ronnie's fishermen went up by train to collect her and steam her back to Newlyn.

In fine weather, they set a course for Padstow on the north coast of Cornwall. After a few hours, at sea they suffered an engine breakdown. The weather turned bad and they found themselves in a storm of south east winds, which drove them over a hundred miles out into the Atlantic. Enormous seas pounded them. Each time they rose to the top of a great sea, they thought, 'This is the end!' But, when the crest broke on them with explosive force, the *Dos Amigos* ran down the face of the wave like a surfboard and survived. She did that time and time again. She showed her true pedigree. She was another St Ives gig, just 2 feet longer than the *Shamrock*. When the storm abated, the fog came down.

After four long days and nights, the lads were freezing cold and very hungry. They were absolutely exhausted. By pure chance, a French trawler found the *Dos Amigos* and she was then towed into St Ives by the lifeboat.

When we heard the news, Mike and I recalled Mike saying, "Don't worry Ronnie, nothing's going to happen to the *Dos Amigos*"!

A Day to Remember

It was a fine morning. The tide was rising, but the little fleet of lobster boats still leaned on their bilge keels on the hard–packed yellow sand of Newquay Harbour. On board the boats, the skippers and crewmen shared the chore of cutting up bait while they waited for the boats to come afloat. There was much shouting and laughter as the men swapped yarns and traded insults.

Young Graham Mountford was on board *Reaper* with us. He often dodged school to come with us. We considered him a cheeky puppy and sometimes, to get our own back on him, we would meet his serious questions about fishing with pure nonsensical answers. This never failed to madden him. However, even at that age, he was a really good hand in the boat and he was great company. Now he too, joined in the banter.

Rodney, skipper of the *Freemans* shouted across to me, "What's the trouble with your skipper this morning Trev? Ee's a bit grumpy innee?"

Mike, who had been quietly working away looked up sharply and shouted, "You'll find out soon enough!"

He turned to the young Moller brothers, who now owned the *Twilight*, which was berthed next to us, "And you two, do your work and get back as quick as you can!" he said then.

"Mind what I say now. This is going to be a day to remember!"

The two lads looked surprised. "Er, yes Mike, OK!" They both nodded in agreement.

Mike addressed Graham and me next. "They're giving gales all round and strong NW gales for this area," he declared. Of course I had been with Mike long enough to trust his judgement but privately I thought, 'Yeh, but not yet eh!'

A short while later, the rising tide lifted the boats and we were able to proceed to sea. The sun shone and the sky was a clear blue. There wasn't a breath of wind and the sea was like a mirror.

Half an hour later, I stood at the capstan hauling on the manila backrope. Mike was boarding and re–baiting the pots and Graham was stacking the pots in their proper sequence for shooting again. When this first string was back in the water, we steamed further off and Graham and I stood forward, waiting for the next dhan buoy to come into view. *Reaper* made a fine bow wave and I realised that Mike was making all speed to get our five strings of pots baited and back into the water before the weather deteriorated.

I noticed just a cats–paw of wind on the surface of the sea, and then another. An area of ripples would appear sparkling like diamonds in the sun, only to fall away again and merge once more into the flat metallic surface of the sea. By the time we had the third string done, the wind was off the land, SE force 3–4. I said to Graham, "If it stays like this we've got nothing to worry about."

I searched the skies for signs of impending doom but saw nothing to give me cause for concern. Mike was very subdued, and when a pair of crawfish came up in one pot, he scarcely announced it. Even Graham's smart–assed remarks failed to get a response from him.

The wind ruffled the water now and was backing and veering between east and south. Thick cloud covered the sun. We had hauled, re–baited and shot all our pots. The first haul accomplished, our intention was to leave the pots fishing for another hour and then start hauling them all again. We took out our crib bags and settled down to the sandwiches and flasks of tea.

Mike was in the wheelhouse and had the engines slow ahead. He gave the wheel an occasional touch, a spoke to port or to starboard and with the help of her mizzen sail, *Reaper* held nice and steady into the wind. Graham and I sat behind the wheelhouse on the small after deck.

Suddenly, we were enveloped in thick drizzle and visibility was reduced to a hundred yards. Reluctantly we struggled into our oilskins. That was just before 10am when the BBC man interrupted the programme to announce a gale warning and we heard him say, "And Lundy NW force 8 becoming strong northerly gale force 9."

"We'd better try and find the *Freemans*," said Mike and pushing the throttles forward he peered ahead into the drizzle. "She's just east of us somewhere. If they didn't hear that last gale warning we had better tell them of it."

The *Reaper* surged ahead. Fitted to the bulkhead, in the wheelhouse, was an old brass barometer. Mike swore by this instrument and he consulted it every day. Now he tapped its face, "My God!" he exclaimed, "The glass has dropped three tenths since we left Newquay Harbour!"

The words were no sooner out of his mouth when there was a tremendous flash of lightning, accompanied by an ear–splitting crash of thunder directly over our heads. We were suddenly aware of a loud roaring noise. Mike shouted, "Quick, get the mizzen off her!"

Graham and I jumped to it, and had the sail halfway down the mast, when a mighty blast of wind from the north hit us and torrents of rain hurled down on us. The wind put a big belly in the sail and we had to grapple with it, until we finally got it down and lashed to the mizzen boom. Mike spun the wheel to starboard and let *Reaper* run headlong before the gale.

With the sail safely stowed, I returned to the working deck and started pumping. Steep seas reared up over our stern. The leading faces of the waves were furrowed like a ploughed field. The tops of the waves were torn off by the force of the wind, so that a mixture of horizontal rain and spray hurtled over and around the wheelhouse and so down into the boat. Our pump had been fitted with a handle like a village pump and using my body weight, I pumped out a lot of water. While this was going on the *Reaper* was travelling faster than at any time since we had sailed in her. She lifted just enough so that the seas roared under us and around us and passed along her sides, while she ran straight and true. I thought to myself that this was all very fine, but where the hell were we going?

The tide was out now and there was only dry sand in the harbour entrance! It would it be another three hours before there was enough water for us to get in. If it kept blowing and the seas were breaking across the entrance it might be five hours, by which time it might be breaking over the north quay and over its green light. Then how would we manage?

I put these thoughts aside and kept pumping while we sped towards North Cornwall's iron coast. A hundred miles of rocks, cliffs and sand without any shelter in a northerly wind. I looked up and saw Newquay Headland, with the seas pounding furiously against it. We passed High Place, with white water leaping up and around it. The engine revs slowed and Mike shouted for us to get the anchor ready.

It was the work of moments. Graham and I made sure that the fifty fathoms of courlene rope was free to run out. We were in the Gazzle. *Reaper* went in close to the old lifeboat slip then turned to face the weather. I was amazed to find the seas seemed less violent.

At Mike's command, we cast the anchor overboard and paid out the rope. As we did so, *Reaper* dropped back, until we were looking up at the towering cliffs just astern. With about six fathoms of water under us and fifty fathoms of anchor rope out, we faced the seas bow on. We hoisted the mizzen sail and Mike put the engines going half speed ahead, to take the worst of the strain off the anchor rope. The high cliff just astern acted as a baffle and broke the force of the wind coming in against it from the sea. Mike had figured things just right. We were in a small triangle of relative calm and the *Reaper* rose and fell over the great lumps of water that had lost their anger. My crib bag was empty but for an apple. I sat eating it behind the wheelhouse, sheltered from the wind and watched the waves raging past, just outside of us.

The first boat to appear was the Burt brother's 40ft *Patsy Anne*. They threw out their anchor but it failed to hold. They retrieved it, steamed off into the weather and shot away again, but again it dragged. *Freemans* appeared and a similar performance took place. The full fury of the storm was missing us and we watched other boats struggling with the elements. Luckily, the wind eased, imperceptibly at first. Then the rain stopped and white clouds raced across the sky, allowing glimpses of the sun. The sea was blue and the waves became confused with white tops crashing off them, or breaking and just fading out. On the high cliff behind us, people from the town had gathered to watch the spectacle.

By the time the tide was high enough to get into the harbour, the seas had calmed down a lot. We hauled the anchor and steamed the short distance to the harbour passing in through the entrance with ease. The Moller brothers moored next to us. They told us that they'd had a terrible time of it and, at one stage, they were on their knees praying. It was indeed a day to remember!

Accident at Sea

There was a terrible accident on board the 40ft *Freeman*. Rodney Lyon was the Skipper and Jimmy Hoare and Mike Morris were the crew. Mike Morris also minded the engines.

On one of their trips, Mike had to go below into the engine room. Now space in the engine room of a 40 footer is always very limited. Since Cornish boats always had two engines, back then, space was very tight indeed. In an old boat, like the *Freeman*, the engine room would be a grim noisy little place full of spinning shafts and whirring belts. Perhaps the winch belt or a shaft bearing was giving trouble.

Whatever the problem, in trying to correct it, poor Mike was badly injured. I believe the sleeve of his overalls got caught in some moving part at the front end of the big engine and he was pulled into it. He was wearing a heavy waterproof apron and this too went into the machinery. The apron strings were made of thin nylon rope and the piece supporting the top of his apron was around his neck. In a flash the damage was done. As Mike was hauled into the machinery, his arm was broken and the nylon rope cut deep into his neck. Because of the engine noise, Jimmy and Rodney were quite unaware of what was going on.

Somehow, Mike managed to get up through the tiny hatch and he lay slumped against the wheelhouse. On seeing him, Rodney immediately put the engines full ahead and raced back to Newquay Harbour. As he lay there, Mike Morris himself bound his broken arm to the deck scrub handle, using it as a splint. There were no radios in the boats in those days and there was no Inshore Lifeboat either. When the *Freeman* arrived at the harbour, the tide was too low and she couldn't get in. It was ages before Mike could be put ashore and taken to hospital.

By the time Mike Lyne and I went to visit him in hospital, he was on the mend. I was appalled at his appearance. He was in bed, his arm was in a sling and he could barely move it. I think his collarbone may have been broken too. He held his head to one side as the result of the terrible wound to his neck. We couldn't even tell a white lie and say, 'You look great!' for indeed he looked awful.

When we stepped outside we both agreed, sadly, that poor Mike Morris would never fish again. Well we underestimated him! Not only did he get better, but he came back as full of beans as ever he was. Within a year, he had bought the 39ft gig *Trevose*, and with his brothers as crew, he pursued the fishing with vigour. That just showed what amazing guts and determination he had.

Getting to Work

Vyrn Cabin was built on a small level patch halfway down the cliff. A stony path led straight from the front door to the cliff edge a few yards away, whereupon it swung tightly to the left. Rising steeply, hugging the rim of the cliff, the path veered to the right until it met the main broader path leading up from George Northey's Boathouse, to the road at the top.

It was lovely on a summer's day to step out of the Cabin door into the sunshine, take in the glorious views of the sea and of the River Gannel below. Bees droned and small birds chirped among the brambles and blackthorn. However, it was very different at three or four o'clock in the morning! I would be standing in the doorway, wearing my crash helmet, black rubber thigh boots and old black oilskin coat. My ex–WD gas mask bag, containing a flask of coffee and two Marmite sandwiches would be slung around my neck.

Many a time I stood and waited for my eyes to adjust to the total darkness and listened to the wind and the pelting rain. At last, realizing that it was too black to see anything anyway, I would launch myself into the night. I knew exactly how far it was to the edge of the cliff and just where the path turned to the left. Reaching that point, I would go on all fours, scampering upwards with the trailing brambles snatching at me and with the crib bag swinging wildly around my neck.

It is only a blessing that no one was ever confronted by me, emerging onto the main pathway. The galumphing noise of the rubber thigh boots combining with my rasping breath would have been enough to give anybody a queer turn. Of course, on those mornings I would be in a right lather myself by the time I reached the road. There I kept my motorbike parked up against George's shed. Sweating and gasping I would pounce onto the bike, switch on the petrol, tickle the carburettor and stamp on the kick–starter. How I hated being late! Kick, kick, kick, perhaps she's flooded. Switch off the fuel. Kick, kick, kick; curse, curse, curse! Switch on the fuel and kick some more.

Plan B: Run her down the road. It is not easy to run in thigh boots but I'd make a fair fist of it, running alongside my trusty steed and flinging myself into the saddle as I let out the clutch with a skill born of long practice. The engine makes a hollow popping noise and we trickle to a halt. I jump off and drag the 'Beast' all the way back to the shed, heaping abuse on it as I go.

Plan C: I can't run very fast in thigh boots but I do my best. Down Pentire Road until I reach the golf links. Away from the streetlights, it is not easy to avoid some of the pits and hollows enjoyed by golfers, but I pick myself up and gallop on across the undulating grass for what seems like miles. I am bathed in sweat because I am overdressed for this carry–on. Out into Fore Street, the going is easier now and the daylight is coming in. I plunge down South Quay Hill.

Ah! There is Mike, as always, trustworthy Mike is never late (in fact he is always a wee bit early) and we are not going to be stuck on the sand by the falling tide. He stands there in the punt. With his left hand, he swings the long oar, which rests in the sculling notch in the stern. In his right hand, he brandishes a large white handkerchief with which he frequently mops his brow.

With buckling knees and rasping breath, I reach the bottom of the hill. Mike gives the oar a quick twist and expertly drives the punt's bow up to the steps. The large white handkerchief does some frantic brow mopping. I clatter down the steps and get aboard the punt. Mike shoves off and, with an expression of excruciating pain on his face, sculls us quickly to the *Reaper's* side.

As I climb aboard, I note that Mike has already put two five-gallon drums of diesel oil and a seven stone basket of gurnards for bait on deck. *Reaper*'s two engines are ticking over nicely and her heavy moorings are singled up, so we only have to tie the punt onto them and we can steam away.

In no time at all *Reaper* steams out through the pier heads and I feel her lifting to the swells. I look back at the wheelhouse as I tip the basket of gurnards out by the cutting board. Mike glances away to port. I edge my knife on the sharpening stone that Harold Bullen has given to us. I call out, "Thanks for remembering the sharpening stone Mike!"

"Pshaw!" he exclaims and turns his face away to look out of the starboard window. Mike never forgets anything.

South Easter

The *Reaper's* engines were ticking over as I split the gurnards with my black–handled gutting knife and threw them one by one into the bait basket. The wind moaned softly, but down in the harbour we were sheltered by high cliffs and the houses that crowded along Fore Street.

Mike leaned out of the wheelhouse widow with the battered little transistor radio pressed to his ear. "Forecast's bad," he said and, after a pause, "BBC Man's dishing 'em out now, south easterly gales for Fastnet, Shannon, Sole and Lundy. We'd better make haste!"

Together we threw off the heavy mooring ropes and chains. *Reaper* proceeded out through the quay gap and away to the eastward, with the wind on her stern.

A few hours later Jack Carne, Newquay's Harbour Master, was watching the weather. He saw the well–spaced lines of surf speeding towards the shore. Each swell steepened and then crashed in glittering foam, making a white arc around the bay towards Porth Island. Jack saw the snow–white foam against the wonderful blue of the sea and the curtains of spray flung high by the offshore wind, the bright sun making rainbows in it. Jack took no notice of the panoramic view. He stared off into the distance, searching for a glimpse of fishing boats.

I pulled my long oilskin frock over my head. For a few moments, I staggered blindly around the swaying deck, with my arms stuck up in the air, until I managed to get my head through the circular neck opening. It was a stiff, smelly, uncomfortable garment but since leaving the harbour, the wind had freshened considerably and spray occasionally curled up over *Reaper's* stern and spattered across her decks.

I finished preparing the bait and looked around. The sea looked ugly, with tumbling white horses all over it and the wind sang in the rigging. Mike eased back the throttles and I went back aft behind the wheelhouse. Together we hoisted the mizzen sail. I went forward again and picked up the boat hook. Mike steered up to the dahn buoy, which I caught and took aboard. I hauled on the buoy rope and threw a turn on the capstan and, from then on, kept hauling continuously throughout the operation.

Up came the metal floats at ten–fathom intervals, while Mike expertly kept the boat above the pots. As soon as the first pot arrived, he was there alongside me. As it broke the surface, he pulled it aboard. He snatched out a lobster and put it in the lobster box. He flung three big spider crabs overboard plus a spotted dogfish. He then took three brown crabs by surprise and whipped them out and into the crab box before they could lock themselves on to the pot with their iron grip. He took out the two mangled baits and quickly fixed in two new ones. He stowed the pot and was back beside me staring down into the water like a gull, waiting for the next pot. So it went.

Reaper was a beautiful boat on the gear. The helm was locked amidships while her great mizzen sail held her up into the wind. With plenty of revs, the propeller thrust us forward and I had an extension to the gear lever near at hand, so I could knock her out of gear if she went too far ahead. I put three turns on the capstan and the pots came zooming up to the boat, despite the increasing wind. Up they came, more spiders, some with legs and claws over a foot long. Mike sent them whirling off into space with a sweep of his arm. He grabbed spotted dogs by the tail and flung them away in disgust. When one wrapped itself around his arm like a snake, he tore it off and banged its head on the gunnel, with a loud curse of 'Bastard' before sending it flying.

Another pot surfaced. "Lobster," he shouted, "No two, three!" he corrected himself, as lobsters crabs and spider crabs all tumbled together in a snapping kicking flailing mass of legs and claws inside the pot. Mike's hands worked at a furious pace to prevent the crabs and lobsters from murdering each other and everything around them.

The next pot came up and Mike could hardly board it. Three great conger eels as thick as a man's thigh were in this one. He turned the pot on its end and grabbed at the congers. They twisted and gyrated, their snapping jaws armed with needle sharp teeth. The congers fought back with their great strength but Mike hauled them out, slimy and gasping and booted them across the deck. All the while, I kept hauling. Pot after pot came up with nothing worth keeping but a few crabs. Mike stowed a pot and skidded back beside me for the next one.

Suddenly he flung himself down on the gunnel. Not one word came out of him! I stopped hauling and, still keeping the strain on the capstan, I took a step forward to peer over his shoulder. Was it a heart attack? I wondered. "Crawfish!" he managed to rasp out. I was amazed to see that he had each hand on a big yellowy crawfish. One clung to the end of the pot and one clung to the top, both on the outside! I reached over and boarded the pot and there was another big crawfish inside. Mike had seen the two on the outside and managed to grab them before they could flip away. The last three pots held two more crawfish and another lobster. As the last pot came aboard Mike changed the baits and shouted, "Leave the dhan out."

He jumped back into the wheelhouse and positioned the boat to run the string of twenty–five pots back across the same spot. We went slowly ahead, the dhan streaming astern of us. Mike watched the echo sounder and when he was satisfied he shouted, "Over she goes."

I threw out the pots one by one. With the engine at low revs, the wind drove us ahead at a fair lick. The pots were twelve fathoms apart on the backrope but as soon as I threw one pot overboard, the rope was coming up tight to the next one. We went off for the next string. There were five strings of twenty–five, which made one hundred and twenty–five pots in all.

Each string proved harder to deal with than the previous one. We would have been happy to head for home, but of course it was now low water and at least another three hours must pass before we could get into the harbour. We drank our flasks of coffee and ate our sandwiches while Mike steered towards one of our dhans. The force of the wind held us off so he had no trouble

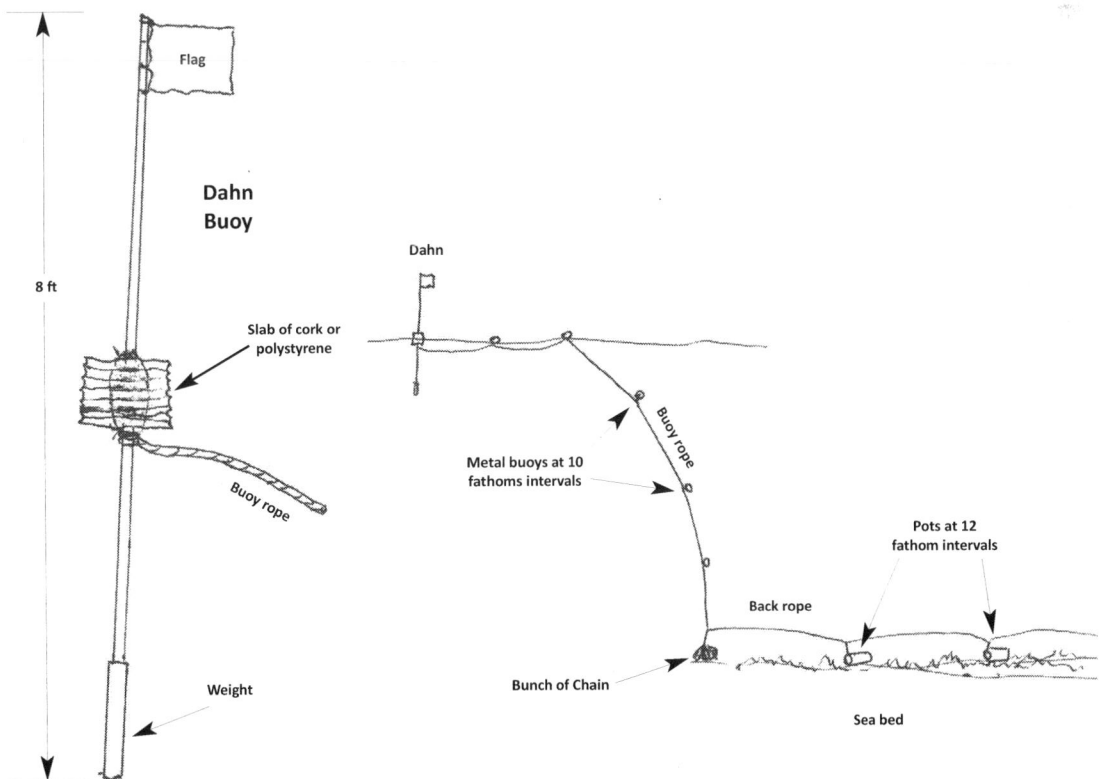

keeping station. White horses crashed and roared all about us. *Reaper's* bow rose and fell and spray lashed against the wheelhouse windows.

Jack Carne looked at the moorings. All the boats were there except the *Reaper*, he noted. He peered over the harbour wall, holding on to his peaked cap. The visibility was reduced to about one mile by the flying spray. Thin, high clouds veiled the sun.

"What have we got?" Mike asked me.

"Sixteen crawfish and fourteen lobsters," I answered.

"Nothing wrong with that," said Mike. "That's good fishing for one haul. There's fresh bait in every pot. We'll have the first string up again, though I doubt very much if anything is moving. This south easter will make mountains of ground sea and the fish will feel it coming."

So it proved. The pots came up empty with the baits untouched. "They're hanging on for dear life down there!" was Mike's comment as he boarded the empty pots.

It normally took us twenty minutes to haul a string of twenty–five pots, but great gusts of wind hit us and even with three turns on the capstan, it took us much longer. We lowered the mizzen sail and shot the pots running before the wind. I lifted each pot chest high and hurled it overboard with all my strength. The wind was trying to blow the pots, heavy as they were, back into the boat. Once clear of the pots Mike turned for home.

Back in the wheelhouse, he looked at his pocket watch, which hung from a nail in the window frame. "If we don't see Newquay Harbour in one hour, we'll be in serious trouble," he said.

He peered into the white wall of spray. Visibility was down to twenty yards. He watched the compass card as it turned erratically due to the violent motion of the boat. Having decided on the course home, he sent the *Reaper* surging forward into the gale. Meanwhile I stood on deck pumping. The spray curled over the bow and hit my oilskin and sou'wester with the force of a fire hose.

Jack Carne was in his little office on the south quay when he heard the announcer break into the programme. "Shannon, Fastnet, Sole and Lundy gale increasing to severe gale force nine or storm force ten imminent".

He picked up the phone and rang Trevose shore station. He explained the reason for his anxiety. "One of my boats is still out. Have you seen her?"

They replied that they had indeed seen her earlier, but had since lost sight of her due to poor visibility. Jack phoned RAF St Mawgan a few miles away and asked if they could send up a search plane. They told him, "Sorry, Not possible! The wind speed is eighty–three miles per hour and everything we have here is tied down."

Jack wondered if he should ask the Padstow lifeboat to launch. Simon Drew, a retired fisherman, had heard the storm warning on the radio. Knowing that the *Reaper* was still out, he got into his car and drove up onto the headland, hoping he might see her from the high ground. After a while, his patience was rewarded. As he told us later, "The first I saw of her was the top of her mast coming through the spray."

That was a tough trip but once again, the *Reaper* had proved herself.

Storing Shellfish

Storing shellfish is always a problem. If you don't get it right, you are going to suffer losses. Lobsters, crawfish and crabs are prone to crunch up their own kind when confined in a small space. We used to cut the tendons in the claws, in such a way that the shellfish couldn't open their claws. The cut claws would bleed but when the fish was put back into seawater, the wounds would quickly seal up. However, if the shellfish were left out of the water, they could quickly bleed to death. That is why the nicking process had to wait until the last minute, before they were stored.

At sea, we kept the catch covered in seawater soaked sacking and placed them away from the sun and the wind, to prevent their gills from drying out. The heavy wet sacking also kept the fish inactive. On returning from fishing we would hitch *Reaper* onto her moorings and put the shellfish baskets, covered with the wet sacks, into the punt. Mike would scull the punt in a leisurely fashion so as not to draw attention. Newquay in the summer was swarming with tourists, only aching for something to gawp at. All we wanted to do was to get alongside the quay to where our wooden store pot, or 'carve' floated, put our shellfish away, secure *Reaper* and get ourselves home for a well–earned rest.

It seldom worked out like that however. Usually we would be spotted and instantly a mob would appear on the edge of the quay, all leaning out and craning their necks to see what was going on. We often had to listen to their daft remarks and even dafter questions.

Nicking lobsters is a delicate operation. If you have thirty or more, your chances of nicking one of your own tendons, or getting a finger crunched up are quite high. We would be wearing thick jumpers, overalls and thigh boots having been out since before dawn when even in summer, it is chilly and the half gale of wind would have kept us cool all day while we worked. Now in the shelter of the harbour, with the sun belting down, the sweat would soon be running off us. Mike and I hated this bit, but we would answer the questions as best as we could, not wishing to be bad mannered.

"Hey Mister! Where did you catch those?"

"Can them things pinch you?"

This, often when Mike had a big seven pound crawfish clamped between his knees and himself and the crawfish were actually locked in what appeared to be an arm wrestling competition. Sometimes, when Mike was nicking a big cock lobster with claws the size of boxing gloves, someone would ask, "Would it hurt you if he pinched you?"

A favourite one was, "How much is that lot worth then?" and "By gum! You must be making a fortune!"

The worst question you could get at this stressful time was, "Oi Mate! Will you sell us a crab/lobster/etc.?"

This was a trap question. Some people love to haggle and since you are too whacked out to argue over pennies, you let the thing go for next to nothing. Immediately there will be a chorus of, 'Me too! Me too!' This will be followed by, 'What do you do with it?', 'What! Boil it alive?' and so on.

One day we came in at half–tide on the flood, when there was just enough water for us to creep up to the moorings. We got ourselves and the baskets into the punt and sculled across to the carve without causing a sensation. I handed Mike the lobsters, one by one. He nicked them

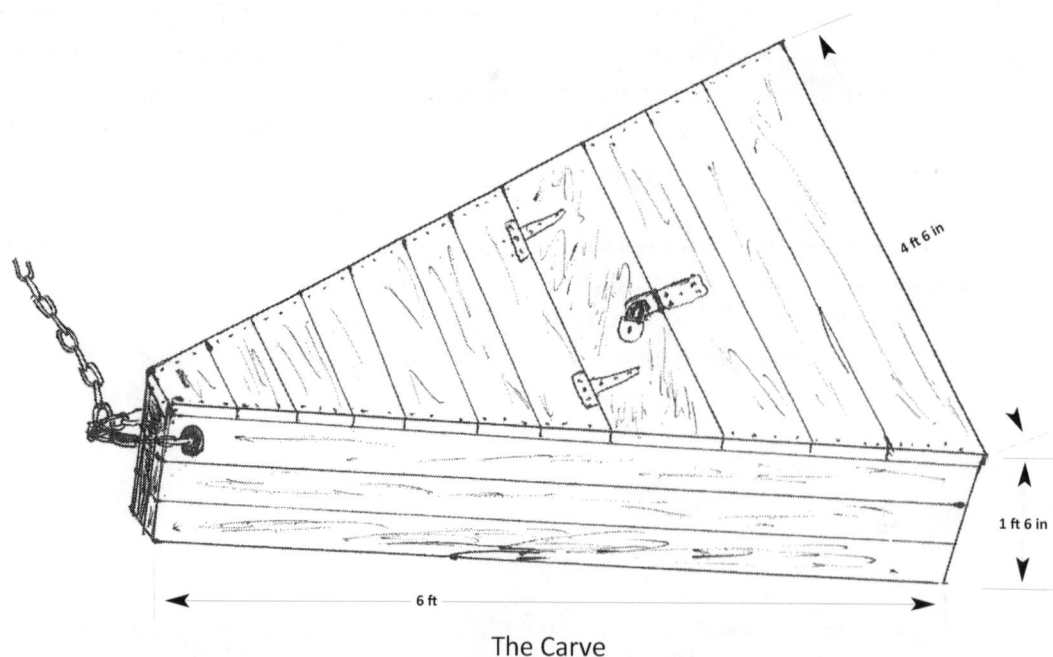

The Carve

and dropped them through the open trapdoor in the top of the carve. We had just started on the crabs when a loud cockney voice shouted, "Cor Blimey! Look at all them crabs!"

People came running. The cockney geezer gave them a running commentary, "See what ees doin'? Ees puttin' them in that box so they'll keep 'til tomorrer. Cor! That's a lovely one innit?" And so on.

More people joined the throng, curious to see what was happening. Our man shouted, "Ow much d'yer want for a crab?"

I kept my head down.

"Oi! Come on mate. I've got the money ere. Sell us one!"

He went on and on and in the end Mike said, "Oh for Christ's sake sell him one," and in a quieter tone, "And make sure and charge the bugger enough!"

'Well yes, perhaps he will shut up then,' I thought to myself. I picked out a nice hen crab of about two pounds weight and held it up to show him. But now the Cockney was centre stage and enjoying every minute of it.

"Nah! That's too small I want a bigger one" I picked up a slightly bigger hen crab.

"Nah! Still too small! I want one bigger than that."

I rooted down in the crab basket, prising the clinging crabs off their neighbours, until I found a jack crab of about three pounds. When he saw it he yelled, "Yeh! That one will do. Ow much is it?"

"Five bob," I yelled back. With a flourish, he threw two half–crowns down into the punt.

"OK!" I told him "We'll bring it to you. We'll be coming ashore in ten minutes."

"Nah!" he yelled, "Frow it up to me."

I stood there holding the crab in my two hands. It was a lively devil too. I looked up at the sea of faces. The edge of the quay was about twelve feet above my head.

"Are you sure?"

"Yeh! Go on frow it!" he commanded, stretching out his hands in readiness.

I steadied myself against the motion of the punt and then lobbed the crab up to him. It was a good throw. He caught it and vanished from sight.

The crabs were all nicked, the trapdoor of the carve closed and padlocked. The crowd dispersed. Ten minutes later Mike and I were walking along the quay, carrying our empty bait basket and diesel can, when the Cockney came rushing up to meet us.

"Look at me bleedin' fumb!" he cried, holding it under our noses as if he was proud of it. "That bleeding crab got me!"

The thumb was black and blue and already swollen. His poor thumbnail was simply corrugated. Mike and I did our best to make sympathetic noises, but hurried on our way before we lost control and collapsed laughing.

About Store Pots

We had two store pots in the bay: a big one made in a cylinder shape, which would hold about three hundred pounds of crawfish. It was constructed in the same manner as the French barrel pot and was made of wooden hoops and laths. We used to bring it on board using the tackle on the foremast. It was a brute of a thing when it was full!

The smaller store pot was made of galvanised steel mesh and that one would hold about one hundred and twenty pounds of lobsters. We kept these two store pots on a heavy anchor quite close to the harbour. They sat on the bottom on the clear hard–packed sand, held by the anchor and marked with a buoy.

The shellfish kept perfectly out there in the bay, but at the first sign of bad weather or ground sea, we had to dash out and bring the store pots into the harbour. Being rolled around by the swells would soon kill the fish and, if it got bad enough, the store pots could be torn off or smashed in that very exposed spot.

Apart from these we also had two 'carves'. These were triangular wooden boxes, about six feet long by four feet wide and two feet deep. They were constructed from heavy planks, tarred black and had a hinged trapdoor in the top. The carves floated in the harbour and each one was secured by a chain to the south quay wall. They would each hold about three hundred pounds of shellfish and were very heavy even when empty. When full of shellfish, they were always in danger of sinking, and we would have to tie trawl floats onto the three corners to keep them on the surface.

The carves were a constant problem. In the summertime, kids used them as rafts or diving platforms. We would sometimes come in from sea and find a carve had turned turtle. Two hundred pounds of crabs, which had been sitting on the floor of the box before the kids capsized it, would now be happily sitting inside its lid. Risking a double hernia, Mike and I would lie with our bellies across the punt's gunnel, attempting to heave the carve the right way up. Often we would almost succeed, only to have the damn thing come churning back over on us, a hundred–weight of tenacious crabs holding on grimly to the lid acting as a counter balance. As Mike would say, "It was a real pile hanger!"

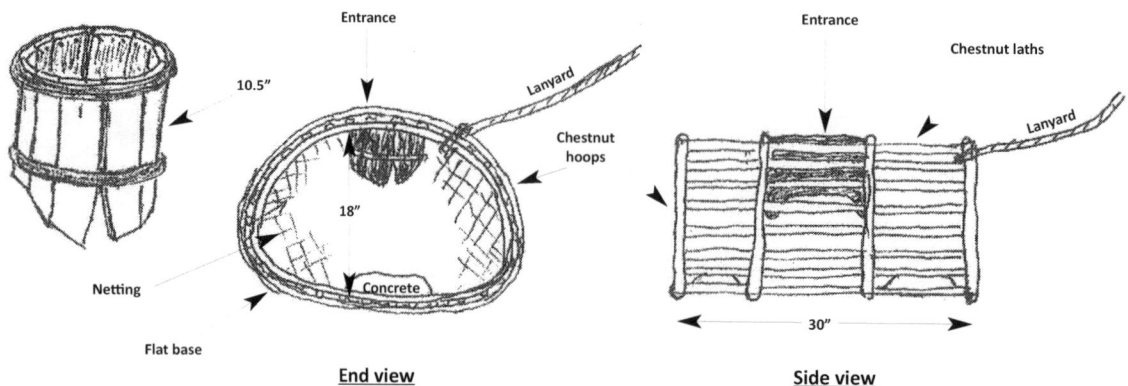

French Barrel Type Craw/Lobster Pot

We made the inside hoops in a steel former first, then fitted the laths using 1¼ inch galvanised nails. Next we added the outside hoops. The nails were clenched and the wooden mouth tied in place. The ends were netted and a dollop of concrete smoothed into each end of the base. (Hoops and laths imported from France by Harveys.)

When the tide went out, the carves sat on the dry sand and the kids made sand castles on top of them. Often lobster's legs and feelers would be poking out through the gaps in the planks and the little horrors would pull them off causing the lobsters to die. One dead lobster could quickly putrefy and that would usually poison a few more. Later, when we came to put our day's catch away, we would find the padlock jammed up with sand.

Putting lobsters into a carve was one thing, getting shellfish out of the carve on landing day was quite another! If the tide was out you walked to the carve, opened the trapdoor and picked the fish out into baskets and carried them up to the waiting lorry. With the tide in however, the carves had to be tackled from the punt. It meant reaching into the dark recesses of the carve and grabbing the lobsters, crabs or crawfish. Even crabs are surprisingly nimble in the water. We stored the different species separately.

We had many queer comments from holidaymakers if the arrival of Harvey's lorry happened to coincide with high tide. We would scull the punt over to the carves, which would now be only a few feet below the level of the quay. One day we had gathered quite a crowd. There was silence as Mike undid the padlock. When he opened the trapdoor and people saw that it was full to the brim with crabs, a great gasp went up. Someone said, "Look at that for a catch!"

Mike and I glanced at each other, realising in that moment that the onlookers presumed that we had come over in our punt to gather our day's catch and that the carve was a kind of shellfish trap!

Mike had his sleeves rolled up as high as they would go and was rapidly handing the crabs out to me. As I was loading them into the baskets, I was amused to hear the discussion taking place. All sorts of theories were offered. Mike handed me the last crab and straightened his back. A voice from the quay asked, "Hey Mister! How do the crabs get in there?"

"In through the trapdoor of course," said Mike, as he put the padlock back on.

"Yes," the voice persisted, "but what keeps them in?"

"Last one in, closes the door behind him!" said Mike sculling the punt towards the steps.

Fern Pit to Penpol

It was January 1965 and the *Reaper* lay at Fern Pit. We had her secured at the little stone quay alongside George Northey's boathouse. It was the ideal berth while Mike had jobs to do on the boat.

I lived in Vyrn Cabin, which overlooked the quay and George was always on hand to keep an eye on things. We planned to move upstream to Trethellan. So Mike and I went to Newquay Harbour and took up our mooring chains. We loaded them into Mike's van and drove to the river Gannel. Selecting a suitable spot at Trethellan, we laid the chains and dug in three anchors in readiness.

We thought the top of the spring tide, which occurred in the evening of 4 January, would be the time to move the boat, but in fact, on that tide, the high water never reached to within two feet of the required depth. This meant we would have to stay at Fern Pit for another fortnight until the next spring tide. Mike was tempted to strip down the main engine and do an overhaul. Fortunately, he decided to put that job off and instead, concentrated on making pots with me up in the loft. We had the youngsters up there skinning hoops and laths. There was Graham Mountford, Dave Trebilcock and Robert, John and Nigel, whose surnames elude me. We never paid the kids but they stayed toiling away with us through many a long evening, so I guess it must have been fun.

On 13 January, we got very heavy rain and a south west gale force 9. The forecast was north west storm force 10. Over the next couple of days the gales continued. We watched the weather and we watched the tide as it approached the top of the springs again. Fern Pit wasn't safe in extreme weather and an error of judgement could spell disaster.

The morning of the 17th dawned with heavy squalls from the south west. Pauline and I were at home in Vyrn Cabin, netting the ends of newly made pots, when Mike arrived.

"We've got to clear out from Fern Pit today," he announced. "There's a hurricane warning – winds northerly force 11 or 12."

From watching the tides, we knew that *Reaper*, drawing four feet three inches aft, would come afloat at four o'clock that evening. After Mike left, the wind increased dramatically. *Reaper* sat high and dry on the sand and the River Gannel was only a stream. Out beyond Crantock Beach however, the sea was a churning mass of storm driven waves.

At two o'clock, I went down to the boathouse. Mike and George were already there and they were discussing tactics. It would not be easy to get *Reaper* out of the berth with the wind pressing her in against the quay. There was also a great lump of rock jutting out in front of her bow. Mike decided that once clear of Fern Pit, instead of trying to reach our moorings at Trethellan, we would head for Penpol creek on the opposite side of the river Gannel. This small creek runs roughly east and west, and the steep wooded hill rising on its northern bank should give us good shelter from this storm.

It was fortunate indeed that we were down at the quay early. To our surprise, a wall of water several feet high came hissing and roaring, sweeping around the bend in the river. It surged ahead filling the whole river bed and *Reaper*, from sitting high and dry on the sand, became instantly afloat an hour and a half before we expected!

Mike started the engines and as George cast off our ropes, there was a danger that one of the big surfs coming in would drive *Reaper* up on the quay. Mike put the main engine astern. With the wing engine going full ahead and the helm hard to starboard, he coaxed the boat around the protruding rock. Suddenly we were charging upstream and we could see the surf breaking on both banks of the river all the way up.

Manoeuvring was very difficult as the wind was so strong. One enormous squall hit us so hard that the boat listed over to port, and the wind held us heeled over for what seemed like ages. During the squall, we could hardly see for flying spray. George told us later that he had lost sight of us when we reached the Corisand half a mile away, despite the fact that our mast headlight was on.

Very soon, we were crossing the main channel and heading into Penpol Creek. Lying in the creek, on permanent moorings, was the hundred foot long ex–MTB, *Ada*. We went alongside her and made fast temporarily. It was amazing the amount of 'run' we experienced there. It was like a mill race flowing up to the head of the creek for minutes on end, before turning and rushing back out again.

At one point, our stern rope pulled a fairlead off *Ada*'s bow. After half an hour, we felt that there was enough water to proceed up the creek, so we let go and moved ahead. Our luck was certainly in because there was Ron Greet in a punt coming out from under the trees to meet us. I climbed down into the punt with *Reaper*'s bow anchor and rope and shot it where Mike indicated. We came back and did the same with our stern anchor. Last of all we took a heavy rope from *Reaper* onto the shore and made it fast to a strong tree.

George Northey appeared at the water's edge. He had driven round to the Crantock side to see how we had fared. Ron ferried him across the few yards of water to join us aboard. When the two engines were stopped the noise of the wind was colossal, but the high land and the trees gave us great shelter. We saw other boats manoeuvring in the river. They were obviously having some problems. After some dodging about, one boat headed up the creek and came alongside us. It was Martin Burt's boat, the thirty–two foot *Cornishman* with Martin and his cousin, Chris on board. We took their ropes and when they were secured alongside, they told us that there was pandemonium up above at Tregunnel, with all the boats dragging their moorings and being driven against each other.

With our boats safely moored, we all crowded into *Reaper*'s tiny forepeak. We had a good fire going in the black iron stove to keep us warm, while the hurricane raged outside. We discussed plans for the morning. The boats would only be afloat for the brief period over the high water. That would be the dangerous time. Anything was likely to happen in those extreme conditions and it was essential that both crews be on board, in case an anchor dragged or a rope parted, so we would be able to use our engines and take whatever action was needed.

We could get aboard the boats in the morning before the rising tide reached them. I elected to go to Trethellen on my motor bike. I'd leave the machine at the bottom of the hill, then cross over the footbridge and reach the boats by that route. Martin and Chris said that they too would use the footbridge. George, who would know the Gannel better than anyone, and Mike figured what time we must be over the bridge before it was covered by the next morning's tide.

Soon the boats were on the ground and the tide had receded enough for us to be able to wade ashore. It was scary going up through the trees, with the noise of the wind and the branches waving madly about. The tempest showed no sign of abating. We reached the road and piled into George's car as he headed back towards Newquay. Before anyone climbed out, Mike said, "Now remember, you have to be at the footbridge by half past five tomorrow morning. Later than that and you won't get across, because the tide will be over it."

"Yes Mike," we chorused.

"And bring a torch to find your way through the woods," he added. "Not a minute after half past five mind! Don't be late!"

"No Mike," we sang reverently.

So that was it. When I got home, I set the alarm accordingly. It seemed that I had hardly closed my eyes when the alarm woke me. After a cup of tea and a slice of toast, I pulled on my thigh boots and started off to Trethellen, finding my way to the footbridge. By my pocket watch, it was twenty past five. The water seemed to be about eighteen inches below the boards of the walkway on the bridge. There is no handrail on the bridge so that boats can pass over it at high tide, so on this black, windy morning, the only way to cross without risking getting blown off, was to go on hands and knees and to grip the boards for dear life. Once over the bridge I crossed the sand and climbed the path until I was opposite the boats. I picked my way down through the trees, walked the few paces across the mud and hauled myself on board the *Reaper*.

A few moments later Mike arrived. It was now five thirty. We stood in the wheelhouse and peered into the blackness. There was no sign of Martin and Chris. Then at five thirty–five, headlights appeared, coming down Trethellen hill at a fair lick. The headlights went out and we could see only blackness. Then we saw the beam of a torch dancing swiftly along the water's edge to, presumably the footbridge. There was a bit more dodging about before it danced erratically back the way it had come. The headlights came on again, seesawed back and forth only to be replaced by red tail lights, which hurried away up the hill and vanished.

"'Tis them alright!" said Mike. "Now look what a bloody job they've got!"

Time passed and the tide reached the boats. That was when the rain started. Yells and curses came from the woods as Martin and Chris came plunging down through the undergrowth. They struggled across to the *Reaper* as the rising water threatened to come over the tops of their thigh boots. Gasping from their exertions, they hauled themselves on board.

"We nearly made it across the footbridge but the effing tide was over it!" they explained. "We had to drive all the shaggin' way round."

"You did?" said Mike, permitting himself a tiny smile.

There would be a few more high waters when we had to mind the boats in Penpol. By the time the storms eased off, we had had enough of the footbridge, the slippery way down through the trees and the sticky mud of the creek bottom.

On high water, the two boats steamed the short distance across the river to Trethellan. *Reaper* went bow in and I picked up our mooring buoy with the boat hook. We brought our chains aboard and tightened them in. *Cornishman* went bow in. Martin and Chris shot the anchor over the stern, but there was nothing to secure them ahead. Martin cured this by tying three ropes into the bushes! We pulled his leg about this and Mike called him 'Brimble' (as for Brambles) – a nickname that stuck for all time.

The Beach Seine

When the weather was right, we would walk the cliffs, hoping to see a shoal of mullet or bass. The ideal conditions were when the seas were calm and the winds light. Of course, you don't get many days like that in North Cornwall in winter. Even when the local weather is fine, there is often a ground sea. This is generated by weather disturbance in the deep ocean. It comes rolling onto the beaches as breaking surf, thus making beach seining impossible.

The beach seine net is usually quite large. There was a massive net owned at Sennan Cove and it took all the men in the village to haul it. In Newquay, Eddie Hoare owned one that was one hundred and twenty fathoms long and five fathoms (or thirty feet) deep in the centre, or bunt as it is called. The net tapered out towards its wing ends, where it finished at four feet deep. Attached to each wing end was a heavy rope called a warp. Each warp was manned by a team of eight to ten men, whose job it was to haul the net and its catch in to the beach. Once the wing ends reached the dry sand the fish could not escape – or could they?

With its leaded footrope, Eddie's net weighed about one ton. He had a 26ft boat kept especially for the beach seine. It was propelled by oars when the net was being shot. Eddie used his motor boat to tow the seine net boat to wherever the shoal of fish was located.

The first time I was involved in beach seining was the winter of 1964. From January on, we walked the cliffs on suitable days. It was a cold job, usually with easterly winds and plenty of frost. We covered every beach and cove from Watergate to Crantock. Some of the lads were real experts in assessing from the cliff tops, the amount and the type of fish present in a patch of 'colour' in the water. Several people reported finding shoals of fish, but when Mick Chegwidden or George Northey or one of the other experts studied it they would say, "No! 'Tis only settlement" or, "That is just smelt" (small sardine–like fish) or, "Yes 'tis mullet, but only a few baskets!"

One bitter cold day in early March, a patch of colour was seen off Whipsiderry. It was estimated to be about ten tons of mullet. Along with a score of other fishermen, I quickly made my way down the path from the high cliff top to the beach. Eddie's motor boat with the seine net boat in tow was already approaching Whipsiderry beach. Jimmy Hoare and other lads had the net laid up and were ready to shoot. Mick Chegwidden stayed at the top of the cliff to act as the 'Huer' and guide the seine net boat around the shoal. Jimmy slipped the tow rope and the seine net boat quietly approached the beach under oars. The end of the warp was passed to the team of ten men, who then held on to it. Jimmy steered out towards the open sea, his crew paying out the warp followed by the wing of the net. Mick waved, signalling for a turn to port. Jimmy put the tiller over and now the crew pulled strongly on the oars, driving the boat swiftly along parallel to the beach.

They were urged on by shouts from Mick, the huer, on the cliff top. He could see the shoal, which was showing signs of alarm and starting to move. At another signal from the huer, the boat raced, with bending oars, in towards the beach. We in the other team of ten dashed out into the shallows to meet the boat. We were dressed in our overalls and working clothes, but a bit of salt spray never worried us when there were fish about. We grabbed the second warp and ran up the beach with it. Now the two teams pulled with all their might and the two wing ends came up onto the sand.

There were excited shouts of, 'Keep her coming!' and, 'We've got 'em!' But then came disaster. Our team plunged headlong and I fell on my knees on the sand. I jumped up to see that the net had parted about ten feet from the wing end and the corks on the headline were drifting back out to sea. The fish were escaping!

I pulled out my knife and cut through the warp close to the net; then tying the warp around my waist with a bowline, I ran into the water. I saw that the net was drifting out away from me. I could only manage a breaststroke because of the weight of my clothes. I had to duck under a couple of waves, but being a trained surf lifesaver, this didn't bother me. However towing the heavy warp made it hard going. I reached the headline and pulled it around my body, and then twisted it around the warp because I realised that when the strain came on the warp, I would be pulled off the net.

Having now secured the net to the warp, I waved to the team on the beach to pull me in. They pulled manfully on the warp, which of course pulled me under water. To add to my problems the torn end of the net where I had turned it around the warp had caused the bowline knot to capsize. The warp was now a tightening noose around my waist, threatening to cut me in two. I was dragged ashore and Martin Burt, seeing me gasping whipped out his knife and sawed through the knot to release me. Chris Moffat grabbed me by the arm. "Come on," he said, "let's get you home!"

My clothes were heavy with salt water. I ran up the beach after him. It was a long way to the top of the cliff. Hard on Chris's heels, I stumbled and tripped and ran and, despite these exertions, I was getting colder by the minute. At the top of the cliff, we were exposed to the freezing easterly wind, as we ran to Chris's car. We climbed in and sped back to Newquay. Chris stopped at a shop in town. He ran in and bought a half bottle of brandy, which he thrust into my hands. Five minutes later, he delivered me to my door, where a warm fire and a change of clothes saved me from freezing solid.

It was a pity that the net had parted because the bulk of the fish escaped. We only got a share of three pounds per man. The following day Mike and I were discussing the whole adventure. I said, "There is something that puzzles me. My legs look as if they've been bruised. My thighs are black and blue."

"Seen it before," said Mike as though it happened every day. "Looks like you've been beaten with sticks. That's just the cold!"

The Beach Seine II

After Whipsiderry, we all went our various ways. Mike and I went back to the seemingly endless task of making the French–style barrel pots. A few days later word came in of another shoal of fish being sighted. This shoal was constantly on the move, particularly during the hours of darkness, so every morning started with a hunt to find out where the mullet were. Tantalisingly the fish just seemed to prefer the rocks, never venturing into a sandy beach where we could deal with them.

Other people were interested in our mullet too. It was rumoured that men from Par were coming, bringing a punt and net on a trailer. One day a rival gang did show up. We were following the shoal, which was moving to the northern end of Porth Island, when the two sides met. We walked up this grassy slope and suddenly there they were. The two groups of men stopped in their tracks. Each team was drawn up in a line facing the other in silence. I could feel the tension in the air. Our people discussed this situation in quiet tones. Someone had seen a lorry with a punt in it down near Porth beach. Someone else recognised some of the interlopers as coming from Sennan Cove. A voice from our side said, "Those mullet are ours!"

"Not if we get them first!" came the rejoinder.

I stepped forward and took a couple of paces towards the Sennan men. I removed my cap and said, "Look! This is the way things are. We have been following these mullet for over a week now and we are going to take them."

A crusty faced Sennan man pulled out his knife and opened its blade. I held my breath.

"See that net you've got?" he said with a sneer in his voice, "If I had that useless old cotton net I'd put this knife through the damn thing."

"Yeh," said another. "Your party will only frighten the fish and drive 'em and you'll get nothing!"

He spat the words out with contempt. He went on, "We've got a brand new nylon net with us that will take twenty tons."

I thought, "Wow! Nylon!" I had never seen a net made of nylon.

Verbal exchanges took place. The Sennan men were full of bluster. The Newquay men were grim–faced and determined. I looked at them all. Not only did we outnumber the Sennan men, but our guys were bigger. It just happens that men from Newquay generally were tall and solidly built. The men from Sennan eventually trooped off threatening, "We'll be back! Then we'll see!"

They knew really that the party was over for them. They had come hoping for a sneaky shot at the mullet while nobody was around. As it turned out nobody caught the mullet. The weather broke and the coast was battered by gales that lasted for weeks.

Mike and I settled in to serious pot making, up in our loft again. We were never short of company because, not only did the youngsters come and lend a hand, but we had Martin Burt as a neighbour on one side and Bill Brown in the other. Someone was always dropping in for a yarn and that relieved the tedium for us. Bill came in one day and talk turned to Newquay, when it was a busy trading port. Bill told us about being crew on the schooner, *Emma*, when his father was the captain.

"It was during World War One," said Bill. "We had taken on a cargo of Welsh coal. We were sheltering in Milford Haven in a south east gale and there were several other vessels there with us. Sometime during the night, we thought the gale had eased a bit, so we left and set a course for Newquay. Other schooners did the same, including the *Faery Maid* commanded by Captain Clemens, who was always known as Captain Todd. *Faery Maid* was a bit smaller than the *Emma*, but she was faster. She got ahead of us. Of course, it was a race to get to Newquay. Whoever got in first unloaded and got a quick turnaround. Because of the war, the ships carried no navigation lights. There was a lot of U–Boat activity in this area then. Captain Todd would come out on the stern of the *Faery Maid* every now and then, holding a lantern because he was afraid we would run him down. It was still blowing hard and if you looked up, you could see our foremast bending like that and our bowsprit bending like that!" said Bill, making shapes with his hands.

"The seas broke over her and she'd be all awash and when she freed herself, we'd dash out and pick up the mackerel in her scuppers! When it came daylight, the two ships were abreast of each other and we sailed through the Quies Rocks together. As we went through, a floating mine, one of them with horns on it, went passing close along our side. Once clear of the Quies, the *Faery Maid* would have beaten us, but suddenly her halyard parted and her topsail came crashing down. We crossed Newquay Bay and were approaching the harbour. Father was at the helm. He looked up and saw Mother waving to him from the headland. He took his hand off the wheel to wave back and with that, a puff of wind came off the cliff and put the sails aback. The rudder kicked and the wheel spun out of his grasp. The *Emma* took a sheer and she hit Listry, the submerged rock, with a great bang. It was so loud that stevedores working in the harbour heard the bang and ran to look over the wall."

"Was there much damage?" I asked.

"No there wasn't," said Bill. "When the tide went out and they had a chance to look at her, they found only one plank had a crack in it, where it was pushed in between two frames. All they did was patch it with canvas and tar and she continued sailing like that, until they were ready to have her slipped and repaired properly. She went to Liverpool to get fixed and the shipwrights there said that they had never seen a ship so strongly built."

More Seine Netting

January 1965 came in and interest in the beach seining was revived. The usual gang patrolled the cliff tops but, as weeks went by, nothing worthwhile was seen. In fact the sea looked remarkably empty everywhere. Enthusiasm waned a bit of course and most of us were lobstermen; and we were busy at this time of year getting our pots ready for the coming season.

There were always people watching for a shoal though, retired fishermen and others who knew a shoal of fish when they saw one. Whoever spotted a shoal of fish and reported it would automatically qualify for a full share of the catch, so that was a great incentive. However not everyone thought beach seining was a good idea. One crisp morning, when the frost lay thick on the ground, this old fellow yelled at us from his garden. "You should leave those mullet alone. If a holiday maker caught one of those it would keep him happy for the whole fortnight!"

Several answers came to mind but in the end, we simply ignored him.

By the beginning of February Mike was putting the Lister, *Reaper*'s main engine, together again, after its overhaul assisted by Graham Mountford, who should have been at school of course.

I spent 3 February working on our last year's pots, up on the stone jetty in the middle of the harbour. These pots would be the first to be used of course. Instead of going home for lunch, I decided to keep working up on the jetty, until the rising tide forced me to leave there to avoid being marooned. I knew that Pauline had made a steak and kidney pudding. This was my favourite dinner and she did it wonderfully well. I stayed on the jetty until the last minute. When I climbed down the ladder, onto the sand, the water was nearly up over my boots.

It was half past three when I walked into the house and I was starving by then. Pauline placed this lovely dinner on the table in front of me. Its centrepiece was this beautiful steaming pudding. As I stuck my fork into it, Jill Northey, who was ten years old at the time, arrived breathless at the door. There were fish in Porth she announced and I was to go up and help George to hitch the punt's trailer onto the car.

I dropped the knife and fork, pulled on my boots and ran up the path to George's garage. When I got there, George had his car reversed up to the trailer. The punt was lashed onto the trailer and George's beach seine was neatly stowed on board. George and I hitched up the trailer. We climbed into the car and George drove us to Porth. David Burt and Alf Waters helped George and I to unhitch the trailer and we all pulled it down to the water's edge. They told me there was perhaps fifteen tons of mullet in the shoal. Now this promised to be very interesting.

George's net was tiny by comparison with Eddie's net. It was about one hundred fathoms long, but only about two fathoms deep in the bunt and tapered down to two feet deep in the wing ends. George only intended it for random hauls in the Gannel estuary, small–scale stuff. Certainly, it was not made to shoot on a specific shoal of fish weighing several tons. However, this was no time for debating the finer points. This was the time for action! George had seen the fish and gathered the crew with all haste. The fish were outside Porth Island again. And George anticipated their next move would be up into the narrow inlet that formed Porth beach.

"We will only get one chance," he told us. "They will come right in on the top of the tide, then turn around and go off out to sea again!"

So we waited, while Mick Chegwidden and Mike Lyne took up separate positions on the high ground from where they could see the fish. Nothing happened until they saw a small part of the shoal split away from the main body and head in towards the beach.

Guided by signals from our huers, George, Dave, Alf and I launched the punt. The beach was very flat there and the boat was fifty yards out from the water's edge before she was properly afloat. George manned the oars while Dave and Alf shot the net. I took the end of the warp and ran back through the shallows with it. My lungs were bursting because I was hampered by my thigh boots. Mike Morris came to give me a hand and then Mick Chegwidden came running down from his vantage point on the island to join us.

Meanwhile the punt's crew had shot the net and, having succeeded in surrounding the fish, they raced in for the beach. Mike Lyne joined in with them, hauling on their warp. We hauled the net as far as we could, but the weight was too much for us. About a ton of mullet went out over the corks with a great whoosh and escaped.

We got the two wing ends in on the sand and we could do no more. Fish were escaping all the time. With a couple of the others, I waded around outside the net, while the rest of the lads held the two wings. When we got to the middle of the bunt, we lifted the head rope up. We were up to our armpits in the water and the net below the surface bellied out against our thighs. The fish pressed against us and as we strained to lift the head rope a few inches higher. The mullet went over our heads like flights of starlings. We stayed like that until the tide dropped back. It took a long time. As the water receded, the mullet became exhausted and the number of escapees dwindled down to a few.

By the time the fish were left high and dry it was completely dark. It was a clear night with a million stars and a big moon. A lorry came with aluminium fish boxes. We carried the boxes of fish up the beach to the road and loaded the lorry. A stream ran down across the beach, just where the lorry parked and the fresh water froze. As we walked on it, the ice broke and tinkled like broken glass. Nora Northey arrived with flasks of coffee and some rum, which saved us from freezing.

When the fish were sold on Newlyn market, they weighed two hundred and two stone. Our share per man was £40. It was most welcome. February is a hungry month!

Yarning

The Newquay men made their own pots back in the sixties. The various boats crews vied with one another to produce pots faster than their neighbours. Each outfit was convinced that their own gear fished better than any of their competitors. Mike and I made the French style barrel pots. The finished pot, made from chestnut hoops and laths fastened with clenched galvanised nails, was lovely to behold. It was stiff and strong, not round like a barrel but elliptical in shape, being slightly flattened at the bottom. Two dollops of concrete went into the bottom to ensure that the pot would sit firmly on the seabed.

Making pots was a good job to be at. In the beginning that is! As time went on and the completed pots began to stack up to the ceiling, you began to wonder if you would ever get to sea again. The only thing that did stave off the boredom for us was the number of people who just came into the loft for a friendly chat.

Looking through my diary for 1965, I see that the year started with a visit from Percy James, who told us of his wartime experiences in the Far East. He told us that when the Japanese overran Burma he was there, in the Royal Navy, but became isolated from the rest of his ship's company and got caught up in the British army retreat. He fought on with them, but for a long time he hadn't even got a rifle. He was running around in the jungle in his sailor suit, armed with a Navy cutlass, until they issued him with the proper gear. That is how he spent the entire war, fighting the Japanese as a foot soldier.

Mike Morris came up and told us about the boat he had just bought called *Trevose*, another St Ives gig, like the *Reaper* but bigger being thirty nine feet long.

Bill Brown came in from the loft next door and told us about taking a party of trippers around the bay. "There I was on the tiller minding my own business and there was this gent sat right up alongside me. He was smartly dressed in a suit and a white shirt. He kept asking me daft questions: 'Excuse me Boatman but what do you do in the winter?' I told him I'm a dentist be trade, only teeth pulling gets scarce in the summer time! Anyway, the mizzen sail had been freshly barked and suddenly the heavens opened up. He was sat directly under it and as the rain poured down, I watched him change colour. His face, his hands, his shirt, the lot, turned bright red!"

The Burt brothers, John, Mickey and David who had a loft quite near at hand, came in occasionally. The talk would be of lobsters, crawfish and beach seining. Our other neighbours, Martin 'Brimble' Burt and his cousin Chris often came in for a chat too.

Brimble was trying to get his boat, the *Cornishman*, out of the Gannel so he could berth her in the harbour, but the weather wouldn't let him. He was out on Pentire every day looking at the sea. As he said, "It was either a guts full of westerly wind or else it was ground sea breaking right across Crantock"

Mick Chegwidden was a regular caller. He was really mad about fishing. In summer, he hauled his few lobster pots and in the autumn, he set bay nets for herring. He was an electrician and fished part time though his heart was down in Newquay Harbour.

He told us about getting an electric shock. He grabbed a live wire by mistake and the current went through his body. He couldn't let go! He said, "I must have been going to black out. All I could hear was this thumping noise. It was getting slower and slower, like a diesel engine slowing down. Someone realised what was happening and switched the power off. What I had been listening to was my heart slowing down!"

Of course, he usually talked about fishing. Like the day he got a basking shark, bigger than his punt, stuck in his bay nets and what a struggle he had with it.

Rodney Lyon was skipper of the forty foot, *Freeman* and like some of the others, he had fished in boats from Newlyn for pilchards or been longlining on the bigger boats. Like the Burt brothers and Mick Chegwidden, Rodney got on well with the 'Frenchmen'. These were French crabbers who came to fish our coast every summer. We were kept up to date with the adventures of boats like the *La Salle*, the *Petit France* the *Emigrant* and others. These boats were family owned and the men had been fishing the Cornish coast for years. They were all from the town of Camaret in Brittany and were always welcome. However, company owned boats from other towns, like Lorient and Audierne, had a very bad reputation. They were always poaching inside the three–mile limit as it was then. It was said that some of them had pulled, or even stolen the Cornish lad's pots. None of the Camaret boats were ever accused of such behaviour.

Some of the Cornish men went over to Camaret on holiday and stayed in the homes of their fishermen friends, who made a great welcome for them. There was a language problem for us all, but we managed! I think only Rodney managed to speak some Breton, but then he was starting to study Cornish and Celtic languages at the time, so I suppose he would!

By mid–February pot making was drawing to a close. It didn't matter whether you made one hundred or two hundred pots, finishing the last five or six would really do your head in. As John Burt said, "The fishing is easy. Making pots is the hard part. If you can stick this, you can stick anything!"

Well anyway, thanks to our many friends, and not forgetting the youngsters who helped us, we had struggled through. The talk had helped. We talked of times past and of those who had gone before. We yarned about fish and fishing. We talked about French men, Padstow men and the men of St Ives. We didn't speak of our women, or gossip about our neighbours. Fishing was our life. We talked shop.

The Predators

Whatever anyone said about Harvey's, they did provide a great service to us Fishermen. Their lorry arrived on Newquay's south pier twice a week throughout the summer, except for the times when our fishing was interrupted by bad weather. Walter, the lorry driver, was a hard worker. He usually arrived alone and as soon as he parked the lorry, we would bring up our crabs, lobsters and crawfish in baskets. During the next couple of hours, the crews would land in turn. Sometimes four or five thousand pounds weight of shellfish would be weighed, receipted and packed into wooden barrels and boxes by Walter.

Some of the fishermen did not make things easier for him. One or two of them would be awkward, while the rest were in a rush to get away to sea. There was a fair amount of teasing and leg pulling going on as well and how Walter kept his concentration during his hectic visits was a mystery. Somehow, he always managed to bring us the news and the stories from the other ports around the Cornish coast.

It was towards the end of the summer of 1963 that we first heard about the skin divers.

"There's Hell up down west!" said Walter as he packed our crawfish into the barrels. "The St Ives men are up in arms about the skin divers landing a few craws."

He picked up another six–pound crawfish by its horns and expertly tucked the tail under the body before placing it in the barrel. "I don't know what all the fuss is about, the bit of stuff they're landing won't hurt anyone."

"Oh well," said one of our lads, "You know what they're like down St Ives, a bit old fashioned." And that was that!

We all hurried off and put to sea before the falling tide could leave our boats caught on the sand. We gave no more thought to Walter's casual remarks. Indeed why should we?

One fine day in 1964, a boat approached from the westward at high speed. We had just shot a string of pots, and were steaming for the next dhan, when the boat's white bow wave caught Mike's attention. It proved to be the *Cornubia*, the Fisheries Protection vessel for the Cornwall Sea Fisheries Committee. She quickly overhauled us and Mike put the *Reaper's* engines into neutral as she came alongside.

In command was Clifton Pender, Chief Fisheries Officer for the Committee. He invited us aboard to show us what *Reaper* looked like on his radar. We climbed aboard the *Cornubia*, which then steamed away from our abandoned *Reaper* at about seventeen knots. Clifton invited us to look into the radar screen. I got a surprise. I did not expect to see this large blob of light on the screen. *Reaper* made as big an echo as a steel freighter. Clifton explained that this was caused by the new radar reflector that Mike had recently mounted on the foremast. After a bit of friendly chat we were put back aboard *Reaper* and they steamed away east. We had met Clifton before of course and he seemed a nice guy.

Shortly after this, John Rhodes, a diver buddy of Clifton, came out with us. We were curious to know what this diving lark was all about. We had our pots in the vicinity of an undersea rock known as Pells. We took our diver there because that piece of ground was always good for a few craws, though it never produced large numbers. In two twenty minute dives, he had a total of seventeen crawfish on board, and they all came from the same spot! Mike and I were alarmed. We realised that if this is what one diver could do, then a few more could make short work of the fishing grounds. John had already told us that he and Clifton often went off in the *Cornubia* and had themselves landed great quantities of craws.

Now we understood the St Ives men! How galling it must have been for them to have to watch this big, fast, high–tech launch working on their fishing grounds. The boat, the fuel and Clifton's salary, all were being paid for by the Cornish ratepayers, which included themselves! Mike and I decided there and then to have nothing more to do with skin divers. Now that we had seen it for ourselves, we just hoped that the divers would stay away.

We were soon fishing at full stretch. We never missed a tide and hauled our hundred and twenty–five pots, three times a day. Newquay's tidal harbour dictated that we must be steaming out of the gap at three o'clock on some mornings. Perhaps that is why we never noticed the sudden increase in local diving activity. I think Bill Sharrock was the first of the boatmen to carry divers. The term 'skin divers' is misleading because these divers wore the full rubber wet suit with flippers and they used compressed air bottles.

Bill fished about sixty wire pots, part time. He would never normally catch crawfish, as his pots were only suitable to catch lobsters. He spent his summers taking holidaymakers on trips around the bay. George King and some of the other boatmen joined in the diving for crawfish business. There was no shortage of divers either. The RAF base at nearby St Mawgan had plenty of them.

At first, they didn't impact upon us at all, and they had little success. However as their numbers increased, things quickly changed. In a few short weeks, the divers also discovered what the fishermen had always known, that the crawfish were in small isolated groups. Between these groups, there were also vast areas of rock, which appeared ideal crawfish habitat but in fact held only a few crabs and lobsters. From the diver's point of view, the answer was very simple. With their time under water limited to about thirty minutes, they couldn't afford to go hunting all over the rocky ground in the hope of finding crawfish. Instead, all they needed to do was to steam until they found the fishermen's marker buoys and then dive on his gear.

Because of the continual hunt for crawfish, each fishing boat often had strings of pots miles apart. This meant that while you were hauling your eastern strings, you couldn't know that divers were busy on your western strings a couple of miles away. You might see the boat alright, but there was plenty of boat activity in the summer, so you wouldn't know if it was a boat with anglers or trippers. By the time you went to haul the western gear, the diver's boat would be gone. They didn't need to take the fish out of the pots. Crawfish, unlike lobsters do not hide among the rocks, but wander about over the small area in considerable numbers. All the divers had to do was to pick them off the rocks with their gloved hands, stuff them into sacks and pass them up into their boat. This put the fishermen in serious trouble because when they hauled their pots and had reasonable fishing, they would shoot back in the same area.

Pots only catch craws that are feeding. They go into the pot, lured by the bait. So you could re–shoot the pots in the same place for several hauls, only ever getting hungry fish in prime condition and leaving any fish that may be off their food, or in the process of changing their shell. The craws moult regularly as they grow and soft new shells are exposed. These harden up in a few weeks, but since the divers took everything they could see around the pots, they took the 'soft shellers' too. Many were so soft that you could poke your fingers through the shells. They couldn't survive being handled and many died. When the tide went out their dead bodies littered the sand in Newquay Harbour. Incidentally, by taking everything, the divers were no longer landing only good quality fish, so the price went down for everyone!

It was no use shooting back if the divers had been on the ground. Suddenly knowledge of the grounds handed on from previous generations and learned the hard way by the fishermen was rendered useless. Now they never knew where the divers had been.

The days were growing longer and the fishermen were working longer hours, as was usual at this time of year. All of them were deprived of sleep and, because of the heavy nature of the work, they were physically tired. They certainly didn't welcome the extra work forced upon them by having to continually load and shift strings of pots again and again, because the areas became denuded of crawfish.

Almost all the divers belonged to RAF St Mawgan's Sub Aqua Club. To our annoyance, we learned that they had their air bottles charged for free and that the purchase of diving equipment was subsidised. They were being helped to destroy our livelihood, with the aid of taxpayers' money! Feelings were running very high. An RAF diver who had been going out with the boatmen now bought the lovely little *Westward Ho*. Considering the raw anger and frustration we felt towards these divers, it surprises me now that nobody actually lost control and rammed a diver's boat. Fishermen sometimes found them bobbing about above their pots loaded with craws. In any other walk of life, this situation must have resulted in bloodshed. I can only believe that, like all fishermen, the Newquay men lived with the constant threat of drowning at sea and so it was not in their nature to put anyone's life at risk on the water. Their instinct would be the very opposite.

Meanwhile most divers had no experience of boats. They would not be aware of the 'rule of the road at sea' nor know that their diving boat should fly the appropriate flag. Most of them were inexperienced divers too! When there was a gang of them, they often wandered away from the dive boat and popped up unexpectedly. That none of them was accidentally run down is a minor miracle!

Back ashore, The Critics were having a ball. Because of their knowledge of all things maritime, they were able to supply the town with up to the minute news items. We would hear back stories of confrontations between fishermen and divers. It was true that tempers flared and hard words were spoken. These incidents were nothing like the colourful stories circulated by The Critics. I wasn't there on the quay the time the police came down. They warned some of the fishermen, "If anything happens to these divers, you are for the High Jump!"

Since nothing had happened, one can only suppose the police were alarmed by all the tittle–tattle. Shortly after this someone stole the rudder from the *Westward Ho*. Naturally, the fishermen were suspected. Whether the rudder was removed while the tide was out, or was taken while the boat was afloat on her moorings nobody knew. It was never seen again and *Westward Ho* was kept in harbour for two weeks whilst a new one was being made.

The price of craws was depressed to four shillings a pound. We blamed this on the divers operating all around the Cornish coast. When the divers wanted to land to Harvey's lorry while we were landing our fish, we objected and Ronnie had to make other arrangements for them. As Chairman of Newquay Fishermen's Association, I wrote to Cornwall Sea Fisheries Committee, The Newquay Chamber of Commerce and to our local MP. I also had letters printed in the local newspaper and the weekly *Fishing News*. The Sea Fisheries Committee ignored us. The Newquay Chamber of Commerce supported us. We managed to arrange a meeting with John Pardoe of the Liberal Party, who was most sympathetic and also with Scott Hopkins of the Conservatives, who was quite snooty and said, "The sea is free to everyone!" He also warned me, "Be careful what you write in the newspapers!"

It did seem that the fishermen had very few friends. Many local people thought that we were old fashioned and diving was the modern method. Only the fishermen were aware of the damage being done.

Feeding Time

Clem Brown owned the aquarium at the harbour. He was a most pleasant man. From his accent, I believe he came from London, but he lived in Newquay with his wife and his daughter, Janet and he had been there for a great many years.

His aquarium was situated inside an old railway tunnel. The tunnel entered the cliff underneath the South Quay Hill and the other end of it had at one time emerged up in the Town. In former times, railway lines ran through this tunnel carrying trucks full of cargo to schooners in Newquay Harbour. These days the rails were no more and Clem had installed his fish tanks in there. He charged visitors sixpence each to walk in and have a look around.

Clem had built the tanks out of concrete with glass in front and had seawater circulating around them. It really was a work of art. Some of the fish knew Clem because it was he who always fed them and, incredible as it sounds, whenever Clem walked close to the tanks, some fish, the bass and the mullet in particular, would press against the glass and try to follow him. They just ignored everyone else.

Every year Clem went away on holiday for a month and Mike and I would feed the fish during his absence. This was easy because twice a week was enough and it was soon accomplished. We used to enjoy it. There was a big open tank that was shallow. It was very natural and it was really like looking into a big rock pool. The water was as clear as gin. This was Clem's lobster tank and we found it very instructive. We would throw a small piece of fish into the middle and watch how quickly even the most distant lobster, became aware that the bait was in the water. We saw that the big brute of a cock lobster always intimidated the others and got the bait first.

Clem was always seeking new specimens for his aquarium. If anything unusual like a cuckoo wrasse or any strange crabs came up in the lobster pots, Clem would pay handsomely for them. Sometimes he booked us for a day's fishing. We hated this, although he paid us well. He would come out in the boat with us and we would have several tubs full of seawater on deck. Each tub had a piece of heavy plywood floating on its surface to stop the fish jumping out. We would get the pollack feathers down but, when the pollack or blackjacks were hooked on, instead of us being allowed to haul like lunatics, we had to haul up the lines slowly and gently. This was to prevent the swim bladders inside the fish from expanding and killing them. Oh! But you could feel the fish getting off the hooks. All the best ones escaped and you'd be left carefully pulling this miserable little juvenile on board and placing it with tender loving care into a tub and covering it up! It was frustrating but Clem would be as pleased as punch.

One day he asked us for a couple of big crabs, so we picked him two beauties from our day's catch. Jack crabs were one and eight pence a pound, but of course, Clem paid us better than that for them. After about six months, the two crabs seemed to have lost interest in life and just sort of sat there looking bored. The trouble was that their complexion had changed, from being a healthy terracotta colour to a sort of grey prison pallor. We told Clem we would release them. We took them and popped them into one of our store boxes for the time being. Of course, when landing day came we let them go up onto Harvey's lorry with the rest. In the middle of landing the crabs, Walter suddenly gave a shout, "Where the hell did you get these?"

He demanded. "They came up in the pots same as the rest," said Mike

Walter plonked the two big crabs down on the deck of the lorry where they shuffled about miserably. "Look at them!" He protested, "They're not even the proper colour. I can't take them!"

"Them crabs are perfect. I reckon those two came off a wreck," Mike argued.

Walter picked up each crab and shook it, listening to hear if it was watery and pressing his thumbs underneath its shell to see if it was soft. It was a point of honour with Walter that nobody got a dodgy crab past him. Mike kept talking and in the end, Walter packed them away with the rest.

The next landing day, as we approached his lorry Walter pounced, "Them two crabs were useless! We boiled them up and there was nothing in 'em only water!"

"Well I'm darned!" said Mike. "Fancy that!"

There was a sea trout in Clem's aquarium. It was about twelve inches long and it enjoyed the freedom of a big tank all to itself. It zoomed up and down and cavorted about, making a great show. It was really a bit of a pet.

Mike and I were longlining at the time and, knowing Clem was eager for specimens, we kept a lookout for anything wonderful and strange. We settled on a monkfish, so when we caught one of about four and a half pounds weight we kept it and brought it in to Clem. He was delighted with it and decided it would look nice in with the sea trout. When he put the monkfish in the tank, it just sat on the bottom like a big fat tadpole, minding its own business. Meanwhile the trout continued its aquabatics near the surface. Despite its sluggishness, the monkfish looked interesting with its camouflage, its staring eyes and with its little antennae sticking up from its head. Three mornings after the monkfish's arrival, Clem entered his aquarium to find the sea trout gone! None of us had considered the Monkfish's antenna, with its little artificial bait, dangling above its innocent smile.

Perhaps the best specimen Clem bought from us was the conger eel, simply because it grew so fast. It was about three feet long and no thicker than a man's forearm when it went into Clem's tank. A few years later however, he was over four feet long and as thick as your thigh. It had made its home in a big drainpipe but now, having outgrown the pipe, it just left its tail inside, while the rest of its powerful body was up against a corner of the tank, where the glass joined the concrete. Clem assured us that the conger did move around sometimes, but we never saw it move away from its favourite corner. It would be breathing gently, with its big mouth slightly agape, head up near the surface of the tank.

Before one of his trips away, Clem was explaining to us how to feed the conger. "He's very finicky. He won't pick a fish up off the bottom of the tank. You have to drop it right on his nose."

So saying he held a mackerel by the tail and dangled it above the surface. When released it landed on the conger's snout. The conger didn't even flinch and the mackerel sank to the bottom.

"See what I mean?" said Clem, "He will take it eventually if you keep trying him."

Clem leaned in over the tank with a six–foot long cane, which he kept handy for the purpose. He hooked the dead mackerel up off the bottom and balancing it on the tip of the cane, he carefully placed it on the conger's snout again. There was not even a twitch out of the conger and the bait fell down once more. Mike and I were surprised by this behaviour because congers were dangerous brutes, who tore the baits out of our pots, munched up lobsters and tried to maim us. They were all action and yet this one, apart from tiny gill movements, could have been dead. Well, after five or six go's, the conger did take the mackerel and his jaws made a bang as they closed on it. Then, with one sudden convulsion, the mackerel vanished down the Conger's throat and all was still again.

"And do mind your fingers!" warned Clem as we left.

Clem went off on his holiday and, after a day or two, Mike and I came in from sea and brought a basket with some mackerel in it, to feed the aquarium fish. Some of the lads were standing in a group talking nearby and seeing what we were about, they got interested. Mike unlocked the door and the gang trooped in after us. Among them was Geoff Morris. Geoff was a great character. You would hear his voice above everyone else's and he wore his white peaked cap at a jaunty angle. He did the summer boat trips and visitors loved him.

Well the boys watched us while I cut up the mackerel and Mike fed the fish, little tiny bits for the grey mullet, bigger bits for the bass and so on. They enjoyed the show and had a good laugh. Geoff was a great comic and his comments were priceless.

Mike approached the conger's tank with a mackerel in one hand and the long cane in the other. He was just about to offer up the mackerel and was repeating what Clem had told us about the conger's finicky eating habits, when Geoff jumped up beside him.

"Gimme that," he roared. "I'll show you how to feed the bloody thing!" and he snatched the mackerel from Mike and thrust it over the tank. Whereupon the Conger leapt up like lightening, its jaws snapped shut with an explosive bang as it snatched the mackerel clean out of Geoff's fingers.

"Oh my God," yelled Geoff, staggering back clutching his chest with both hands. He sat down on a concrete step and rocked back and forth saying, "Jesus Christ! I thought the fucker had me!" a couple of times. Then, counting his fingers, he gradually recovered his composure.

We all had a great laugh over that.

Time Flies When You're Enjoying Yourself

That spring of 1965 was a time of frantic activity. The pressure was on to get the pots and gear ready for sea. Painting and refitting boats and engines speeded up as the daylight hours stretched. Any day that the wind came off the land and the sea died down a bit, we would walk the cliffs, searching for a shoal of mullet or bass. Generally, the weather was awful though.

On 10 February, we learned that the Cornwall Sea Fisheries Committee had decided to accept divers as bona fide fishermen. They also declared that there was no evidence of over fishing of crawfish stocks. Rodney Lyon, Newquay Fishermen's Association's secretary, wrote to the Cornwall SFC demanding that they meet with the traditional fishermen. As the Association's chairman, I wrote to the local and national newspapers describing how divers were destroying the crawfish.

On the 6 March the *Reaper* lay alongside George Northey's little Quay at Fern Pit. Mike and I were on board finishing off the last minute jobs before heading for our berth in Newquay Harbour. We were surprised when Pauline came down the cliff path to tell us that Nora had received a phone call from Rodney Lyon. The message was that there was a very important fishermen's meeting taking place that day in the Seaman's Mission in Newlyn. My attendance was required.

I ran up home to Vyrn Cabin and changed out of my overalls. Mike then drove me to John Burt's house. John and Rodney were already waiting in John's van. I climbed in and we set off at once. As we pulled away from Newquay, we all agreed that we must avoid going drinking. We knew that with so many fishermen gathered there, the temptation would be enormous and we were all just too busy getting ready to fish to let ourselves get involved. We would go to the meeting. We would say our piece and we would head for home immediately.

We arrived at the Seaman's Mission in good time. The place was packed with fishermen from all around the Cornish coast. When I got a chance to speak, I attacked the Cornwall Sea Fisheries Committee and their Chief Sea Fishery Officer, Clifton Pender. I also gave the Government Man, Geoffrey Woolaston, who was present at the meeting, a good few broadsides too. I was a bit sorry about this, because Geoffrey was actually a nice bloke, but these things really needed saying.

I read out our association's Resolution, which met with shouts of approval. On foot of this, the meeting voted unanimously to attend the forthcoming meeting between the Cornish Sea Fisheries Committee and the Cornish Fishermen en mass! A strategy was then agreed by the Fishermen. It was decided that if things went against us, then I would propose a vote of no confidence in the Cornwall Sea Fisheries Committee and their Chief Sea Fisheries Officer. The Skipper of the 50ft *Renevelle*, Jimmy Madron from Mousehole, would second the proposal.

As soon as the meeting ended, we nipped out and got into the van. With John at the wheel, we were soon threading our way through the crowd of lads emerging from the Seamen's Mission. We were almost clear when Geoffrey Woolaston came up to the window of the van.

"I say! Would you chaps join me for a small beer?" he asked.

We looked at each other. In that split second, we knew we were doomed! We had given poor Geoff such a hard time and yet here he was offering the olive branch. How could we refuse? To do so would have been churlish in the extreme. John parked the van and we walked across the road to the pub called The Swordfish (or Stringbag as it was known). We soon saw that the bar was crowded with fishermen already.

"We ain't going in there," says John Burt. "We'll never get home. Let's go into the snug instead."

He led the way in through the other door and into the snug. It was the very same in there; it was packed. We squeezed in and Geoffrey managed to battle his way up to the bar and get in a round of beer. It was like Christmas and New Year rolled into one and the atmosphere was simply magic. There were so many lads we knew from the different ports. I found myself next to Jimmy Madron, who was great company. He told me about his boat the *Renevelle* and Ernie Steven's boat the *Sweet Promise* when they were both herring drifting from Dunmore East in southern Ireland. Meanwhile, the beer kept flowing and it was quite a while before we managed to extricate ourselves. After lots of farewells and handshakes, we got back in the van and trundled out of Newlyn on the road home. We congratulated ourselves on having escaped the worst of the mega piss up, which was obviously taking shape in the Stringbag.

Now it happens that after a few miles the road passes the Hayle estuary. Passing through Hayle, we saw some French crabbers against the wharf.

"Hey, there's the *La Salle*!" said Rodney.

"Yes," said John, steering the van towards them, "and the *Emigrant*. We'd better go aboard and say hello!"

We climbed aboard the *La Salle* and the Frenchmen invited us down into their tiny cabin. They didn't speak any English and we had no French, but that didn't matter. Rodney had picked up a few words of Breton (he would) so that was a help. We were made most welcome and in no time at all, out came the bottles of red wine. A variety of chipped and battered tin mugs were lined up on the table and we drank a toast to, er, Cornish/Breton good relations or something and we plonked our empty mugs down on the table for a refill. We drank another toast to something similar and after one or two more, having democratically arrived at a consensus, mainly through sign language, we trooped across the decks and all squeezed into the *Emigrant*'s cabin.

"Ah!"

"Greetings!"

"Bon Soir!"

Out came the tin mugs and bottles of red wine.

"A toast!"

"Another toast!"

Bottles of brandy suddenly replaced the bottles of wine. Brandy sloshes into the mugs. Language is not a problem. Rodney's Breton is improving by the minute. I start singing, "Frerer Jacka Dormy voo," and all the Frogs join in. Somebody opens a seat locker and brings out dry salted herrings. Using their sharp, wooden handled gutting knives our hosts side fillet the herrings. They saw up hunks of bread. The herring fillets are firm and tough. The flesh is yellow. Bread, herring and best French cognac, what could be nicer? I didn't realise I was so hungry. I ate a few sides of herring and the brandy sloshed into the mugs again.

"Merci! More herring? Don't bother to fillet it Mate. I like the head, the guts and the bones as well."

Nobody seemed surprised at my preference. It was that kind of an evening! At last, it was time to be on our way. We bade fond farewells in French, English and Breton, and exchanged hugs and handshakes and, "see you agains".

We stepped onto the wharf in the darkness. The rain pelted down on us. We climbed into the van and John started up. The van seesawed back and forth.

"We're stuck," said John. "You'll have to get out and push!"

Rodney and I got out. Hayle Wharf was also a coal yard and the van was bogged down in the deep ruts and puddles in the coal dust. We pushed while John revved up the engine. The wheels spun, spraying muck and black water. We pushed harder. Suddenly the van shot ahead and I sprawled full length into a big black puddle. I picked myself up and, wringing wet, climbed into the cab beside Rodney.

"Well, Dammit!" said John. "We're late as it is. The damage is done. Let's go to St Ives to round the night off!"

"'Ess, Good Idea!" said Rodney.

So off we went, hauling up outside the pub called The Sloop. We went in and ordered up pints of bitter. I was glad to sit down; the salt herring was beginning to affect my sense of balance. When Rodney went up for the third round of bitter, I called out, "Not for me Rodney. I've had it!"

John said understandingly, "It's alright Trevor. We know how you'm placed!"

After my companions had finished their pints, John drove us home. The drink didn't seem to affect him at all. I promised myself that I would never again get into drinking pint for pint with John Burt, because of his awesome capacity. (I have forgotten this vow, to my detriment, several times since that night.).

Anyway, while we were carousing our women were worrying. Auntie Mollie came down from her house, "Weona" to tell Pauline that Mrs Burt had been on the phone, because Mrs Lyon had rung her to see if there was any news of us. An hour later, Pauline was up at Fern Pit calling Mrs Burt on Nora Northey's phone, to know if she had heard anything yet. So it went, their anxiety mounting: had there been an accident or what?

At midnight, Pauline went to bed. Somewhat later, I staggered into the bedroom, disrobing as I approached the bed. I was about to slip quietly between the sheets, when Pauline suddenly awoke. If her face bore an expression of horror, then I never noticed it.

"You're surely not going to get into bed like that?" she said gently.

"Like what?" I asked her.

"Well!" she answered, picking her words carefully, "You are, sort of, black. I mean look at yourself!"

I glanced down at my hands and forearms, "Ye Gods! How did that happen?" I yelled in surprise. My arms, my legs, my feet! I stared at them in amazement.

"Go on. Look at yourself in the mirror," she continued. "You need a bath!"

The be–whiskered face, streaked with black like war paint, was strange and terrible indeed. Of course! It was the coal yard, the black dust, the rain, the puddle I fell into when the van was bogged. It all came flooding back to me. I discarded the socks and underpants and stepped into the shower.

"What kept you so late?" she called.

"Late?" I queried.

"What time do you think it is then?" she asked.

"I dunno about nine o'clock," I burbled.

Dear Diary

I started keeping the diary to record the weather and the numbers of crawfish and lobsters we caught. Basically that, together with the areas we fished, was supposed to be all of it. It just kind of grew then so that before very long, I was adding scraps of information about what was happening to other fishermen besides us. As the year advanced, more and more details were added. Snatches of conversations were included and sometimes stories recounted to us by other people, were faithfully written up.

A diary is a peculiar thing, especially if, like this one, it is left in a box in the attic for forty years. Just reading through it has triggered so many memories. Sometimes a single sentence will transport me back to Newquay. Suddenly I am down the harbour. The tide is out and I am standing on the yellow sand. The sun is baking the seaweed on the harbour wall. It smells good. Reading on, other scenes are evoked. The boats are all wooden and smartly painted. As the tide floods into the harbour, they slip their moorings and head out to sea. Their mizzen sails are of barked canvas, red–brown in colour. Rope is made from manila or sisal. The men are young and strong.

The diary is not a complete story but at least it shines a small light on our working lives at that time. In some parts, the diary is very patchy indeed. It tells the beginning of an interesting story, but then there is not one more word dedicated to it.

For example, the entry for 26 January states, "Sammy Malone's motor boat *Silvia* was leaving harbour. Sammy and his son and another youth were going to take the boat to Padstow, to have some work done to her. Unfortunately, Mick Chegwidden's punt's stern rope went into the *Silvia*'s propeller. In so doing *Silvia*'s propeller shaft was pulled out of its coupling."

That's fine, but it doesn't complete the story! That's my crib with it. You can flip through the remaining three hundred odd pages and there is not a peep about it. The diary leaves poor Sammy and the two lads standing dejected and forlorn on the quay. Poor Sammy is left in limbo land with his boat in tatters. This is most unkind! Anyway, there is nothing to be done about it now so, despite the diary's obvious shortcomings, we have to proceed and make the best of it.

On 23 February, Rodney Lyon wrote to the Cornwall Sea Fisheries Committee demanding that they meet with the Fishermen to discuss the problems caused by divers.

15 March

Weather has been terrible. Gale force 8–9 with continuous heavy ground seas. We decided to go to Harvey's with our shellfish. Four of us went to Newlyn, George Northey, Mickey Burt, Mike and I. After delivering the fish to Harvey's, we called in on Tom Cotton, Clerk to the Newlyn Harbour Master. We talked to him about the divers and felt that he was very much on our side. We discussed the attitude of the Cornwall Sea Fisheries Committee and he was full of sound advice.

Leaving Tom Cotton's office, we went to the office of the White Fish Authority to see Geoffrey Woolaston (poor Geoffrey), to further discuss the problems caused by the divers. We were all pretty steamed up about the whole business. The answer we had received from the Committee stated that there would be a meeting in the County Hall, in Truro, on Wednesday 17 March, but only a sub–committee would meet us. Members of the press were to be excluded.

16 March

Rodney Lyon and I met in the Cadoc Café to discuss the Resolution, to see if we could improve it, but we didn't come up with any new ideas, so we left it as it stood. I was very wound up all day, in case I had to propose the vote of no confidence at tomorrow's meeting, as we'd agreed at the big meeting of fishermen in Newlyn.

I was very conscious that I had no experience of big important meetings of this scale. I was daunted, because many of Cornwall's most respected and experienced fishermen would be present, though I was not one bit afraid of the civil servants, scientists or politicians who might be there. I was afraid of making a hash of things, of missing something vital, of letting the side down.

In the evening, I phoned Jack Worth of Newlyn and read him the Newquay men's Resolution. He liked it, so I asked Auntie Molly (Molly Wride) to type it for me. I took courage from the fact that I knew, from talking on the telephone to 'Groupie' Lombard and Trevor England from Padstow, that we had the support of the Padstow men. George Northey was selected to go with me. I was glad of that because George was intelligent and reliable.

17 March: St Patrick's Day

It being a full moon, I wonder was there something weird and esoteric going on? I rather think it was merely the 'butterflies–in–the–tummy' I was feeling that morning, as George drove us to Truro in his Morris Minor Traveller.

When we arrived at the County Hall in Truro, we found a great crowd of fishermen already gathered there. I saw many familiar faces, but there were far more men who were strangers to me. County Hall contains a large room, with all the seating forming a semi–circle facing in towards the podium or top table. In fact, it is a proper custom–built Council Chamber. We filed inside and took our seats there.

The first two hours were taken up by a meeting with the Ministry of Agriculture Fisheries and Food (MAFF) scientists, Mr Basil Hepper and Dr Simpson, with Mr Williams as Chairman. A very warm discussion took place. The fishermen asked some very direct questions about diving and the effects on stocks. At first, it seemed the scientists were going to flannel their way out of giving direct answers, but the fishermen weren't having it and refused to be side–tracked. I took no interest in this. I cared little about the migrations of brown crab or the life cycle of Palinurus (crawfish). I was just glad of the two hours meeting because it was giving me time to acclimatise myself to the big occasion and the large crowd.

At the end of that meeting, Mr Williams vacated the Chair and his place was taken by Commander W.B. Luard, Chairman of the Cornwall Sea Fisheries Committee. Beside him, on one side, sat Clifton Pender, the Chief Sea Fisheries Officer for the county with Mr Verger, the Committee's Secretary, seated on the other side. This then was the sub–committee, which now sat facing us. At a table drawn up next to theirs sat seven divers, who also faced the audience. This arrangement struck me as being very strange indeed!

The meeting started quietly enough. George and I sat side–by–side, saying nothing and just listening to the proceedings. One fisherman after another stood up to make his point. The divers kept butting in on whoever was speaking. Commander Luard didn't interfere or call them to order in any way. The most vocal of the divers was a man called Cowan–Dickie. There were some very good speakers among the fishermen. In particular, there was a man called Penberth, another was Hunkin from Mevagissey and there was Charley Laity from Portleven. There were many others who could have contributed so much to a sensible debate, but instead of that, the meeting was deteriorating rapidly. The divers continued interrupting as fishermen tried to speak. Unrestrained by the Chairman, they seemed to be enjoying themselves.

The fishermen next turned their attention to Pender. When he dodged their questions, they pulled him to pieces and let him know what they thought of him. The Chairman now admonished the fishermen continuously. I felt that the dreaded moment had come. I couldn't see my seconder, Jimmy Madron, but just hoped he was somewhere in the hall. I stood up and shouted, "Mr Chairman, I propose a vote of no confidence in the Cornwall Sea Fisheries Committee and its Chief Fishery officer Clifton Pender!"

Immediately I heard Jimmy Madron shout, "And I second that!"

I saw him then over on my right. It gave me a great lift. Pandemonium broke out. The Chairman shouted, "Order! Order!" Turning over pages quickly, he declared, "The next item on the agenda is …"

I cut across him and repeated, "Mr Chairman, I propose a vote of no confidence." Jimmy jumped up again with, "I second that!"

The Chairman did his best to bluster his way through it. I jumped up for the third time and yelled, "I will not be shouted down, Mr Chairman," and again I repeated the proposal. Straight away, I heard Jimmy yell, "I second that!"

The noise increased as fishermen shouted their support, "You've had your proposer and your seconder!" they were saying.

The Chairman seemed confused and nervously shuffled his papers. Pender sat staring into space. The divers sat there, the seven of them facing us immobile and silent. Somebody shouted, "Carried unanimously!" and a great cheer went up.

With that, we all walked out of the County Hall and into the sunlight. On the broad steps outside were the reporters and the TV crew. Some of us gave interviews. It was a great relief to me that it was over. I am eternally grateful to Jimmy Madron. His instant response was crucial. It has to be remembered that I was only a whippersnapper compared to Jimmy, the greatly respected skipper of the *Renevelle*.

The entry in the diary finishes thus, "Putting the proposition was a frightening experience."

By the way, I can't remember and the diary doesn't tell me anywhere, just what the Newquay men's Resolution was!

Dear Diary II

On Thursday, 18 March 1965, I spent the morning up in the loft with Mike, working on gear. I took the afternoon off and went home to Vyrn Cabin. At about half past four Martin 'Brimble' Burt arrived. He was wondering if it was possible to get his boat, the *Cornishman*, out of the Gannel. We went to ask George Northey for his opinion. George stood watching the sea for a while. He sucked quietly at the pipe clenched between his teeth as he studied the patterns of the waves breaking on Crantock beach. Suddenly he made his mind up, "Yes you can do it alright, but you'd better whip on. It's almost high water now."

We jumped into Brimble's van and young Dave Trebilcock came with us. We sped off up to Tregunnel where the *Cornishman* was berthed. She was only barely afloat, so it was easy for us to cast off her bow moorings and scramble aboard. We hauled on the two stern ropes and boarded the anchors. Brimble quickly got the engines going and we headed down river with all haste. We passed over the footbridge at Trethellan, with plenty of water under our keel. We passed Fern Pit and headed for the open sea. A couple of steep threatening seas met us at Salt Cove and some heavy spray came aboard but then we were clear. We steamed around to the harbour and moored up. As the diary states, "Brimble was delighted."

Cooker Mountford and Bobby Broderick came out for us in the punt and brought us ashore.

The next morning the wind had dropped away to almost nothing, but there was a big ground sea running. It would have been impossible to leave the Gannel in those conditions!

So it continued until 24 March, when it blew a full force nine. This was the beginning of a period of west to north west gales, which kept the whole fleet penned in. We were not idle during this spell of bad weather. Most days there was a tremendous run in the harbour. Mooring ropes and fender lanyards chafed through, so the boats needed frequent attention. Even our punts were at risk of suffering damage and so they had to be minded too. Any spare time was given to the endless task of making new pots. We were also repairing the old pots. Nobody liked this bit. When you'd finished replacing broken laths and mending holes in the net ends there was no satisfaction in it. You were still looking at battered old pots, but the job had to be done. These were the pots we could take risks with in the early part of the season.

On 26 March, the AGM of the Newquay Fishermen's Association took place. Mr Lord of the Fisheries Organisations Society attended. It was resolved to ask the Ministry to ban diving for Shellfish. It was also resolved to ask the Minister to hold a public enquiry into the affairs of the Cornwall Sea Fisheries Committee.

Members expressed their concern at the Newquay Urban District Council's proposal to build a restaurant on the centre jetty. In the Council's own words, the restaurant would be 'cantilevered out' on both sides. That would obviously prevent vessels from berthing near the jetty. This scheme, if it came to pass, would take away the safest berths in the harbour and would make the place untenable for the thirty– to forty–foot boats. (Did the Council want to get rid of us or what?)

We asked Mr Lord to seek from British Rail, a copy of the agreement whereby the Great Western Railway Company had given the harbour in Newquay to the people of the town. He promised to do so. I later wrote to the Newquay UDC, pointing out that generations of Newquay fishermen had been "using those berths since time immemorial."

It gives me great pleasure now to see that the harbour has, so far, escaped this particular piece of vandalism.

The bad spell of weather, during which we often had westerlies of force eight, nine and ten lasted for several days. On 30 March, we awoke to a shift of wind, a south east gale force eight. Off to sea at last! All the boats carried their pots out and, over the next three days, we were able to haul several times and gather up a few craws and lobsters. At times, the south easter blew a real smoker, but we were sheltered by the land.

2 April marked our first landing to Harvey's lorry on the quay. The wind had dropped away to nothing and, as we proceeded to sea, the fog closed in. Of course, there was a big ground sea. This was to be expected.

Ground sea follows a spell of south east, just as night follows day! As the morning progressed, the fog thickened and the seas grew bigger. Off in seventeen fathoms the seas were smooth, rounded hills of water, which loomed suddenly out of the fog. They hoisted *Reaper* up several feet before letting her gently down and passing silently on their way. The combination of swells, alternating with periods of calm, and being enclosed by a wall of dense fog was, to say the least, confusing to the senses. When we were hauling or shooting the gear, the boat would maintain a steady course; then the swells arrived on our beam and *Reaper* rode sideways up and over them. That was ok. The motion of the boat was quite pleasant as our stem sliced through the blue water. No, it was when I was hurriedly cutting up gurnards for bait, between each string of pots that things got to me. Sometimes I wouldn't know whether I was on my head or my heels!

Meanwhile, Mike took us from one string to the next. He studied the compass and peered out into the dense fog. Noting the time on his watch, he knew to the minute, precisely when the next dhan should appear. When he missed a dhan, he continued on the same course for another two minutes. Then he spun the wheel and returned, steering the opposite course at the same high speed. Sure enough, exactly two minutes after our high–speed turn, *Reaper's* bow came up to the dhan.

Apart from Mike's skill at finding our gear in the fog, which he demonstrated many times while I fished with him, there was always the element of luck involved. If, for example, the next dhan had been chopped off by a passing ship, then the system of using compass courses which had been jotted down in his notebook the previous day, would have been disrupted a bit.

Another reason why you needed luck on your side, while fishing in the fog, was the danger of collision. In order to reduce steering error caused by the tides, we steamed at full speed, in direct contravention of the rules of seamanship which advise, 'proceed slowly'. It was only luck on these occasions that we didn't meet one of our neighbours doing exactly the same thing. There was always the chance of running down a becalmed yacht, or middling a steel coaster.

It didn't do to dwell on such things in the days before GPS and small boat radar. On this particular day, visibility was down to hardly more than the boat's length by the time we finished the first haul. This was really too thick to do anything with, so Mike headed for Newquay. When we knew we were close to the harbour, and the echo sounder showed twenty feet of water under us, a sea broke with a crashing roar almost on our stern. We quickly headed out to sea until we saw the Old Dane Rock looming out of the fog. We then crept carefully into the Gazzle and dropped anchor.

The fog thinned a bit and we saw the French crabber, *Petit France*, come and anchor near us. A bit later, in came Mike Morris's *Trevose*, which also anchored. When the fog finally lifted, we could see John Burt's *Patsy Anne* anchored off Towan Beach. By then the tide had risen and so we all entered harbour.

The fog persisted for a couple more days until a westerly wind came and cleared it; however, a big swinging ground sea continued. We knew it would be useless to fish with that going on. So the first week of April slipped away. On 6 April Mike, George Northey and I went to Mevagissey to buy longlines with 3,000 hooks and whiting lines with 3,800 hooks, from Ainsley Hunkin. We met more of the Mevagissey lads, including Harry Barron and spent a nice afternoon there.

In the evening Rodney Lyon, John Burt and I went to a Newquay Chamber of Commerce meeting, held in the Victoria Hotel. Members asked us a lot of questions, which we answered rather well, I thought. They resolved unanimously to support the fishermen's campaign to get diving for crawfish banned in Newquay. They would write to the Newquay UDC, the local MP, MAFF and the Cornwall Sea Fisheries Committee.

After the meeting, John Burt and I went to the bar in the Central Hotel to meet Pauline, Janet, Nora and George Northey. Richard Gillies and Edgar Veal were there too. It was a happy gathering as it was George's Birthday. He was fifty, which seemed incredibly old to me at the time.

What's in a Name?

Most of the nicknames you hear today have come from the television, which is a pity. A few years back, nicknames were very imaginative. Often the nickname fitted the person so well you would have a job to remember his real name. Of course, many were simply a surname altered in some way, as in the case of Jenkins the plumber who was always 'Joey Jenks' or the Burt brothers who were the 'Burtie Boys' of the *Patsy Anne*.

On the other hand, there was 'Beat 'em Burt' and his burly son, 'Bim Burt', who were the town's blacksmiths and there was 'Brimble Burt' of course, named during the hurricane in the Gannel.

On the Padstow boats calling into Newquay there was David Chapman 'Chapper' and 'Hoss', a giant of a man. There was also 'Dasher', Meanwhile the Padstow Fishermen's Association Chairman ex–RAF Group Captain Lombard was known as 'Groupie'.

Back in Newquay, Pat Kennedy, the schoolmaster was 'Mr Toad' who liked messing about in boats. 'Cap 'n Bones' had sailed in the schooners in his younger days. An obsequious town councillor was known as 'Cringin'.

I nearly forgot Mickey Burt, or 'Boots' so called, because when he was about nine years old one of the fishermen gave him a pair of his old sea boots with the tops cut off. Of course, Mickey was thrilled and wore the boots all the time, even though they were miles too big for him.

Fred Pierce an old retired fisherman didn't pronounce his R's and so was referred to as 'Fed'. Fed went crew for a chap who had a neat little 23 footer with two gleaming Petter diesel engines. He only went to sea about once a week in the summer time and he owned a gents outfitters. He was 'Tailor's Dummy'.

Graham 'Cooker' Mountford was so named because of the hours he spent in the kitchen of his family's restaurant.

The Moller brothers, Graham and Kelvin, did get their nickname from television, a children's programme called *Bill and Ben, the Flowerpot Men*. It was because they were always running around the place with their thigh boot tops turned down, resembling the flowerpots that landed the two boys with 'Bill and Ben'. Nobody ever said which was which, but it stuck to them anyway.

We called George Northey 'Gilson' because of his huge strength. If you had him in the boat, you didn't need a tackle to lift heavy weights. 'Gilson' somehow changed to 'Gingey' later on.

Rodney Lyon was 'Courtney', which over time became 'Courtee' and Jimmy Hoare was 'Starchy' (I hate to think about it!).

We had 'Toofy' on account of the fellow's unusual front teeth and 'Hasty Jake' who was inclined to be slow footed.

'Heel and Toe' was a guy who bounced along the pier rather than walked. A man who joined the crew of the *Freemans* had made a trip on one of the Grimsby deep sea trawlers. He was 'Bear Island Bill'.

Shortly afterwards he left the *Freemans* and joined Alfie Waters' 24 footer, replacing Alfie's previous crew, a girl whose frizzy hair tossed about by the sea winds, earned her the name of 'Golly'.

Jack Carne, the Harbour Master was named 'Forenoon' because he never used the words, 'This Morning'. Instead, he would say, 'If you'd been here this forenoon you would have seen it all' and so on.

Simon Drew, retired fisherman, boat repairer and sailor was 'Drewdrop'.

It's funny how nicknames occur really. Mike called in to see us when we lived in the house in Alma Place. Our eldest boy Martyn, who was cutting his baby teeth at the time crawled out from behind Mike's chair and fastened on to his ankle. Mike recoiled in shock and horror yelling 'Potrick' thinking he was being attacked by a large spider crab. So Martyn had his nickname before he could even walk.

Mike himself had a nickname. If anyone asked if we had any lobsters or craws he usually answered, "No, poor enough you, only a few 'Cabs'."

So that was it: 'Crabs' with a silent R as in 'Fed'.

A boatman friend of Mike earned the name 'Shyster' when he carried skin divers.

A nickname that I thought most unkind was 'Rangatang', implying that a good friend of mine came from the forests of Borneo. I should hate for him to be offended. Even now, forty years later, he is still powerful with strong hairy arms! Oh yes we even had a 'King Kong' as well. I heard old Edgar Carter referred to as 'Gramps'. It fitted him well because he was about the oldest boatman still working.

Some nicknames were of a temporary nature as with the two guys, both named Malcolm, who palled around together. They were cruelly dubbed, 'The Malcolm Sisters'.

I am unaware of any nickname attached to me but I am certain they didn't miss me out. Nobody was safe!

What about 'Gruesome Grose', who was actually a handsome young man?

My favourite was Mike Morris who became 'Hungry Horace?' His nickname fitted like a glove. Later it was shortened to 'Hungry Hor' and finally to simply, 'Hor'. Hor was always convinced that everyone else was catching more fish than he was. This wasn't always true of course but instinct told Hor that someone else's pots were right in amongst the craws and lobsters. Meanwhile the strings of pots that he had so carefully set that morning were in a virtual desert. He couldn't wait to haul them and shift over to where someone else was fishing. As soon as the tide eased 'Hor' would start work, moaning at the crew the whole time. When a few empty pots came up he would say, "There I knew it! We should have been further west with the Burtie Boys. They must be loading up."

He would get three strings of pots on board and race ten miles west to join the *Patsy Anne*. Racing ten miles east again after shooting near the Burt's gear, Hor would suddenly decide that Bill and Ben were slaughtering fish a couple of miles inside. Urging his crew to haul faster, he would explain, "They've got their pots on the best piece of ground for miles around. It's black with them there at this time of year."

So saying, he would board the other strings of pots and make all speed for Bill and Ben's gear. Hor's method of fishing could be described as 'hot pursuit'. You just never knew when he would turn up. It became a battle of wits. If we fell into a good spot of fishing, then Hor mustn't get wind of it, or he would surround us with gear.

Actually, there was no badness in Hor; he just couldn't help it! If he even suspected you were getting fish he would surround you with gear. One day we were working east of Park Head and we were getting a lot of crawfish. The day was wonderfully fine and we were keeping a weather eye open for Hor. We would see him in the distance from time to time. We'd know him by the plume of black smoke from his racing diesel engines. Anyway, after the second haul, we had a box of lobsters and 36 crawfish below in *Reaper*'s fish room. Mike stopped the engines and we just drifted. In half an hour, we would need to start hauling again. We took out our crib bags and thermos flasks and sprawled out on deck, enjoying the sunshine. Suddenly we heard the sound of racing engines and soon saw Hor approaching us rapidly. He came up alongside and greeted us with, "Well, any Crawfish?"

"Not even one," answered Mike. "Half a dozen lobsters is all we've got."

With the two boats drifting side–by–side, it was so awfully quiet. Hor hung over the gunnel with his head actually over *Reaper's* fish room boards, beneath which 36 crawfish were sitting around loose. Any moment I expected one of the craws to hop and fall over on its side and start flipping its tail like mad. If this happened, it would panic the lot and there would be bedlam, with an unmistakable chorus of slapping tails accompanied by that awful creaking noise the craws make with their horns.

Hor showed no sign of leaving and we yarned about all sorts of things. We discussed the weather, the prices, the skin divers and still he showed no sign of departing. Meanwhile his beady eyes darted everywhere. I was sure the craws would start up and give the game away.

At last, Hor seemed to come to a decision. The corners of his mouth turned down and his eyes narrowed. "Brimble has been outside there for a couple of days without shifting," he said, staring into space as if thinking aloud. Suddenly, he jumped up and leapt into the wheelhouse and steamed away at full revs. A veil of black smoke drifted over us.

I asked Mike why he'd told Hor we had no craws. Wouldn't it have been safer to admit to two or three in case he heard them flipping?

"Not likely!" said Mike, "If I said we had two and he only had one, he would have been here like a shot!"

I guess he was right.

'65 was a Difficult Year

Spring turned into summer and with the longer days, we were able to haul our one hundred and twenty five pots three times a day, tides and weather permitting. Our fishing improved simply because of the increased number of pots hauled each day. Mike and I were catching about thirty fish but the crawfish were scarce. This affected our earnings because one crawfish weighed the same as two or three lobsters.

The scarcity of crawfish and the frequent spells of bad weather resulted in many divers losing interest and vanishing from the scene. The other side of the coin was that the gang that were still diving for crawfish, and who had put money into the job, were becoming desperate and more inclined to dive on our gear in the hope of finding enough to make it pay. What we had predicted was coming to pass and we knew in our hearts that the crawfish were really finished.

In what little spare time we had, we went to the loft and worked on our newly acquired longlines. We replaced the worn snoods, the lengths of twine that held the hooks to the back line and we fitted two thousand new swivel hooks. We had help of course, Cooker Mountford who should have been studying at the Tech, Dave Trebilcock, his younger brother Philip 'Tich', and other youngsters as well. Looking back now, I wonder where we found the energy!

The fishing itself was demanding enough. There was a plague of spider crabs in those days. They loved our fresh gurnards and our French pots with the ten–inch entrance. That was the first year we landed spider crabs because Harvey started exporting them to France. We packed them into tea chests, which each contained 100 lbs and we got eight pence a pound for them. At our first landing, the spiders weighed 566 lbs and they were all big cock fish, no hens!

Once the summer came in properly, we had to abandon the spiders because we needed all our storage pots and carves for the crawfish, lobsters and crabs. So, since we couldn't keep the spiders they went back into the sea. As soon as he boarded the pot, Mike just whipped the spiders out and flung them overboard. We knew this wasn't a good idea because 'a feeding fish' will go straight into the nearest baited pot. Chapper had a better solution. He used to keep them on board. Chapper and his mate would be knee deep in spider crabs aboard the *Mon Rêve* after one haul.

Often, if it was fine enough, *Mon Rêve* and *Reaper* would anchor in a small cove, Porthcothan, and lay side–by–side waiting for the tide to ease. While Mike and I got stuck into sandwiches, Chapper and his mate went hitting the spiders with iron bars and killed them all before tossing them out. Chapper actually received a letter from the Council telling him to stop this practise because the visitors going swimming at Porthcothan beach were stubbing their toes on dead spider crabs.

That year all the boats had trouble. I think it started when *Reaper*'s main engine had a burnt out exhaust valve, which meant we were tied up for a couple of days while Mike and his friend, the engineer John Julyan, dealt with the problem and got us going again. After that, it was like a virus going through the fleet. The next one to suffer was Alfie Waters' new acquisition, the lovely 44ft Looe lugger, *Seagull*. He'd only brought her round from Mevagissey a couple of weeks before, when we got a northerly gale. The short steep seas sweeping into the harbour repeatedly hoisted *Seagull* up and slammed her keel down on the hard packed sand. It happened to be neap tides so it was ages before the tide left her high and dry. This was due to the lugger's fine underwater profile.

During the same period, the gigs merely pounded a few times and then sat on the sand lying comfortably over on their bilges. Of course, on the flooding tide the *Seagull* received another prolonged pounding before she became fully afloat. When she was high and dry again, you could see the water running out of places along her seams. As soon as the gale moderated, Alfie steamed *Seagull* to Padstow, where the harbour bottom is mud and after that, he fished her from there.

Unlike the gigs, the lugger was not designed with Newquay and St Ives harbours in mind. Shortly after the *Seagull* incident, the *Freeman*'s quarter engine manifold cracked. They had it repaired but then their batteries died. The virus was spreading!

In John Burt's *Patsy Anne*, the Gardner main engine fuel pump packed up. Dave Chapman's *Mon Rêve*'s main engine gearbox got smashed. Mike Morris's Lister main engine in the *Trevose* got cracked cylinder heads and the Moller brothers lost a week's fishing when their winch packed up.

Despite our busy schedule, we kept the pressure on to try and get something done about the divers. Rodney Lyon and I wrote letters seeking support from politicians, local councillors, Chambers of Commerce and other organisations for a ban on diving for shellfish. We were partially successful, it would seem, because a report in the local newspaper had the chairman of the Cornwall Sea Fisheries Committee accusing the members of parliament of 'political chicanery'. The following week the same paper printed pieces from Peter Bessel MP and Greville Howard MP, in which they robustly responded to the chairman's accusations.

Fishermen from all over Cornwall attended a series of meetings. It was decided to form The Cornish Inshore Fishermen's association. Charlie Laity from Porthleven did most of the talking and Group Captain Lombard from Padstow bought most rounds of beer. Meanwhile we read that Clifton Pender, the Cornwall Sea Fishery Officer had reported that divers were catching significant numbers of crawfish off Pendeen. Walter, of Harvey's lorry, refuted this and told us that there were hardly any crawfish being caught anywhere.

The Newquay boatmen who had been carrying divers now turned to other things. George King put out lobster pots in August. He got caught out by bad weather with the pots too close in and lost half of them. Bill Sharrock went trawling. His trawl came fast and he parted the warps. The following day he was waiting for Jim the Diver to come and search for his net.

'65 was the year the *Galleon* arrived. A towing vessel brought her into the harbour. She was originally a Baltic trading schooner we were told. With three new dinky little masts fitted and square sails, together with a bit of artistic paintwork, she made a passable galleon. There were even a couple of gents got up as pirates to take money off the emmetts!

A digger was brought down to the harbour and a great trench was dug in the sand. When the tide came in, the *Galleon* was shoved as far up towards the high water mark as she would go and so she was beneaped and stuck there for the summer.

'65 was the year we got the lifeboat. It was the inflated inshore type (RIB). Mike and I were sceptical at first, but actually, the RIB proved to be very effective. Among the crews who manned it on subsequent rescue missions were Graham 'Cooker' Mountford, Pat 'Mr Toad' Kennedy, Martin 'Brimble' Burt, Mick Chegwidden, Mickey 'Boots' Burt, Harold Bullen (the local gravedigger), Bob (a pirate off the *Galleon*) and many others.

That was the year that a v–bomber crashed somewhere in the Newquay Bay area. The pilot had managed to bale out. Apparently, the plane was experimental and full of the latest technology. One morning, as we were steaming off to haul our pots, Mike saw a patch of oil on the sea. He took landmarks of the position and when we returned to harbour he gave the Harbour Master the details. As a result, the RAF sent us a radio buoy. This thing was a cylinder, about six feet long and one foot in diameter and fastened to it, was a length of nylon rope. On the other end of the rope were two steel ammunition boxes full of brass nuts and bolts. These boxes weighed about half a hundredweight each. We were asked to take the radio buoy to sea with us and shoot it on the spot where Mike had seen the oil patch.

"Stand back when you launch it," we were told, "because four stabilising fins and a radio antenna will spring out."

Fair enough! Next morning as we passed over the place where the oil had been Mike gave the word and I heaved the buoy overboard. As it sailed out of the cylinder, the fins and the aerial did pop out and indeed, you could get a nasty clout off them if you weren't watching yourself. The buoy bobbed about, no doubt bleeping away merrily for a few seconds – until the ammunition boxes dragged it below the surface and it plunged down out of sight. The RAF had not given us enough rope! Considering the v bomber they hoped to recover was worth one million pounds they were very stingy with their nylon rope. The following year the buoy washed ashore on Towan Beach covered in barnacles. Stormy weather had chafed its rope through.

Anyway, a couple of weeks after we released the buoy two ships arrived in the bay. One was a lifting ship called the *Barglow* and the other was a Royal Navy minesweeper. *Barglow* was fitted with under water television. It seems they located the wrecked plane but then they were ordered away again. A couple of days later *Freeman* came in proudly displaying their booty. Two sinkers made of solid lead, weighing one hundredweight each and several fathoms of wire rope, topped with six lovely 8–inch yellow plastic trawl floats. We presumed that they were left there marking the wreck. We don't know if the Navy ever came back. We never saw them again anyway.

'65 was also the year of the walkie–talkie radios. These were made in Japan, a little box about 6 inches high and 4 inches wide. It would fit neatly into the pocket of your donkey jacket. They were of course highly illegal. In fact, if you were caught with one in your possession the Postmaster General promised you dire consequences. It really makes you wonder what all the fuss was about. These radio sets were a wonderful innovation. For the first time ever the small fishing boats had contact with each other and with the shore. This was a tremendous advance from a safety–at–sea point of view. There was only one channel on them but that was all that we needed. All the boats bought one and the skippers called each other from all points of the compass. It was a lot of fun too of course.

'65 was what you might call 'incident packed'. Things happened all the time. It seemed that none of us got a moments peace. The breakdown virus kept doing the rounds. Our Lister had to have a new cylinder head. Mike Morris's main engine in the *Trevose* gave more trouble and then he bent his shaft and propeller. John Burt travelled up to Dursley in Gloucestershire, for parts for *Patsy Anne*'s Lister quarter engine. Martin Burt's main engine bed bolts sheered off.

There was bad news of a different kind when somebody poured engine sump oil into our lobster carve. This must have been done during the night, when the tide was out. As luck would have it, the day was too fresh for us to go to sea, so we decided to drive to Harvey's with our fish. When we opened the carve we discovered the felony. The lobsters would have all been killed had they been left in the carve another day. As it was, we threw a few buckets of salt water down on top of them and they were all perfect. Naturally, we suspected the divers.

One evening we came in from sea to find that the transom of our punt had been stove–in. We wondered who had done the deed. Martin Burt pointed out the culprits to us: a couple of holidaymakers with a plastic boat and outboard. When we challenged them, they admitted guilt and said they would pay for the repairs (I don't remember if they ever did!). The problem was, how would we manage without the punt? Anyway, Malcolm Brown went to work on it and he did a lovely job, so that the punt's stern was stronger than before.

These emmetts fooling around in the congested little harbour were a great nuisance. The wash created by their outboards made our boats heave about violently on their moorings and slam into each other causing the fender lanyards to chafe through. It made the lobster carves jerk at their chains and hit off one another causing mortalities among the crabs and lobsters.

One evening after our day's work, we went in the punt over to the lobster carves. While we hung over the side of the punt, putting our catch away, this tubby little plastic boat with two tubby little men in the forward cockpit was zooming around the harbour. It had a tiny outboard, which was revved up to the last. Every time it passed us, our punt and the carve hopped around so violently that I expected Mike to end up with his head in the carve. How he cursed them! With the lobsters safely locked away, Mike sculled us in to the steps. As we moored the punt, the tubby little plastic boat made yet another circuit, its little engine sounding like an angry bee. I think they meant to weave their way between the tier of moored punts, but one of the punts' bow ropes caught the pair of them under their chins.

One guy was yelling, "Stop the engine! Stop the engine!"

The other guy was screaming, "I can't! I can't! Me accelerator's stook!"

We nearly witnessed a dual hanging. Perhaps Mike's curses are more potent than I'd imagined! Anyway, it gave us a good laugh.

Even rotten old '65 had its hilarious moments. Like the time Mike Morris was adjusting his punt's moorings. He had his thigh boots on and was up to his knees in the water. He gave the stern rope a mighty pull, whereupon it parted and he sat down, plonk in the tide. The air was blue!

The first two weeks in September were marked by severe gales and really big ground seas. On 22 September, we put the six baskets of longlines on board, with a total of two thousand No 4 Mustad swivel conger hooks, which we baited with pilchard. For the next three weeks, we fished the lines. We used every opportunity to explore Watergate Bay, Whipsiderry and Bedruthan. We went west, down off the Madrips and across Perranporth. It was a pleasant change from the pots. Sometimes Brimble Burt and Chris shipped on and sometimes George Northey came. Cooker Mountford was almost constantly helping out. We had 15 to 20 stone per shot, mostly of rays with sometimes 10 or 20 stone of spurdogs as well. We also drifted for herrings without having any great success. By mid–October, Mike and I decided that longlining wasn't paying and so we went back fishing the pots again.

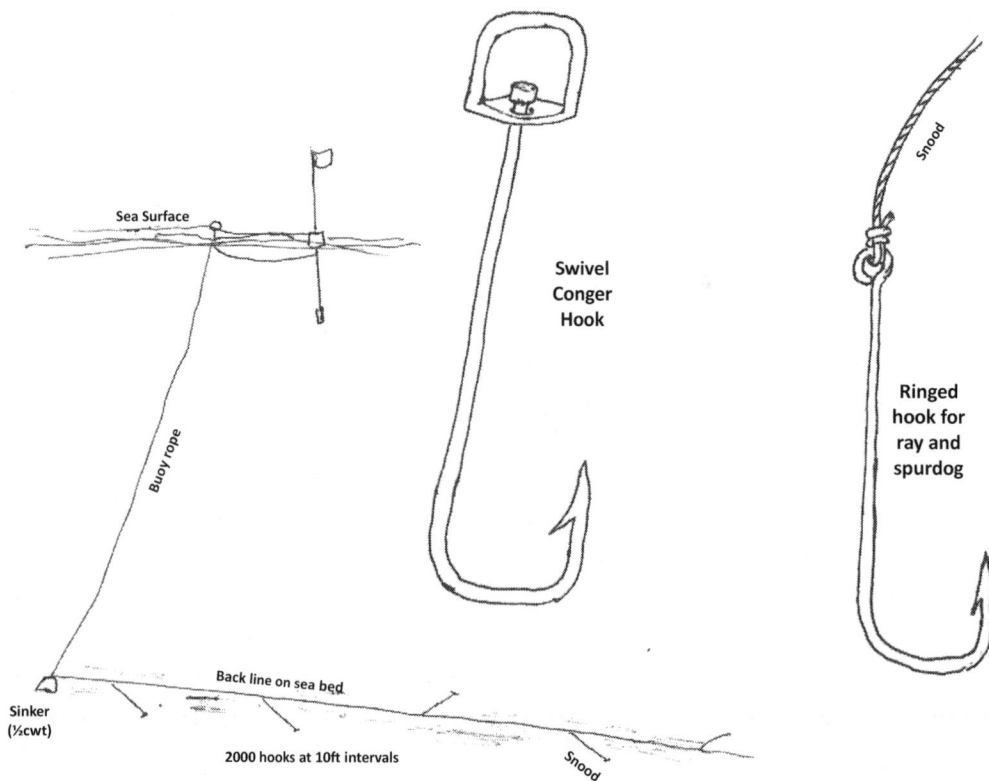

Sea Surface

Buoy rope

Sinker
(½cwt)

Back line on sea bed

2000 hooks at 10ft intervals

Snood

Swivel
Conger
Hook

Snood

Ringed
hook for
ray and
spurdog

Well we laughed when Mike Morris sat down in the tide but, on 21 October, it was my turn for a wetting. We left the dock at 5.30 am on a falling tide. We dodged around in the bay waiting for daylight and then headed off for our nearest string of pots, which was about a mile and a half away. This was some of last year's gear and the pots were fragile and the rope worn and chafed. When we reached it, I boarded the dahn and put the rope on the winch. I soon realised that the backrope had parted so that only the first pot came up. The other twenty–four pots were left lying on the seabed. Mike and I dropped the mizzen sail, intending to go to the dahn on the other end of the string of pots. As the sail came down an extra–strong puff of wind hit us and put a big belly in it. The sail pushed me clean over the side!

The wind was from the south east and the *Reaper* lay broadside on to it. I was now in the water on her lee side. I still had the mizzen halyard in my left hand. I was surprised at the rise and fall of the *Reaper's* hull, as seen from my fish's eye view. When she lifted on a wave, I was looking at her quarter propeller and when she came down the boat seemed to be falling on top of me, so that I had to shove myself away from her.

Within seconds, Mike was kneeling on the after deck and he reached down and grabbed me. I had on a brand new pair of thigh boots, which had cost me £4.10s. I kept my toes curled up to prevent them from falling off. Now I normally weighed about ten–and–a–half stone but with wet clothes and thigh boots full of water I weighed much more. Mike was a naturally strong guy and as he dragged me up, I got my two hands on the boat's rail. Together we heaved. The boat lurched about. I hung there. For a split second, we were nose to nose. I looked into Mike's eyes and burst out laughing. Mike was laughing too. We shouldn't be laughing; it was making us weak. We gathered our strength and one more combined heave did the trick and I flopped onto the deck. Mike went into the wheelhouse and headed for the dahn. I took up the gaff and caught it. We hauled the string of pots, knotted the two parted ends of the rope together and shot away again.

Although the sea in October is reasonably warm, the air on that particular day was fairly cold. By the time we'd finished with that string of pots, I found myself getting colder by the minute. Mike suggested I go down into the engine room. I stripped off and squeezed myself down into the tiny space warmed by the air–cooled Petter engine. I wrung out my sodden clothes while Mike headed for the harbour at full revs. The tide was still too low for us to attempt to enter harbour. I put on my wet clothes again and Jimmy Hoare came out in his punt and brought me back in to the quay. I went home to Pentire and changed into dry clothes and I felt fine. I went back down to the harbour in time for us to land our fish into Harvey's lorry.

Around this time, the 40ft *Freeman* was put up for sale. Jimmy Hoare went off to Hull to join a trawler bound for the northern fishing grounds. Rodney Lyon joined the French crabber *Emigrant*.

One day, as we were hauling pots, *Emigrant* came up alongside us and Rodney was on deck. It was good to see him togged out the same as the rest of French crew. He fitted in so well with them and was obviously enjoying himself.

A 40ft French crabber called *Nicole* appeared in the dock. Some Cornish fishermen had bought her. We noted that they had some of their pots shot near ours. Later the *Nicole* left the area. Then an article appeared in the *Fishing News*:

> "After their 40ft Lobster boat *Nicole* ran aground on rocks in a heavy sea five Cornish fishermen, Barlow and David Richards, Frank Noall, Joe Sealey and Arthur Ware spent the night in an abandoned house on a deserted island off the Breton coast. Their boat's engine had failed while on their way to Audierne to sell their catch. They were rescued when a Lighthouse tender spotted their abandoned vessel."

On 7 November, *Reaper* left for Padstow. We had Cooker with us. The trip took two hours. We left the boat with John England, who was to install our new Parsons Pike 48hp to replace our aging JP2 Lister. We all returned to Newquay by car.

On 23 November, Cooker came to Fern Pit and picked me up. He was driving his dad's car. We went to Padstow and boarded the *Reaper* and Mike took us out on the river for a test run. We were all amazed at the power and speed of the boat with her new engine. We saw the Padstow lifeboat leave and we heard later that the 38ft *Deo Gratias* had not returned from trawling in Port Isaac bay. The crew, Raymond Provis and Hoss Bailey (the gentle giant) were taken off the boat before she foundered in a westerly force 8. November ended with storms of wind and forecasts of 9s and 10s.

On the 30th, *Westward Ho* parted her moorings. She drove up the beach and sank. On her way, she struck Bill Sharrock's boat and bent its shaft severely. Another diver's boat, *LA Puce*, parted and was damaged. As someone said, "Three divers in one hit!"

A terrible event occurred on 3 December 1965. Mike and I were watching for an opportunity to bring the *Reaper* back to Newquay from Padstow. The weather for the previous seven or eight days had been atrocious.

On that Friday morning, it was blowing NW force 9–10. At ten o'clock, I decided to go to the harbour to see if our punt was alright. There was a lot of rainwater in her so I bailed her out and then headed for home. I stopped on Pentire Hill to look at the sea. There was a really big ground sea running; each sea broke about two miles off and its great mass of white water rushed all the way into Fistral beach. It was awe inspiring! I worked in the shed at home making lobster pots and then left to check up on the punt again. It was 4.20pm when I reached North Quay Hill.

In the gathering gloom, I saw the flashing light and heard the noise of a helicopter. I joined the crowd of onlookers. The helicopter went down low on the water and moved slowly across Towan Beach, whilst an RAF Shackleton circled overhead. The helicopter made its way back to the harbour and hovered over the entrance. It gradually descended so that from our position on the hill we were looking down on it. Its blue flashing light was a bright contrast to the darkening sea and sky. That and the loud clatter of its rotors are the enduring memories that remain with me. One of the other onlookers told me that someone was lost.

I drove the motorbike along Fore Street and down the South Quay Hill, where I met up with some of the lads down there and they told me that it was Edgar Carter who was lost. I watched as the sea flooded into the harbour making the boats plunge and strain at their moorings. I watched it dragging at the boats as it poured out again like a sluice. Out it went, swirling like a boiling cauldron; out through the quay gap to meet the onrushing power of the breakers, as they tore past the gap, to spend their fury on Towan Beach.

So that was the story. Edgar had gone to pump his boat out. He had cast off his punt and sculled out towards his motor boat the *Lady Gwen*. Old Edgar, expertly sculling with a single oar over the stern as he had done year in, year out, was suddenly defeated. Just a few more sweeping strokes of his oar would have carried him to the *Lady Gwen* and safety, but the powerful surge caught the punt and dragged it swiftly to the open sea. Despite his efforts to turn her bow and drive her back in towards the boats, the current bore him out through the quay gap where his punt was overwhelmed and capsized by the breaking surf. The alarm was raised. Tom Rowse and others ran along the South Quay to the gap.

"Quick!" they shouted, "The lifebuoys! Get a lifebuoy!"

The lifebuoys were missing! They'd been removed by the Council at the end of the summer for painting! Edgar's death cast a gloom over everyone. There was fury over the lifebuoys.

The punt washed ashore on Towan Beach, only slightly damaged. There was no sign of Edgar's body, though people searched the shore every daylight hour. Just before noon on Wednesday, 8

December, I was making pots up in the loft when Bill Brown came in. He told me that Mike Lyne had found Edgar at the Bothwicks Rocks on Great Western Beach.

Edgar Carter's funeral took place on Saturday, 11 December and was well attended.

On Sunday 12th, the *Lady Gwen* along with a few other motor boats was hauled up the slip onto the hard, as was the usual practice at that time of year. For years after, whenever I heard the sound of a Helicopter, I would be filled with a dreadful feeling of apprehension.

The stormy weather continued, preventing us from getting *Reaper* back from Padstow.

On 21 December, the wind had eased, so we went by car to Padstow and brought *Reaper* away. Cooker came with us, of course.

On 22 December, with Cooker on board, we steamed round to the River Gannel. A great sea passed under us on the bar and broke ahead of us and then we were safely in and we tied up at Fern Pit. It was the end of a tough year.

Apart from the couple of weeks longlining and netting, we had fished 126 days, pulled 19400 pots and caught only 543 crawfish. It had taken us the whole season to catch what crawfish we'd normally expect in a month. That was it; the crawfish were gone. We bought another hundredweight of wire and started making lobster pots!

Etiquette

The first page in the 1966 diary begins with, "The New Year blew its way in with a westerly force nine."

The next page gives it as, "Force nine or ten with heavy rain during the night."

By 3 January, there is obviously some improvement, because it tells of Mike coming to deliver a big bundle of withies he had cut. These withies would be used by me to weave the entrances (mouths) of the wire pots. Pauline came down the steps to George's Quay and boarded the *Reaper*. Mike gave the new Parsons Pike engine a run and Pauline declared herself, "Most impressed."

Now, with the arrival of the freshly cut withies, I threw myself into the making of the wire pots. In order that the pots would be uniform in size and shape, I had various jigs and formers to help me bend the wire into the required shapes. These were very basic tools, mostly made of wood, but they were, in fact, very effective. It meant that all these lovely little inkwell–type pots, built to my own unique measurements, were identical.

Several months later, an event occurred which demonstrated the need to pay attention to detail where pot making was concerned. It happened towards the end of summer on a warm sunny day. There was enough south west wind to keep us tied up. Mike, who had been out along the south quay said to me, "Hey! Trev! Did you know that there are nine of your pots on the quay?"

I told him that this was impossible because, apart from a few spare ones at home, all 125 pots were out at sea. Mike insisted that we go together and look at these pots. Well, when I saw them I did at first think that they were some of my own manufacture but then I got down on my knees for a closer look, "No! No!" says I with some satisfaction. "See the way the wire standards are turned up there, and there? I'd never do it like that. It just wouldn't do."

"Oh so they're not yours then. Well whose are they?" said Mike looking closely at the shiny new pots.

"Haven't a clue!" I answered, straightening up.

"I'll tell you whose pots they are!" announced Mike suddenly. "It's some bloody part–timer or a blasted skin–diver and I'm not having him picking your brains!"

With that, Mike sent his boot crashing down on top of a pot with all the force he could muster. I stood there unbelieving. The pot caved in to half its original height. Mike stamped on the next pot, and the next. "Bastard! Bastard! Bastard!" came from between Mike's clenched teeth as each boot descended on a pot in his relentless march of destruction.

I glanced around nervously. There were people everywhere. Emmetts, locals, fishermen and dog walkers but nobody seemed to notice my mate. His six foot of solid bone and muscle was doing a sort of goose–step on top of the tier of lobster pots. Upon reaching the end, Mike did an about turn and stamped his way back again. This was too much for me and I burst out laughing. The pots were as flat as pancakes as Mike marched off, grim faced, towards his shed. I tried to stop laughing, but when I glanced back at the flattened pots and then at his retreating back, it set me off again. As I walked along the pier, I was conscious of people looking at me hard. They must have been thinking, 'What's the matter with that lunatic?'

But wait, I am getting ahead of our story and must take us back to January '66. In those days, in spite of frequent fallings–out and some quite entertaining rows, we fishermen actually got along very well together. When a skipper was taken ill or a boat was broken down, other boat's crews and skippers were always ready to help out by hauling the stricken boat's gear and carrying it off into the safety of deeper water. As well as that, we also worked as a team when it came to beach seining. There was a great camaraderie and togetherness there but even so, we were very tight with information.

The men all had their own favourite fishing spots, the locations of which were guarded jealously, but it went much further than that. For instance, if I wanted to know the size of the mouths in the pots my neighbour was making, I wouldn't dare to ask him. No, I would have to wait until one day he would just up and tell me all I needed to know. It is what is called 'etiquette' I think. Naturally, before that time came, I would, if I had any cop on at all, have already measured his pots every which–way, when no one else was around!

A climate of secrecy prevailed, in which rumours flourished. The big one going around towards the end of '65 was that the Burtie Boys were selling the *Patsy Anne*. Word came back from Newlyn that Ronnie Harvey was interested in buying her but that the asking price was too high. Within the week word filtered back that Ernie Stevens of St Ives was interested in buying the *Patsy Anne*. It was the Stevens who had had her built several years earlier under the name of *Sweet Promise*. The Burtie Boys remained tight–lipped!

The next rumour caused a great stir. The Burtie Boys were buying a fifty–foot French crabber! The news emanated from somewhere west because there was still a total news blackout in Newquay, which was Burtie Boy area. Out of the blue came another snippet. Rodney Lyon and Mike Morris were going to join the new boat as crew. I thought this was exciting news, but was it true? Curiosity was killing me, but I felt I couldn't ask. One day I was at the harbour talking to Mike Morris when along came Eddie Hoare. Big, bluff, tough old Eddie, who always called a spade a shovel! Without as much as a hello, he stopped and looked Mike Morris in the eye, "I heard you are going with the Burts!" he said.

Mike Morris was clearly taken aback. After a long drawn out "Ehhhh?" he recovered somewhat and said, "I'm not going to France!"

"No! No! No! I mean aboard this boat they're having!"

Mike spluttered something like, "I'd be the last to know anything around here!"

But Eddie gave a big laugh and wandered off in triumph. So the cat was out of the bag! That's the trouble with people like Eddie; etiquette is not really their thing!

New Year, New Life

Mickey Burt and I sat at the top of South Quay Hill, in the green painted shelter called Rose Cellars. It is a lovely spot, with views across the harbour and the bay, and it gave us protection from the chill January wind. Mickey was telling me all about their new purchase, the fifty–foot French crabber. Much of what he told me, I already knew because scraps of information had been flying around for weeks. It was nice to get the story direct from Mickey as it enabled me to sort the facts from the fiction.

I smiled, thinking of some of the wilder rumours still doing the rounds. I thought back to when Mike Lyne bought the *Reaper* (*Shamrock* as she was then). That was a time when The Critics really had a field day. As soon as we entered Newquay Harbour they predicted, 'Two men will never work she' and, 'Whatever was ee thinking of, buying a great thing like that!' They said much more besides! Of course, Mike and I never heard these comments at the time but, Newquay being what it was, our friends faithfully repeated them for us at a later date. Now I thought, 'Here we go again!' Only this time the Burtie Boys were getting all the flak. Mickey told me the new boat's name. She was called *Bacchus*, which Mickey pronounced as the Frenchmen did, "Bar–coose."

I wished Mickey good luck with their new venture and said I was sure they were doing the right thing. I would not be so churlish to even hint at what The Critics were saying. They were giving the Burtie Boys no chance at all. "What do 'em think they'm gonna do with a bloody great Frenchman?"

No, I wouldn't mention one word of the Critic's statements. Not yet anyway, but sometime later I would give Mickey, David and John Burt the whole bit about who said what!

Bill and Ben, (Kelvin and Graham Moller) called in to see me. They were making wire lobster pots and had got into a mess, they said. Their hands were killing them. All they wanted to know was, did I straighten the wires or did I cut pieces from the coil and use them curved? I was happy to show them the whole process and off they went fired with a new enthusiasm.

Someone broke into our shed down the harbour. When I got down there on the Monday morning of 10 January Mike was already giving a statement to the police. Two coils of pot rope had been taken. It doesn't sound much now, but apart from the inconvenience of it, a coil of one–and–a–half inch circumference Cuprinol treated manila rope cost £8/10/– or the equivalent to what many a person carried home for a week's wages in 1966.

Throughout January, we were very busy, sometimes working at the pot–making until midnight. Often we had to be up early in the morning to go down to George's Quay and tend on the *Reaper*, when bad weather threatened to shove the boat up onto the quay. Mike burned off *Reaper's* hull removing all the old blue paint with a blowlamp and a scraper. He then painted her a lovely deep yellow/orange, with black topsides. She looked very smart and the boat's lovely shape was picked out by the contrasting colours.

The weather was awful. We had some small showers of snow and lots of days of heavy rain, with plenty of force 8's and 9's from all directions. Work on the Newquay Fishermen's Association took time as well. I wrote articles and letters to newspapers about the diving problem and I put together our *Report on Diving for Shellfish*. Chubbs, the printer, ran off 200 copies. Pauline and I handwrote 40 letters to accompany copies sent to councillors, MPs, journalists and anyone else we thought might be useful.

On 15 January, Bill and Ben collected Pauline and me and drove us to Truro. We went there to meet the Cornwall Sea Fisheries Committee in Truro County Hall. Commander W.B. Luard was the Chairman, Reed Johns Vice Chairman and somebody called Hoare was the Secretary and of course, Clifton Pender was there as Chief Sea Fisheries Officer. On our side was Group Captain Lombard from Padstow, Alfred John Pengelly from Looe and Bill Hocking from Mevagissey. All these performed very well. The CSFC were up to their old tricks but (says the diary) we made them toe the line!

On 22 January, the Burtie Boys and Mike Morris left for France. Rodney Lyon stayed in their loft making pots.

On 25 January, I drove my Frances Barnet motorbike to Truro for my driving test. This time I promised myself, this time I will pass. I sat in the dingy waiting room for ages until this friendly little man came and called my name. I followed him out into the street where my gleaming green and chrome bike rested on its stand. I had fitted a new spark plug and a set of points, in preparation for this ordeal that I and my bike were about to endure. I straddled the bike, and Mister said, "Start your machine."

I trod on the kick start, kick, kick, kick; tickled the carburettor; more kicking; perhaps she's flooded; shut off the petrol, more kicking; switch on the petrol, frantic kicking born of desperation; Suddenly, a hand on my shoulder, I paused, my foot raised.

"Time's up. You've failed!" announced the examiner with obvious delight.

I slumped down onto the saddle utterly dejected. The swining bike had carried me seventeen miles without missing a beat. Now it had died on me. I gave it a half–hearted kick and it sprang into life! I drove back to Newquay against the wind and the horizontal rain thinking murderous thoughts like, 'When I get you home, I'll borrow George's sledge hammer and after that I'll throw you off Pentire!' and stuff like that.

On 26 January, Bill and Ben's new boat the *Evelyn Meyrick* arrived in Padstow from Wales.

I drove the bike to the harbour on 27 January. When I wanted to go home, the bike wouldn't start. It took me a whole hour to get it going. I should have murdered it while the mood was on me, but I realised that I could not afford to buy another one. I spent the rest of the day pulling the bike to pieces, taking off the flywheel and removing the coil.

In the evening, I went to Blystra Hall for the AGM of the Newquay Lifeboat. Only about twenty people were there. The same day the Burtie Boys came back from France.

The following day Pauline and I took Martyn to Truro on the bus to get new parts for the motorbike. We took the opportunity to make a 'day out' of it. We saw a bargain price pram, which we bought for the soon–to–arrive baby.

In the evening, I soldered all the magneto wires and the next morning I reassembled the bike's engine and in the afternoon rode the bike to Truro for the AGM of the Cornish Inshore Fishermen's Society in St Mary's hall. It was a very good meeting with thirty–eight fishermen there. The motorbike performed very well.

On 1 February, I finished the fortieth new wire pot.

On 2 February, Mike and I were working in the loft when Bill Brown came in. Mike had just had some teeth taken out and was feeling a bit shaky. "Teeth out!" said Bill. "That's nothing. In the old days they tied a piece of string to the tooth and the other end to the door handle and they slammed the door!"

"These days they can even X–ray your teeth," I remarked.

"X–rays!" Bill yelled. "I'll show you effin X–rays" with this he half stripped off to show us the operation scars on his stomach. "Look at that! They put me on the slab and they gutted me like an old pollock!"

At 9am on 12 February, Mike Lyne, George Northey and I went up on Pentire headland. Mike and George both had their two–way radios. They were trying to contact Bill and Ben, who had left Padstow aboard the *Evelyn Meyrick* and were hoping to be able to get up into the river Gannel. The reception was very bad, so Mike and I drove in Mike's van to Newquay. There, at the Huer's hut, Mike got a good contact with Bill and Ben and told them to make for the harbour, as it would be too dangerous to attempt the river. Mike stressed that the ebb was away already and there was too much sea. Mike heard the boys say 'ok', they understood. How useful these illegal sets were to us!

When they brought the *Evelyn Meyrick* into the harbour I went down to have a look at her. She was a fine Scottish built 28 footer, with a 30hp Lister engine. In the evening, John Burt and I went to Truro in John's van for a meeting of the Cornish Inshore Fishermen's Society. MP's Wilson and Scott–Hopkins were there but Charlie Laity the Fishing Skipper from Porthleven was definitely the star of the show.

For the next few days, we worked at the pots as the gales of wind and rain from the SE persisted.

At midnight on 17/18 February, Pauline was getting pains every five minutes so I went up the cliff path to "Weona" and phoned Nurse Harris. She arrived at 12.30am in a SE gale with driving rain. She griped about the weather, the cliff path, the place, the puddles, Pauline's blood pressure, my boots and anything else she could think of but she did a good job and at 7.40am Jenefer Mary arrived, weighing eight–and–a–half pounds.

Auntie Mollie had stayed with Pauline throughout the night and she was a great support. The next day Bill and Ben called in. When they saw the baby, they were amazed at her smallness, never having seen one so new. Many more friends came to see the new arrival. Cooker called ostensibly to borrow a book. I pulled the cover back and while he was peering into the pram, Pauline walked in. Cooker jumped back all embarrassed and denied looking at the baby at all!

It was a happy time for us.

Myth and Legend

The last week of February 1966 was remarkable for the amount of rain that fell. It was a time of strong winds, which veered and backed between SW and NW. On 27 March the diary gives the wind, W–SW Force 6to 8 and in large letters I had alongside it, NO RAIN TODAY!

Mike and I were down at the harbour. Our punt was upside down on the hard and Mike was painting it. I was close by, repairing one of our lobster carves. George Sollice came along and Mike said, "Here, tell Trevor about the time Dick Gill came in from sea and told of seeing all these crawfish swimming on the surface."

"Well," says George, "it was the end of September, which in those days meant the end of the lobster fishing season because everybody brought in their pots and they cleaned out their boats ready for the herring season. On this particular day the weather was so fine, there was hardly a ripple on the shore. Dick and his mate had just finished hauling a string of pots aboard and were about to head in for Newquay, when suddenly they saw all these crawfish around the boat; shoals of them up on the surface swimming away to the westward. They reckoned the crawfish were clearing out ahead of the weather because the following day there was a mighty ground sea, as big as you ever get and then came a storm that raged for several days!"

This story stayed with me all down the years, mainly because it defies all logic. To my mind there is no single crawfish or lobster capable of getting itself up to the surface from ten or fifteen fathoms, because they weigh heavier than the water. Indeed they can swim, and rapidly too, by flipping their powerful tails. This is a useful means of escape as they leap backwards in a series of jerks, but they quickly become exhausted and having no swim bladder, they soon drop back to the seabed. Therefore I reckon it was impossible for shoals of crawfish to migrate westward on the surface. What really intrigued me was that I was certain Dick Gill wasn't telling a fairy story. He was simply reporting something as he'd seen it!

Like many stories from the past, though they seem fantastic, they are nearly always based on true fact. About thirty years later, I had an answer to this crawfish story when I opened a book and saw a coloured photograph. It was taken from above and showed a squid just below the surface of a crystal clear sea. The squid was exactly the colour of a crawfish and its two extra–long tentacles stood out from its head like the horns of a crawfish. I could imagine a shoal of squid near Dick Gill's boat, while the pots were being hauled. Suddenly they are startled by a change in the engine revs. Their means of escape? Jet propulsion! As they squirt water, they make a series of backward leaps. I am convinced that this is what the fishermen saw on that September day. Perhaps one day, marine scientists will solve the riddle of how Jonah survived his trip in the whale!

Another man with a strange story to tell was 'Ossie'. The first time I met him, Mike and I were measuring off coils of manila rope that would form our backrope for the pots. It was a fine spring evening and quite a few visitors were sauntering about. I saw this man walking quickly towards us. He was of average height, lean and bony, with fairish hair that somehow stood up on his head. He was like a man on a mission, appearing to be very tense with a wild look about him. He stopped alongside us and exchanged a few words with Mike, who casually enquired about his health.

"Aw they nearly got me last night!" he responded.

"They did?" Mike said, sounding surprised.

"Aw yes, they almost had me but I beat 'em by God!" said Ossie talking quickly. "The worms were all over my body. I could feel 'em!"

He trembled with emotion and he glared wildly into our faces, as if to make sure we were paying full attention.

"Last night they were even under my finger nails!" he grated through clenched teeth. "Look at that!" he cried, extending his hands towards us. Dutifully we peered at his nails. "I could feel 'em moving, but I fought 'em. I wouldn't let 'em get me!"

"Er, what kind of worms are they?" I enquired, half–afraid to interrupt his flow. (Well one never knows does one?)

"I got 'em in Africa! They're in the fresh water. They're in the snails. They're everywhere! That's where I got 'em, in Africa!"

"'Tis a good job you're a fit man Ossie," said Mike.

"Aw yes, they'd have got me a thousand times over if I didn't keep fit and fight 'em"

"He runs every day y'know," said Mike addressing me.

"I ran sixty miles last week," added Ossie enthusiastically.

"Yeah, he chases after the china clay lorries, as they come away loaded from the pit."

"I do!" Ossie asserted, "and I do the yoga too. I have to or the bastards'll get me!"

"That's right! Trevor you have never seen muscles like Ossie's!"

Ossie jumped up on a quayside bollard and, balancing there, he undid his belt and wriggled his trousers low down around his hips, then lifting his shirt up high, he did peculiar things with his stomach muscles. Those on the right hand side of his tummy bulged out while those on the left were sucked in. Ossie reversed the process and did it several more times. A crowd gathered. Little old ladies paused, gasped in awe and toddled swiftly past. Children stopped licking ice creams and giggled. I gazed in wonder as the top section of Ollie's stomach muscles bulged out and the lower half down to his, just visible pubic hairs, sucked inwards.

"Well I'm damned!" said Mike, "You'm some fit man!"

Afterwards Mike told me that Ossie had spent several years working in Africa. However, the general consensus was that the worms were a figment of his imagination. Perhaps because he got a sympathetic audience, Ossie seemed to seek out Mike. It appeared to me, judging from subsequent encounters, that Mike was able to get the best performances out of Ossie.

Many years later, I watched a TV documentary, which included a piece about a hideous creature known as the guinea worm, which burrows its way into the human body. It lives in certain rivers in Africa and easily gets into people. I remembered poor Ossie and his paranoia. Perhaps he was right all the time.

Spring Fever

On Friday, 4 March 1966, Mike and I went to Padstow in his van. There we met the Manager of Clayton Love the fish merchant. Many lobster fishermen from Padstow, Newquay and Port Isaac were there too. The manager was asked what plans he had for collecting the shellfish and his answers were most reassuring. Clayton Love had contracts to supply the great Cunard liners with lobsters and therefore could afford to pay the highest prices, "Which quite frankly make Harvey's prices look daft," he said.

We discussed this on the drive home and agreed that things were looking good. It was time to get *Reaper* out from George's Quay and to start fishing. Some small things still needed to be done to the boat and to the gear but as Mike said, "If we wait until we're completely ready, then we'll never make a start."

Home again, Mike and I went down to the boathouse to tell George about our meeting. George and I quickly got into an argument and as usual, the essential points of the argument were somehow lost and we descended into taking cheap shots at each other.

George said, "Huh! You don't think Clayton Love is going to come all the way from Southampton for your little bit of fish?"

I fired back, "Yeah! It's because of old stick–in–the–muds like you, that fishing here is in the doldrums!"

George and I had plenty of ammunition of course. Mike said nothing while we had a go at each other. Only when the argument flagged did he shove his oar in and get us going again.

At 3pm on 6 March, I walked out on Pentire with my small son Martyn. For twenty minutes, I watched the surf breaking on Crantock Beach and across the mouth of the Gannel. I decided that it would be possible to leave with one more hour of flood tide so I took Martyn home to the Cabin and made my way down to the boathouse, where I gave Mike my opinion of the sea conditions. We cast *Reaper* off from George's Quay at about 5pm and had a smooth passage out.

The *Patsy Anne* left the Gannel later that evening and had a rough time of it, even though the wind was only 4–5. She had been sold and was bound for Newlyn.

On Monday, at 8.30am, the ebb was away but there was still plenty of water under the boat. We spent time adjusting the moorings of both the boat and the punt. By lunchtime, the boats were all high and dry and Swindon and his wife were grovelling around in the sand. 'Swindon' took his nickname from the town of his origin. He and his father owned a converted ship's lifeboat, which they kept berthed up the Gannel. They had worked on it for years and whenever anyone asked about it, Swindon would reply emphatically, "We're coming out of the Gannel this year!"

I'm sure he really meant it but though the old tub was a hive of industry every winter, somehow she never quite made it. I remembered seeing Swindon in the spring of 1965, as he crawled from underneath the boat. His hands, face and overalls were streaked with paint and the sweat was pouring off him.

Mike said, "She must be nearly ready for sea!"

"Yes she is," answered Swindon triumphantly, "I've just given her a second coat of anti–fouling!"

Mike, without a hint of a smile said encouragingly, "Ooh, She'll go now boy!"

Well of course, nothing happened as usual and the boat remained up Gannel on her chains, as if she grew there. That is why we were so surprised now to see Swindon was putting down mooring chains in the harbour. He was covered in sand and muck and was soaking wet and shouting a kind of running commentary, in a voice that would frighten the crows. He was never known to speak quietly!

Swindon must really mean it this time, we decided, because 'tealing chains' was an awful job. The bridles, large linked, heavy chains that stretched across the harbour were maintained by the Council. All the boats' mooring chains were shackled into these by the boat owners but these bridles were buried under the sand and could be very hard to find.

Well anyway, there he was with his missus, dragging his own big hanks of heavy chain that were heavy enough to hold a destroyer. The next day we were busy ferrying our pots, twenty at a time, from the loft down to the quay in Mike's van. It was a day of drizzle and sunny spells and we could see Mr and Mrs Swindon running up and down the beach, wielding spades and digging up piles of sand, so that it looked like the place had been mortar bombed!

"I'm going home for a bigger shackle," Swindon yelled to his missus as he raced up the beach.

Half an hour later, he raced back down again clutching an enormous shackle to his chest. He went down on his knees in the wet sand and struggled to join two hanks of chain together. Mike and I were sitting in the van about to go for another load of pots. We paused, eager to see the drama played out. We heard a sudden cry of anguish and Swindon's raucous voice, "Aw! It's too bloody small!"

He jumped up with the shackle and sprinted up the slip towards his car. We had to leave it there. Mike turned the van and we drove up South Quay Hill. As it turned out, the converted lifeboat didn't come out of the Gannel to pick up her moorings that year, nor indeed the next year either!

The next morning, 4.30am, saw us down the harbour. We cut up half a basket of gurnards and then hauled it up on the jetty, where we baited the pots. Just as we prepared to load the pots into the *Reaper*, we heard the BBC *Shipping Forecast* on Mike's little transistor radio. "Sole, Lundy and Fastnet, south west force six or seven," the man said.

We stopped work and thought about it. The tides were still very strong and we weren't sure what would follow the south wester. Only one thing for it: we decided we had to take out the baits again! We went through the fifty pots and put the hundred baits back in the basket to be salted again back in the shed. As we lowered the basket into the boat, Mike's radio, distorted by static, screeched the popular song, *Michael row the boat ashore Alleluia!* Mike took this very personally, "God help anyone who says the wrong thing to me today!" he raged.

We went to the shed, dealt with the bait and measured off rope for another string of pots. Mike only cheered up when Digger Greet arrived and told of his proposed trip to the Mediterranean.

Bill and Ben managed to get the *Evelyn Meyrick* out of the Gannel and into Newquay that evening, before strong westerlies, up to gale force, kept us all in harbour for the next few days.

On 11 March, I had a day of tidying up the loft and getting rid of rubbish. When I was parking my bike back home at Fern Pit, I met George coming out of his net room. I gave him an update of the news and then asked what he thought of the prices being paid by Clayton Love.

"Won't do you any good!" he said. "No wonder the fishing died out here, with attitudes like yours!" I shot back and so we continued the old argument as we walked down the cliff path together.

Chris Moffat had bought Alfie Waters' previous boat, the 23ft *Morning Star*. Chris brought her back to Newquay from Padstow to go at the lobster fishing.

One morning, when the tide was out, Ben Maile the famous artist came down the harbour. Mike was laboriously painting *Reaper*'s name on her bow. He persuaded Ben Maile to do it. Ben completed the work in a few seconds and made a fine job of it.

On Sunday, 15 March, we baited and loaded the two strings of wire lobster pots, the wind having dropped away to a NW 2–3. We steamed off to St Columb Rock and shot them there. Cooker was on board helping. The diary records, "He was full of nonsense as usual!"

We came back and loaded a string of 25 French pots ready for morning again with Cooker's help. Bad weather never seemed to bother Cooker. He saw some savage days out with us and yet, if he could manage it, he would be there on the quay the following morning, as keen as ever to come fishing with us. Once, when we were leaving the harbour on a falling tide, Cooker was late, which was most unusual. We hung on as long we dared, with the two engines running and then we had to clear out before our keel would be caught on the sand. Mike opened up the throttles and we headed for the quay gap. Suddenly there was Cooker running along south quay as hard as he could go.

"Jump Boy!" shouted Mike.

I thought he must be joking, but without a moment's hesitation, Cooker ran the last few paces and launched himself off the end of the pier. He sailed through the air and landed on his feet in front of me with a loud bang. He pitched forward onto all fours with his crib bag hanging around his neck.

"The rotten old sod," he gasped, "he wouldn't even ease her back!"

I was simply amazed that Cooker was uninjured. Coming from that height, it was a wonder he didn't go down through the boards and out through her bottom!

The season had started for us. George Northey and Bill and Ben got their pots fishing too. The Burt's Frenchman *Bacchus* pulled into Newlyn. The weather went wonderfully fine and we had around 20 fish a day for the first few days, which was very encouraging; all except for 18 March when we had to come in with winch trouble. John Julyan came aboard and did a job on it for us. I went into the shed to cut up bait in preparation for the morning. Harold Bullen came in for a yarn at 7.30pm and Mike, seizing his chance slipped away home.

Harold was, according to Mike, the only man who could talk indefinitely without ever drawing a breath. Grave digging was not only a job with him it was also his hobby. It is quite amazing what one can learn while cutting up ten stone of gurnards! I had imagined that a grave was simply a hole in the ground but, apparently, that is not so at all. In fact, the digging of it is highly technical and your shovel, pick and mattock have to be just right. Also, it is amazing what the shovel turns up, particularly in an old graveyard! Harold I suppose was as much an archaeologist as a gravedigger. Not only could he identify fragments of timber from decaying coffins of great antiquity, but he also knew which bit of bone came from which bit of a body. I didn't mind being stuck with Harold and found him most entertaining. Kelvin Moller thought very differently, that kind of talk from Harold about corpses and graves used to freak him out and he always darted away as quickly as possible whenever Harold approached.

Saturday, 19 March, the wind was light and variable and the sea was calm. Our winch was only barely holding together where John Julyan had done a temporary job to keep us fishing. Around midday, David Chapman and his crew in *Castle Wraith* steamed about three miles to where we were fishing just to have a yarn. They approached with a series of bugle calls and as they came alongside, they finished off with a rather ragged Last Post. We were invited aboard to see their conger eel. It was a fairly big one that had come up in one of the pots. They had it swimming around in a big tank of seawater, which they normally used for storing shellfish. Ted, one of the crew, laid hold of the conger by the tail, which caused it to thresh violently and give us all a good wetting. There was always something different about Chapper!

We managed to complete two hauls, despite the dodgy winch and finished up with two crawfish and twenty lobsters. When we returned to the harbour, we heard that Chris Moffat had been working with a gas cylinder, which had exploded. He was unhurt but badly shaken. Although the weather continued fine and we hauled our gear twice a day, the lobster fishing dropped off alarmingly, possibly due to the ground sea which had already started.

On 23 March, we had a WNW gale and the wind stayed in that quarter sometimes reaching force 9. It was 30 March before we got to sea again. Luckily, we had carried our wire pots off into 20 fathoms and brought the French pots into the harbour, and hauled them up onto the centre jetty on the day before the breeze began.

On the 30th, we spent all day getting the pots fishing again; all nicely placed with fresh bait. Bill and Ben had some of their gear all in a heap. We saw them hauling one string with the pots coming up in bunches. All they could do was to cut the pots away from the tangled mass of rope and bring them aboard in ones and twos.

The next few days were remarkable for the hard work we put in, and for the very small returns we all got from it. Our winch was playing up again and I had strained my back. Since I was winch man this was not a good combination. All day hauling the backrope on the capstan head was agony and lobbing the pots overboard in rapid succession wasn't much better. John Julyan had been unavailable to tackle the winch this time because his job with Holman Mining Engineers had taken him on a problem–solving trip to a mine in South Africa. Mike resorted to another outfit who described themselves as marine engineers. The job they did on the winch was useless so we had to manage as best we could.

There was a sudden change in the weather. In the evening, the wind was a light northerly but by morning, we had a rising SE gale. We left at 8am and George Northey came with us. We hauled our string of French pots and shot them closer to home, and then went off to haul two strings of wire pots, which we kept on board. During this time, the south easter increased. We went in under the cliff and hauled two strings of George's pots. They were close in; in the places they called Pronter and Zarvan. Getting George's gear aboard was quite exciting; rock dodging at its best! We came back with spray flying over us as the wind got up to force 9. We shot George's gear across Towan Beach so that his dhan was close to the quay gap. We went into the harbour then and put George into his own boat. It was a simple job for him to then board his pots from the shallow water and bring them in.

Meanwhile we went out again and boarded the string of French pots, which we had placed close in to the harbour earlier, and headed in with three strings aboard. This was a rescue operation and soon the three boats, ourselves, Bill and Ben and George, lay our boats alongside and pulled the pots up onto the jetty. This was to lighten the boats before the expected ground sea came and gave them a good pounding. If this whole thing sounds complicated, well it was! It did take some forward planning and yet, there was so little time to plan anything. This was the down side of working from a tidal harbour!

Bill and Ben had had to leave one string of pots out and so did we, because the wind had freshened so quickly. We all hoped that they were in water deep enough to be safe. George had also been forced to leave a few pots out as well. The ground sea came and although we were expecting bad weather, we didn't expect it to be so bad or for it to last so long. We were tied up for days and the diary tells of gales of wind and enormous seas.

The whole month of April was a disaster as far as landing fish went. Almost everyone else lost some of their gear, but we were lucky and got away with our pots intact. We got some few days fishing during the first two weeks in May but nobody did any good, due to what the diary records as "Big Ground Sea" and "Enormous Ground Sea" and more gales of wind! It was near the end of the month before we had any good catches of 20 or more lobsters for a day's fishing.

It was during May that Cornwall's Chief Fishery Officer, Clifton Pender resigned. This was good news indeed, considering his support for skin divers! On 29 May, we worked down as far as St Agnes, and over the next few days we shifted our gear around in that general area. At last, a few fish were moving and we had 30 or 40 lobsters and a few crawfish as well. Mick Chegwidden came out with us one day when we had 58 lobsters and five crawfish. That was a beautiful day with the sea smooth and the weather sunny and warm. Cooker came out with us on another day and disgraced himself by breaking the stick of a dahn that Mike had made just the evening before!

The *Freeman* had been sold and Hoss Bailey was now fishing her from Padstow. Mike Morris had *Trevose* up for sale and she was up in the Gannel awaiting a buyer. Brimble was offered £1,000 for the *Cornishman* but he wanted £1,200. Cavell the diver repaired his boat and launched her down. Those of us who saw the workmanship thought she would sink under him. The *Bacchus* had been working just outside our gear but she had now moved west down off St Ives.

On 5 June, there was a "very steep gulch". We were just clear of the harbour when a huge sea broke in on us. It even washed our bucket overboard and Mike had to ease her down while we pumped out. The wind where we were was only westerly force 5 at the most but the awful confused seas came rearing up at us from the north west. This we believed came from gales in the Irish Sea. Despite *Reaper*'s wonderful stability the gulch on that day made working almost impossible and it nearly rolled the pots out of the boat.

Mike and I struggled our way through the morning and though we could hardly speak over the racket, we managed to have a row about Groupie! Mike said he was a prat and I said he was a good guy. *Reaper* leaped violently about and wouldn't stay up on the gear. The mizzen sail was useless as we fell into deep troughs and teetered precariously up on wobbly crests. Now the pots were coming up under her keel. Each one hung under our bilge and Mike nearly had a hernia dragging them up and over the rail. The exertion, the sun and the temper reddened his face.

"I still say Groupie is a prat," he shouted above the noise of sea and engines. I couldn't answer because *Reaper* swung away to port 90 degrees and the backrope was singing with the strain. I reached down to the gear lever extension and knocked the engine out of gear for a moment, letting the rope surge on the capstan until the strain came off. I shoved the lever forward and, as our bow swung to starboard, I hauled as hard as I could and three or four pots came swiftly up, each presenting itself nicely for Mike to board and deal with. He dragged out crabs and spider crabs with such haste that they shed legs and claws as he flung them overboard. He lifted out a big 6 lb lobster and cradling it like a baby, he fell backwards to sit among the pots. He scrambled to his feet. Stuffing the lobster in the box and throwing the wet sacking on top of it he leaped back to his position at the rail, but by now the pots were under the keel again. The strain on the capstan was mighty. It was awfully hot with the sun belting down and I still had my stiff oilskin frock on.

I shouted, "What the hell do you know about Groupie, anyway? I'm the one who goes to the meetings, not you!"

Mike opened his mouth to answer but I yelled, "We're fucking fast!"

He spun round and charged back to the wheelhouse. I declutched the capstan and Mike opened the throttle. Spinning the wheel, he brought the boat back in position over the string of pots. I put another turn on the capstan. Between us, with Mike at the helm and me at the winch, we worked together manoeuvring, teasing, coaxing the trapped pots away from the jagged rock which held them in its iron grip.

The flooding tide was strong. The gulch was getting worse. If we got it wrong, we would smash the pots and part the rope. We worked together, not needing speech or signals because each knew what the other would do next as the situation developed. With a sudden jerk, the pots were free. We hauled them aboard and leaving the dhan out, we towed it east for a couple of minutes. When Mike satisfied himself that the pots would land on good ground he called casually from the wheelhouse, "When you've a mind to!"

I lobbed out the heavy bundle of chain followed by the pots one at a time. Over went the last pot, the bunch of chain and the buoy rope with its floats. I threw out the dhan as if it was a harpoon. I was relieved to hear Mike say, "That's it Boy! One haul will do us. Let's get the hell out of it!"

I made sure the few lobsters were protected from the sun and wind and then staggered aft along the heaving deck. I took off the dreadful oilskin frock and sat on the doorstep, sheltered by the wheelhouse. Mike steered for Newquay. It had been a long morning and I was suddenly hungry. We opened our crib bags. We were at ease with ourselves. We had battled the elements and done our work and every pot had two fresh baits in it.

Mike said, "Groupie's ok really, except …"

I said, "I know what you mean. He does behave like a prat sometimes, but …"

THE TERRIBLE OILSKIN FROCK

This garment, worn with the sou'wester, kept torrential rain and heavy spray off you but if the sun suddenly came out, you would nearly melt. Also, you needed to be an escapologist to get out of it.

The Trammel

Back in January, I had been helping George Northey to mend his trawl. More truthfully George was teaching me net mending! Nets fascinated me and I wanted to learn more about them.

I met Jack Phillips, who was Bridport Gundrys' Representative, on the quay. I bought three hanks of net from him. These nets were destined for Lake Tanganyika but the order had been cancelled, so they came to me very cheap. They had quite large meshes compared to the herring nets, which we were more used to, and so I mounted them as a trammel net. Of course, I hadn't a clue about trammels, but George knew about such things and he showed me how.

Later on, when we had all our pots in the water and we were properly settled into the fishing I wanted to give the trammel a try. However, Mike was not at all keen. Eventually, one evening Mike brought the completed trammel net, together with a couple of anchors, dahns and ropes down to the quay in his pick–up. We got it on board and we laid up the net ready for shooting. As the headline with its floats and the footrope with its leads passed through our hands I marvelled at its construction. It was a really cunning fish trap. I just could not understand Mikes' lack of enthusiasm. As we worked, I was hinting at the fish we might catch. I said that with big meshes like this you just never knew. We might get Turbot and plaice and hake, even bass and sea trout, really high priced stuff.

"We'll be in the money." I assured him.

Mike said nothing but I could tell at a glance that that he was not enjoying himself one bit. He was like a fellow in pain who was just wishing it would go away.

We steamed a short distance out and shot the trammel in the Gazzle, just off the old Lifeboat House, then returned to the harbour. That night in bed, I was picturing Mike and myself hauling the trammel, rehearsing it in my mind really. When I fell asleep, I dreamed the net was full of fish. We were dragging big cod and pollock and fish of all kinds in over the rail. I kept waking up and dozing off again and my dream kept coming back. Each time it returned it seemed sillier than the time before. When the alarm went off, I woke up feeling exhausted.

Of course, that morning we had to steam past our trammel and spend the day hauling our pots. That was agony for me because I was dying to see what our 'killer net' had caught. I didn't dare suggest that we haul the Trammel first because I knew that Mike would explode at the very idea. Never mind, I consoled myself, just wait until he sees what we catch. That will change his mind for him.

It was a long day and I thought it would never end. We entered harbour and put our shellfish away. Mike naturally had to tip diesel into our fuel tanks, but eventually we were free to go. Out through the quay gap we went and within a few minutes, I was picking up the dahn. Now we would see, I told myself. As soon as the anchor reached the surface, Mike was there to board it.

When the end of net came up it was well adorned with seaweed of various kinds, prominent among them was oar–weed, which takes the name from its broad flat ribbons. Fishermen call it stick–weed though, after the thick, tough yard–long stick with its gnarled and twisted 'roots' at the bottom. A student of botany could have gained much from the first few fathoms but there was nothing to excite us there. We kept hauling and the weed got more plentiful. A spider crab, hopelessly entangled peeped out at us from the mass of weeds. A few more fathoms and a couple of hen crabs had knitted themselves into our trammel, further on again a spotty dogfish twisted amongst meshes. As we neared the end of the net, I saw that we had caught two small plaice.

"There's my tea anyway". I said, trying to put a little humour into things.

Mike said nothing. We hauled the other anchor and buoy on board and placed it with the rest. We stood for a moment gazing at the great hump of assorted weeds and stuff sitting in the middle of the deck. I was looking at Mike. He was still looking at the trammel. Then he said slowly. "Well old man, before I'll pull that thing again I'll go to fuckin' prison!"

Sea Stories

If Mike's shed could talk then it would surely tell some stories. The shed came to Mike through Joe Burt, the local boat builder who had recently retired. It was a lean–to built of timber with plenty of small–paned windows to let in the daylight. It was attached to the wall next to the old railway tunnel and it was a wonderful asset, being one of only four fishermen's sheds in the whole harbour. It had an ample workbench and we stored our diesel cans and bait barrels in there.

Fishermen from other ports often came into the shed for a yarn and a week of bad weather was guaranteed to bring men from all over Cornwall. From Newlyn and Mousehole and Porthleven and Mevagissey they came and from Padstow, our nearest neighbours. The Newquay kids all came into the shed too and they listened to the talk. They heard romantic place names, many of them referring to rocks and reefs known only to the fishermen. They heard about the heroes and the fools, about the good times and the bad, so that the history and the traditions of the fishing trade seeped into their very souls. Many of them went on to become fishermen.

Cooker could have been a Member of Parliament, or an auctioneer or something sensible, but too much exposure to the sea stories had him ruined. Stories were important and it seems to me that people had not acquired the short attention span, due to TV saturation, like they have today. No indeed, they listened politely without butting in right until the story's very end.

Like the time when Cooker was telling us one of his stories. The three of us were in the shed and Mike and I worked on gear, while Cooker sat on the bench with his feet up on a coil of rope. He had his knees up under his chin and, engrossed in his tale, he wound a piece of pot rope around his legs and practiced tying knots: first a round turn and two half hitches, next a clove hitch, then a rolling hitch. He made a hash of that one though and tried again. Mike and I glanced at each other. Cooker's second attempt turned out perfect with his two legs bound together just as his tale reached its exciting conclusion. He looked up at us, seeking some sort of reaction. I grabbed him and held him head down in the bait barrel with his nose only inches above the brine. Well! I reckon they could hear the roars out of him up on Mount Wise. Did Cooker run away and join the army? No, of course not: he was hooked, just like David and Phillip 'Tich' Trebilcock and the rest, and he would go full–time fishing whatever it took.

By the middle of June we were fishing very well but the pressure was on us now because we had lost so much fishing time. We gave it all we'd got. My motor bike, which had been going perfectly, now decided to pack up! I tried all the usual cunning tricks, but nothing worked. Going on foot was tough because these were long days; it was all early mornings and late nights; we were hauling three times a day.

The first morning that the bike failed, I ran across the golf links, only to find the shortcut beside the Breden Court Hotel had been closed off by a fence. This prevented me from nipping across Tower Road, through Travena Terrace and so on to the south quay. Instead, I had to charge all the way down to the tennis courts and, after emerging onto Fore Street, run sweating and panting back to the South Quay Hill. This fairly whacked me out.

Now it was Mike's turn to strain his back! Each day it got worse and he really needed to rest it but the weather was fine and we were catching plenty of stuff. He just had to tough it out but I see could the pain in his face.

My mother and father came to stay in Newquay for the summer and Dad, who was a good mechanic, checked the bike out for me. He discovered lots of water in the petrol tank and declared that, in his opinion, this was an act of sabotage. Once rid of the water and with fresh petrol in the tank the bike was as good as new.

At around the same time our bait strings, which were hanging in their usual place near the winch, got slashed through by somebody with a knife. However, we got over these things. We just made up a couple of hundred new ones and stowed them away each night.

Mike's back improved and he was soon at full strength again.

The fishermen all received demands from the Newquay Urban District Council for car parking fees for leaving their vehicles at the harbour. This was quite unexpected and the letter warned the lads that unless they paid up pronto, their cars would be towed away. I wrote to Mr Lord of the Fishermen's Organisation Society, giving him the details. I also wrote to the Council on behalf of our members. Meanwhile our members took evasive action and parked up at Red Lion or some other place. This diktat from our political masters was a great nuisance to us while it lasted. It seemed it was ok for the emmetts and all and sundry to bung up the harbour with their cars and vans free of charge, but the local fishermen must pay for the privilege. Well, we would see about that!

The fine weather brought the divers out. They soon discovered what we already knew, that the crawfish were virtually gone. Diver boat's catches now consisted of two or three crawfish and a couple of bags of sea urchins, which were sold to the emmetts for souvenirs.

King Kong came up to me on the quay one morning, his face all angry looking. He said, "You've reported me for having Royal Air Force gear on board."

"Have I?" says I.

"Yes, and you will be getting a solicitor's letter," says he.

"Oh really, that's nice!" I answered and kept walking.

That evening, after the day's fishing, Mike and I had to cross King Kong's boat to get ashore. He mumbled something about a solicitor's letter and I told him, "Shut your face!"

That worked like a charm. It seemed to us that the divers were less popular nowadays. It followed then that those old friendships, which had been sundered by the fishermen vs. divers argument, were gradually patched up. Simon Drew gave Mike a metal trawl float he'd found washed up on the beach. We knew from small gestures such as this that we were back in favour.

Towards the end of June a couple of days of heavy ground sea cut our fishing right back. Chris Moffat and Dave Sleeman were out hauling pots aboard the *Morning Star*. They were in about ten fathoms when a big sea broke into her and half–filled the boat. Not a nice experience. To make matters worse, due to the surge in the dock, a stone went up through the bottom of Chris's carve and fourteen lobsters escaped.

All season the price of lobsters and crawfish had been equal but now lobsters were fetching eight shillings per pound whilst the crawfish, despite their scarcity, had fallen to six shillings. It was obvious to us that the divers, by landing soft–shelled crawfish, many of which would have died in transit, had destroyed market confidence. This dramatic drop in price was unprecedented.

More annoying still we came across the *Westward Ho* with Cavell and two other divers very close to one of our strings of pots. We thought Cavell might be trying to provoke an incident, and we figured that he must be getting short of money to operate his boat by this time. Therefore, we calmly watched them steam away instead of going over and giving them hell.

On 26 June, we hauled our gear once and when the tide turned, we hauled one string a second time. The south west wind was freshening and thick mist and drizzle closed in, so we turned for home. On this day, we had fished for thirty–four consecutive days. We were tied up with a south west gale for two days, which gave Graham Moller and me the chance to go to Truro in his van, to attend a meeting of the Cornish Inshore Fishermen. Groupy was Chairman and a girl named Peggy was Honorary Secretary and among those present were Trevor England, Warwick Provis, Bill Hoskin, Dick Sampson, Cedric Staples and John Vinnicombe It was a very good meeting and we learned that the new Sea Fishery Officer was an ex–trawler skipper by the name of Broundan Tonkin. Those who knew him said he was very good man for the job.

One evening Martin ('Brimble') and John Bawden came up to me, all very concerned. King Kong had told them that I had reported him and he had a sample of my handwriting to prove it. "Now," they said, he is "after your guts."

This gave me a good laugh. A couple of days later, King Kong was aboard his boat at the steps and even though I took my time crossing his deck to get ashore, he never opened his mouth.

John Cuthill came out with us for a trip on 3 July, a glorious day with a light westerly wind. Between hauls, we anchored in the Sound of the Madrips. It was just beautiful in there in the clear calm water, beside the great, black pinnacle of rock, which was home to thousands of sea birds. We caught fifty–five lobsters and two crawfish on that day. We had good catches all the next week, including one day with seventy–two lobsters.

Throughout July, our French pots caught hardly any crawfish but, in fairness, we were concentrating on the lobsters. By the 26th, we had spent only five days in harbour out of sixty–four. We had a hard time just keeping everything going and general maintenance of the boat and gear kept us very busy. The stitching on the mizzen sail started to come adrift and I repaired it with the needle and palm. As fast as I stitched one seam another would start to unravel itself.

The belt driving *Reaper's* main engine cooling water pump and alternator was prone to break and Mike had spare belts tied in place. When the last one of these broke, we came home on the small engine. The tide was low so Mike put me ashore at Fly Cellars. I got to the motor bike and drove off to buy another belt while Mike dropped anchor in the bay and set about dismantling the winch shafting to gain access to the pulleys. It proved a bigger problem than we had thought because the alternator bracket had been damaged when the last belt broke, and so it was 9.30 that evening before *Reaper* nosed her way into the harbour. Mike was black up to his armpits or, as he would have said, he was "lampered"!

For the most of July, there was an acute bait shortage and Harvey's did their best to make sure we all got a fair share of what was available. Sometimes they organised bait from far away and then it became very expensive. Any conger eels, pouting, wrasse or bream that came up in the pots were, there and then, cut up for bait. Big congers were tough to tackle because of their violent struggles, their slime and, let's not forget, their teeth! Never mind, they too fell victims to our big black–handled bait knives. We also feathered for mackerel and pollock at every opportunity and we often ate our crib holding a sandwich with one hand and jigging the line with the other. The trouble was that when the fish hit the hooks, you jammed the sandwich in your teeth and hauled the line with both hands. In the ensuing battle, the tastiest bit of the sandwich was often lost overboard. It's a hard life!

An article appeared in the local paper with a photograph of Ben Maile's painting of Newquay Harbour. It featured mainly the *Reaper* and Bill and Ben's *Evelyn Meyrick* lying against the jetty. The painting, the article said, would be presented to HM the Queen. We basked in the reflected glory for a tiny moment!

Bill and Ben, the least aggressive of people, came in from sea one day in an awful rage. They had come upon Cavell with some of his RAF friends and they were diving directly on their pots. When challenged by Bill and Ben the divers only laughed at them, they said. They phoned the Department man, Geoffrey Wollaston. Geoffrey told them that there was nothing legally to be done about it but that he himself would speak to Cavell.

A couple of days later, the *Westward Ho* was seen hanging on to one of Bill Sharrock's dahns, while Cavell and his friends were diving. We had little sympathy for Bill since he was one of the first to bring out divers. The fact that he no longer carried them cut no ice with us. A boat we had not seen before with group of divers on board came in and tied up to the north quay. There were some crawfish on the deck so Mike went over and warned them. He said, "If you dive on our pots I will ram you."

They were gone the next day and we never saw them again. The next time we heard about Cavell the story was that Alfie Waters had come across him diving on his pots. It seems that Alfie, aboard the *Seagull,* steamed around the divers at high speed and that Cavell is saying that he is going to report him to the Fishery Officer.

Jock Bleakly, Jimmy Hoare and Mike Carmen went to Plymouth to collect Jock's latest purchase, a 26 footer. They sailed for Newquay on 30 July but got into trouble off Cape Cornwall and were towed in by the St Ives lifeboat at 2am. They apparently had a tough time of it with Jock saying that he never expected to see land again!

August brought strong winds and although we got to sea most days, we did, at last, get a chance to do some of the more urgent jobs that were screaming for attention. Despite interruptions due to weather, the lobster fishing was holding up very well.

Meanwhile, George Northey was getting itchy feet. George had most of his pots ashore, which left him free to work his ferry across to Crantock Beach. This was normal practice with him every summer and he was happy dealing with the hordes of emmetts who streamed down the cliff path. Now however, as the emmetts became scarcer, George wanted to be back into the lobsters and, since he never did things by half, this meant, 'Go for it'. In other words, get–every–last–pot–out–there–fishing–NOW! His only problem was gauging the optimum time. Supposing August stayed wet then the beach trade would surely tail off; but what if it came sunny and the lobsters went scarce? George grappled with this conundrum and, to aid him in his decision–making, he would meet me as I parked my motor bike against his shed after the day's fishing.

'Well what's the story?' was our usual form of greeting to one another, then for a few moments, we would chat about things until we got down to the nitty–gritty.

George, drawing softly on his pipe would watch me carefully as I gave him a blow–by–blow account of the day's catching, ending with something like, "The last string had seven in it so we finished up with thirty six."

George was a good friend and I knew that he wouldn't blow our business around. Even so, I usually reduced our score by ten or a dozen, so as not to excite him too much really!

One evening as I leaned the bike up against his shed George appeared suddenly. "Well what's the story?" I greeted him.

He shrugged his massive shoulders, "Humph, some story! That gang from Southampton that was paying the big prices, what d'ya call 'em?"

"Clayton Love," I said.

George paused and allowed himself a big smile. "The story is that they went all down the coast buying shellfish and they had this big truck like a furniture van."

Sensing bad news and thinking, 'retaliate first', I asked, "What did you expect, a bloody Morris Minor?"

George let out a great guffaw. "It seems the blokes on the lorry hadn't a clue and they threw the lobsters and the craws in first and chucked the crabs in on top of them, the bloody lot died and nobody got paid".

"Yeh George. That's probably an exaggeration! I gotta go; actually, I'm breaking my neck for a piss. See you tomorrow!"

With that, I made my escape and bounded away down the cliff path to the Vyrn Cabin.

1963. Newquay Harbour.

1963. Newquay Harbour. Top left is Pendrellen House with Atlantic Hotel above that. Foreground has Mike Lyne with basket of crawfish; Edgar Carter, sitting (drowned 3rd December 1965); Dick James, standing. Trev in punt sculling (out of sight behind Dick James).
This image is from an old Harvey Barton postcard in the author's collection. Copyright unknown.

1963. *Twilight*. Hauling Pots. "Dammit! We're fast!"
Trev tries to free it while Mike changes a bait (wire pot).

February, 1963. Baby Martyn on the north quay, watching Eddie Hoare mending a net. Shadow of
Eddie shows netting needle, held in his mouth while he cuts meshes.

1963. *Twilight*. Hauling Pots. Trev at capstan (withy lobster pot).

1963. *Twilight*. Mike Lyne at helm.

1963. Trev on *Twilight* entering Newquay Harbour.

1963. *Twilight*. Trev at the capstan. Mike boards and baits the pots (wire lobster pots).

1963. *Shamrock* (as *Reaper* was then known). Stern showing rudder, two propellers and mizzen.

1963. *Shamrock* (bearing the Penzance port of registry) up Gannel, with Pauline and Martyn.

1964. Newquay Harbour. *Reaper* (formerly *Shamrock*, the port of registry has now changed to Padstow) and *Freeman*.

1964. Newquay Harbour. *Reaper*.

1964. Up Gannel. Mike on board *Reaper*.

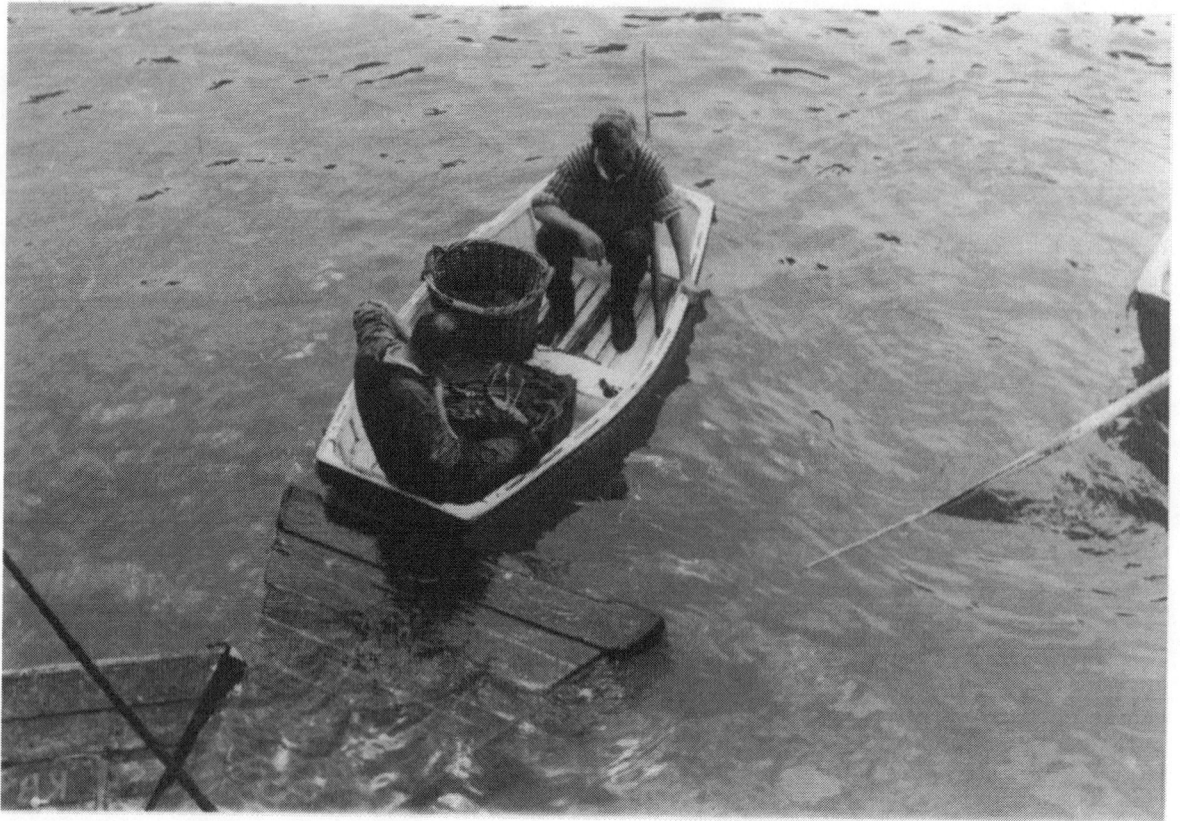

1964. Mike and Trev aboard.
Mike nicking a crawfish and putting lobsters and crawfish into our carve.

March 1965. Newquay, Cornwall. Left to right: *Patsy Anne, Freeman, Reaper*.

1965. View looking up River Gannel from Vyrn Cabin. Martyn with Trixie.

1965. Newquay Harbour. *Cornishman* (Martin Burt), *Evelyn Meyrick* (Moller Brothers), *Reaper* (Mike Lyne)

1966. *Reaper*, hauling wire pots. "Another fine Lobster!"

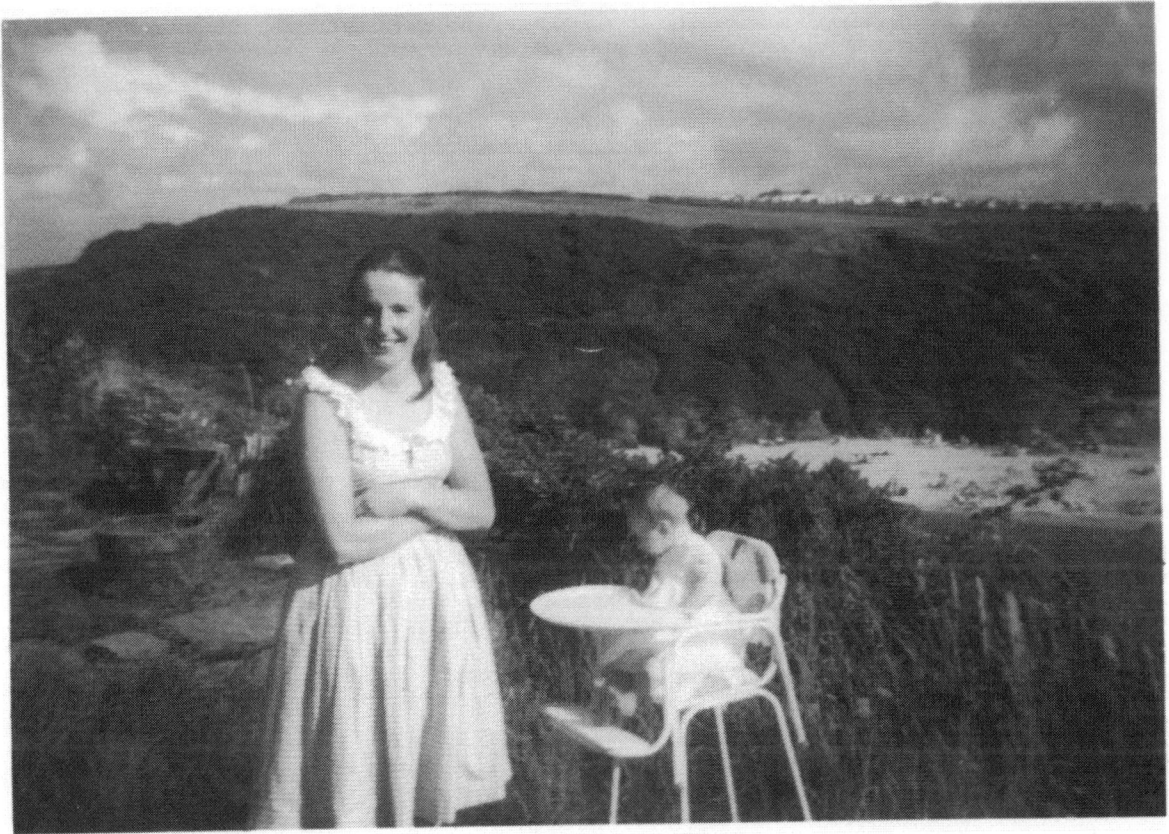

1966. View from Vyrn Cabin across River Gannel to Crantock. Pauline with Jenny.

1966. Vyrn Cabin. View up River Gannel. Trev and Pauline with Jenny and Martyn.

What Price Cat's Meat?

By some good fortune, the date for my next driving test occurred on a blowy day. The auspices were good. The green and chrome Francis Barnet purred sweetly along Trevemper Road with a strong tailwind. I had read the Highway Code many times and I was feeling very positive. I was confident that this time, THIS time I would pass. 'What a difference passing this test is going to make to us,' I told myself as I bowled along. 'I will trade in this bike and get a bigger one with a sidecar and then we will be a truly mobile little family. On my days off, we will go touring all over Cornwall. But hang on a minute!' Something was niggling at me. It felt as though I had a bit of a flat tyre. I pulled in to the side of the road and had a look and sure enough, the back tyre had gone soft. Well that was a nuisance but I had plenty of time and I would get a puff of air in it at the next Garage.

Ten minutes later, I was bowling along nicely when the throttle started playing–up. Now this quickly got worse! Changing gear became very difficult as the revs became so erratic. The journey was a bit of a nightmare but, at last, I reached Truro and pulled into Collin's Garage. I pumped the tyre again and bought a new throttle cable. I fitted the new cable but that didn't help one bit. No indeed, the problem must have lain somewhere deep in the bikes' rotten little mechanical guts! Between the garage and the Driving Test Office, I stopped a few times and fiddled with the carburettor and its wretched cable. All I got for my efforts was a pair of very black hands and a terrible feeling of impending doom. Sitting in the waiting room, for what seemed like ages, did nothing to improve my mood. Nervously biting my fingernails was not a good idea! Some of the blackness had most likely been transferred to my face.

The examiner came out of his office and, after the usual questions about the Highway Code (I could have quoted him chapter and verse) he invited me to mount my machine. The engine started at the first kick. As I drove up the street, the revs increased with a suddenness that took even me by surprise and the bike shot forward. I was fighting for control and franticly working the clutch, the twist–grip and the gear pedal while the bike responded with repeated kangaroo hops. The engine revs knew only the two extremes; it was either dropping to stalling speed or it was climbing to absolute maximum.

I don't know where the examiner was when this happened but to the pedestrians of Truro I must have appeared as the Biker from Hell! Next thing I knew the bike was stuck in bottom gear and the revs were stuck at maximum. This had a strange compensating effect and the bike seemed content to travel at a sedate fifteen mph, albeit emitting a noise like a diving Stuka Dive bomber. Due to the brisk following wind, I was soon enveloped in a pall of thick, pungent exhaust smoke.

The streets comprising the test course formed an acute triangle. Approaching its apex, I noted that some workmen were busy opening a large square hole in the road. They heard me coming and paused, leaning on their picks and shovels. As I roared slowly around their excavation, I lay a dense smokescreen over them. For their part, they waved their caps and gave me a great cheer.

As I motored away down the other street, I found the bike more difficult to steer. I soon realised that the problem was a serious softening of the back tyre. But I am not a quitter! By the time I reached the road works, on my second lap, the back tyre was really soggy and the engine was at screaming pitch.

The four workmen, entering into the spirit of the thing, had climbed out of their hole to cheer me on and waved enthusiastically as if they were spectators at the Isle of Man. As I left them behind me, I could feel the heat from the exhaust pipe burning through my rubber boot. I fought for control as I approached the hidden alleyway (which everyone knew about), where the examiner would be lying in ambush to test my reaction for 'The Emergency Stop'. Suddenly he leapt out to the kerbside and stuck his hand out but I was ready for him! I crammed on the anchors and stuck the bike to the road. I congratulated myself with the thought that I got that bit right anyway! I looked up at the examiner. He raised his eyebrows as the engine blew back through the carburettor with a series of loud detonations and stopped abruptly. The examiner shook his head and departed. I had failed again!

I stayed in the saddle while the bike cooled down, listening to the peculiar ticking noise the engine made as it contracted. I waited until the spark plug was cool enough to touch and then removed it, cleaned it up and replaced it. I got the tyre pumped at a nearby garage and started for home. It had been raining on–and–off all day but my departure from Truro was a signal to the Gods to really turn the taps on. I rode into the teeth of the gale, lashed by torrential rain. Very soon, I was ploughing through flooded roads, often unable to see the grass verges. Every few minutes I would have to stop and remove the spark plug, which would be searing hot and I'd clean it and then suffer the burnt fingers when trying to screw it back into the little hole in the cylinder head. I arrived home at Fern Pit with the engine screaming, white smoke billowing and the exhaust pipe burning through my boot. The back tyre had lost its air and we bounced over the stones on the wheel rims and into George's shed.

The following morning, the weather was too bad for us go to sea, which suited me fine because I was feeling wrecked. Later that day I saw a BSA Bantam motor bike for sale. I got it cheap and it proved to be a little beauty.

Meanwhile, John Julyan went on board and worked on the winch. He improved its performance for us.

Johnny Bellman bought a boat, an awful looking tub! People who really knew about boats, Simon Drew, George Northey and others made disparaging comments when they saw it. It had a slow revving engine, perhaps it was a single cylinder job. When Johnny had it running in the harbour, it made a loud thumping noise and the whole boat shook. Great gouts of black smoke shot rhythmically out of a hole down near her waterline and oily soot settled on the water. Old Brownie said, "If Bellman moors that thing next to my boat I'll nail a sheet of galvanised iron over his bloody exhaust."

A couple of days later someone said Johnny had given up his job and was going full–time lobster fishing. The general opinion was that it was a toss–up which happened first: either Johnny would get killed by that terrible mangle he called a winch, or else he would go off to sea and drown himself!

On Saturday, 6 August, a young man of seventeen had to be rescued from the tide pool at Fern Pit. George Northey was in his boathouse when the alarm was raised. The lad was already under water and had the appearance of being dead when George reached him. George had radioed the harbour using his walkie–talkie and, within minutes, two carloads of Fishermen arrived at Fern Pit. As it turned out the young man was resuscitated and made a full recovery but incidents such as this showed the dire need we had for these little sets. Yet George risked prosecution by sending an SOS. Some Bullshit!

August was not shaping up very well for weather and we had some very testing times. The lobsters were still feeding, despite the drag in the water and our catches were good.

Johnny Bellman turned his van over and had to go to hospital. It was reported that Gruesome Grose had shipped on as mate with Johnny. As one wag remarked, "Troubles seldom come singly."

A couple of weeks later the same wag said that Johnny had been fishing for a fortnight but had only been to sea twice: that was, out one day to shoot the pots and out again, two weeks later, to try and find them!

Our good earnings throughout this period were constantly threatened by the recurring bait shortages. A lorry, bearing the name Ross Group, arrived from Hull with frozen blocks of grey gurnards. Harvey's had organised it and we were glad to get it, even though it cost us fourteen shillings a stone, almost three times the price of the favoured fresh red gurnards we usually got from Newlyn. It was a short–term solution but it was either that or stop fishing. One evening, Johnny Bellman came into the shed while Mike and I were salting in our precious bait. He was short and sturdy, dark haired and had big gruff voice.

"How much do they gurnards cost?" he asked. (No doubt, he knew the price already.)

When I told him, he let out a great laugh. "Haw! Haw! Haw!"

He went, "What are you boys thinking of? You ain't gotta clue! What you want for catching the lobsters is Kitty Kat!"

He then showed us two cat food tins, which were completely empty. One end of each tin was torn in a jagged hole with sharp pieces protruding outwards.

"See," he said, "you only have to punch a couple of holes in the end of the tins and the crabs will do the rest. The tins last a whole week before the meat is all gone."

Johnny was so enthusiastic about this great discovery of his that we couldn't get rid of him. Mike and I, taking care not to encourage him, just agreed with him. Eventually he ran out of steam and wandered off. It sounded like a good idea but investing in one hundred and twenty–five tins of cat's meat, one for each pot, didn't appeal to us at all.

A few days later Johnny and his mate, Gruesome were arrested for breaking into the grocer's shop, Jenkins Supply Stores in Fore Street. At around the same time the bait shortage came to an end and Harvey's could give you as much fresh red gurnards at five shillings a stone as you wanted.

Ah well! Life is full such little ironies.

Shorter Days

August was coming to a close and Mike and I still fished as hard as ever, but we no longer had to get up at quite so ridiculous an hour. This was because of the darker mornings. Our evenings were shortened too.

Another consideration was the sea fleas. These little beauties come in two sizes; the big ones look a bit like large woodlice. Their smaller cousins are hardly a quarter of an inch long but both kinds occur in vast numbers in the fall of the year. As soon as the sun goes down towards the horizon, the sea fleas go into a feeding frenzy. These are the soldier ants of the seabed and they can eat all the bait out of a whole fleet of pots in minutes! Therefore, late in the summer it was a waste of time shooting pots after about 4pm.

The shorter working days and the breaks in the weather gave us a chance to live normal lives. I took Martyn down to the western end of Fistral and we fished for blennies in the rock pools. I realised that this is the kind of thing that dads do. I promised myself that we would do it more often.

The days of making three hauls were over for this year. It soon became a race to get all five strings of pots hauled and shot for the second time before the evening closed in. This reduced the number of pots hauled per day from three hundred and seventy–five to two hundred and fifty. In real terms, our fishing effort was cut by more than half, as more disturbed weather came in from the Atlantic. This forced us to move our pots away from the best bits of ground and into deeper, but less productive areas.

We still took advantage of any lull however, and would load up three strings and dash close inshore with them. This was a chancy business and rapidly worsening sea conditions often found us hauling the last few pots out of the broken water, and clearing out of it with only moments to spare. Happily for us, our earnings held up very well and most days we caught around thirty lobsters. Also, the price of lobsters was going up. We did catch a few crawfish in our fifty French pots but no matter where we shot them, or how many times we hauled them, the story was the same: apart from a few stragglers, the crawfish were gone!

Despite this scarcity, several divers were still operating. Their activities didn't affect us quite as much now, as they found the lobsters harder to catch than the crawfish. However, we were heartily sick of these 'rubber suited parasites' as we called them. The divers remaining were bolder and more determined than before. There were even more incidents of them diving on pots. We all knew how much it cost to run a boat and reckoned that some of these guys may have 'spent the money before they got it' so to speak, and were now driven by desperation. After seeing the *Westward Ho* hovering around our dahns Mike confronted Cavell on the quay. He told him, "If I catch you diving on our gear I will mince you up with the propeller!"

We found it increasingly hard to sit tight and control our tempers. I got pretty worked up about things myself, which may help to explain what happened next; though for a change, the divers were not at fault. Several mornings over the past fortnight we had found one or other of our strings of pots had been messed about with. When we hauled the buoy rope, there would be a great strain on it. Up would come four or five pots and the bunch of chain all together in a lump. That was a fine start to the day, with the pair of us hanging over the side struggling to clear it.

Early on, we had realised that our problem was being caused by one of the angling charter boats, whose skipper was hanging onto our buoy rope and using our pots as an anchor. The pots were being dragged around by five tons of boat at the mercy of wind and tide. This trick saved him from going to all the trouble of shooting his own anchor, the lazy git. We were certain we knew which skipper was the culprit and on this particular morning, as we wrestled with the tangle of pots and ropes, we found an angler's trace with three hooks and a lead stuck fast in our gear.

"That's done it!" I said to Mike as I freed the angling trace and put it to one side. "I'll read his bloody horoscope for him when we get ashore."

Later, as we came ashore carrying our diesel can, bait basket and bits and pieces, I saw our man standing in front of the PSA. He was yarning with a gang of the local lads around him. This suited me fine because there were plenty of witnesses. We could have our row and get it over with and the message would go out, loud and clear, to all and sundry. I went up to him and showed him the trace.

"I believe this belongs to you," I said.

He gazed at it. "It could be mine," he agreed.

"Well stop hanging onto our dahns and use your own bloody anchor in future!"

Sparks began to fly. He denied touching the gear but I wasn't having any of it. Suddenly the situation changed. This other guy barged in, almost getting in between us.

"Don't you accuse my mate," he snarled. I did my best to ignore this and continued the argument but alarm bells were ringing in my head.

I had seen this guy around and heard he was in the Merchant Navy, but I had never spoken to him. He was about my height but he was stockier in build. He was getting more aggressive by the second and the next thing I knew he was offering to give me a hammering. Mike, being a sensitive soul, interrupted my argument and said, "Trev, he's challenging you!"

Now I could see that this guy was going to blow his gasket any moment. I turned slowly away from him, and watching him out of the corner of my eye, I answered Mike loudly so that all could hear, "Ignore him; it's only the beer talking."

The haymaker, had it connected, would have demolished me but I stepped inside it and shot a left and a right into his face. Neither punch was very hard, but they had a certain shock effect and I stuck a couple more in for good measure. We got into a clinch but the gang pulled us apart.

"We don't want no fighting down here," shouted Mick Chegwidden and the rest took up the chorus: "Yeh! No fighting!", "Whatever is it coming to?" and stuff like that.

'Hypocrites!' I thought because, looking at their faces, I saw that they had enjoyed our little spat!

My adversary had detached himself and gone off somewhere but now he was calling me by name from the yard in beside the PSA.

"Come here Simpson, I want to talk to you," he shouted several times.

Chris Moffat said, "Don't go Trev. He's bad news."

But I saw that we had unfinished business and I went in to meet him. He saw me and came towards me holding out his shirtfront in an attempt to put me off guard and saying. "Look, you tore my shirt."

Then he rushed at me with fists flying. I got the left and right into his face again, a bit crisper this time, and drove him back against the wall of the PSA. I thought. 'It's in the bag; I will now systematically beat the crap out of this guy.' With that in mind, I got in close with a flurry of punches.

However, it didn't work out like that. My opponent grabbed the back of my thick woolly jumper and pulled it over my head so that I was the one who was in the bag! It was damn hot in there too. I couldn't see a thing. All I could do was keep on thumping and hope to break his iron grip before I ran out of oxygen. Suddenly I was hoisted backwards by strong hands as the gang hauled us apart and there was Mick Chegwidden's disapproving voice, "Now then, that's enough o' that!"

So, all ended happily. By some coincidence, both the angling boats and the diving boats seemed to give our dahns a wide berth for the rest of the year.

The Reaper's Mouse is Missing

The French crabbers usually carried a youngster in their crew, who they referred to as their 'Mouse'. The entry on the last day of August in the 1966 diary carries a footnote. It poses the question, "Where is Cooker?" and continues, "We have not seen him for several days now."

The footnote offers three possible answers. He has got the sulks. He has run away to sea. He has eloped to Coventry with Wendy. Mike and I are genuinely concerned for him because he is working in his family's restaurant and he is mad to go fishing. We think he should hang on there and not do anything daft. In a few short weeks, the emmetts will be gone and then he will be free. Chris Moffat reckons Cooker won't stick it for even one more week. The fishing bug is hard to kill!

A couple of days later the diary records a positive sighting when Cooker is seen at the wheel of a Mini. Wendy is in the passenger seat. Next day, the panic is over for the time being. Cooker is reported to be still making spaghetti bolognese. It is Friday. Cooker shows up and he is all excited. David Chapman has offered him a berth in his, recently acquired, 50 footer, the *Castle Wraith*. Cooker wonders how he is going to tell his Old Man that Chapper wants him on MONDAY?

The first couple of days of September were fine, but Atlantic low–pressure systems sent powerful ground seas, so that we kept the boats on their moorings. All we could do was watch the great swells break out beyond Listry, roar past the quay gap and spend themselves on Towan Beach.

Some of Bill Sharrock's pots washed ashore in bits. All the part–timers lost gear during this spell because they had left most of it in fifteen fathoms or less. Some divers made a few dives but we heard that they had no success. Due to the disturbance, the water was too thick for them to see anything on the seabed.

On 5 September, storm force ten was forecast for sea area Shannon and the centre of the depression was an intense low of 959 millibars. The next day, Pauline and I took the kids up on Pentire headland and we watched the tremendous surf. It was all the more spectacular because the morning was warm and sunny and the wind a light force three or four. The big seas continued all day and at high water, the runs were going right up the River Gannel and breaking on both shores. We had our pots off deep, so we were able to pick up where we had left off when the sea died down on the following day. One of our strings of pots was heaved together so that the two dahns were close to each other, but the pots came up clear when we hauled it and they were undamaged.

During these spells, I continued making wire lobster pots in the little shed next to Vyrn Cabin. Pauline and I fitted the netting on to the wire frames in the evenings, sitting indoors by the fire. When a batch of completed pots was ready, Mike carried them to the loft in his Morris Minor pickup. At other times, he went cutting withies for weaving the pot entrances and then he brought them out to me.

I spent hardly any time at the harbour because Mike minded the boat, the punt and the shellfish in the carves, and in bad weather this was almost a full–time job. This left me free to work on the pots but I took time out to be the family man as well. I took Martyn down to the boathouse and we swam with young Jill and Gerald Northey. "Good fun," according to the diary.

That was part of the beauty of living at Fern Pit. When the south east wind made most places miserable, the River Gannel below Fern Pit was sheltered and, if the sun was shining and the tide was out, it was glorious down there. The tide pool was deep but there were lots of lovely swimming places in a tracery of pools and streams. It was a broad expanse of crystal clear water and soft yellow sand, which teemed with life. Shoals of shrimps and tiny fish and sand eels scattered ahead of us as we waded through the shallows.

Pauline and I were so contented living in Vyrn Cabin, which overlooked this idyllic spot. The cabin had been built with loving care by George and his father Dick Northey. The main portion of the cabin was made out of pit props recovered from the sea. Perhaps they were being carried as deck cargo and got washed overboard during a storm. Whatever the circumstances of their loss, the Cornish did a spot of beachcombing, as they have done for generations and so, the bulk of the cabin's building materials were dragged up the cliff path. The pit props gave the little house the appearance of a log cabin and the apex roof was clad with cedar tiles. The inside walls and the high ceilings were lined with pine boarding so that it had a warmth and a quiet peacefulness about it, rather like an old country cottage. Best of all we were among friends and we were prepared to live there forever.

For the first time in our lives, we had a settled home and we were not being expelled to make way for the emmetts in the first week of May. We even had a go at gardening, without much success, since we hadn't a clue about it anyway. We got ourselves some chickens and we fared much better, not because we were brilliant at it but more because George advised us which kind of birds to buy. I dismantled some wooden fish boxes and used the timber, together with a few battens and a bit of wire netting, to make an ark to house them. We bought six point–of–lay pullets. Their feathers were of a reddish colour and they were called Thornbers 404. To our surprise and delight, they soon started laying and amazingly, they obliged us by leaving the eggs right there in the nest box which, directed by George, I had built for that very purpose.

The enterprise was doing well but then we noticed that some of our chickens were getting bald patches. After careful observation, we saw that one bird was responsible for all the damage. It was obvious really, because she was the only one left with a complete set of feathers! We christened her Henrietta Feather. We decided to build a bigger chicken house with a nice big chicken run so that our birds could stretch their legs a bit. As soon as this was ready, Henrietta would be left by herself in the ark and she could peck the feathers out of her own arse if she wanted to.

The next time it was too rough to go fishing we set about constructing the new chicken run behind the cabin. This meant climbing a few yards up the rocky slope to reach a reasonably flat bit of ground. I marked out the area and, using a lump hammer and a bar, I punched four holes in the rocks. These were intended to receive the corner posts but as I hammered the bar down into the last hole, water came bubbling up.

"A spring!" I shouted in my excitement, "Pauline, I've found a spring".

We watched in fascination as the water gushed down the slope. It was a healthy stream and it twisted its way between the boulders in a most charming fashion. We were both thrilled at this discovery because we had always dreamed of having a garden with a stream running through it. One exclaimed, "Look! It's making a natural waterfall. We can make a fish pond there."

"Yes and we will have a couple of fishing garden gnomes," agreed the other.

"What about some fairy lights?"

"Could we have a fountain?"

Pauline said, "Let's have a cup of tea to celebrate, I'll go and put the kettle on."

As she made her way down to the cabin, I sat on a grassy tussock and marvelled at having the luck to hit, what was possibly the one and only spring in the whole of Pentire. Pauline's voice interrupted my thoughts, "Trev, I turned on the tap and nothing came out. The water is off!"

I sat there for a moment, not comprehending but then I sprang up and stared at the hole with the water gushing out of it. I dashed down to the shed and got the pick. Within a few minutes, I had exposed the pipe that normally supplied water to the cabin, only now it had a hole punched in it! It took a while to fix that leak. It involved bits of copper pipe and bits of plastic pipe and insulating tape and some jubilee clips and lots of strong language. I never did tell George, our landlord. Call me Chicken if you like!

Wire for making the pots became scarce locally, which just showed how many people were beavering away at the job! Mike, George and Dave Sleeman went off in Dave's car to Trago Mills and to Phillips to buy wire, but they were astonished to find that Bob Perrington had been there ahead of them and bought the whole lot! The following day they went to Newlyn looking for wire. George was very keen to buy some special split cane, which, he claimed, was better for weaving pot entrances than the withies. He was absolutely amazed to learn that Bill and Ben had got there first and yes, they had bought every last bit of it! It is indeed a small world.

We got a few days fishing which gave us a week's money before another bad spell closed us down again. Mike and I were down at the boathouse, talking to George, when Cooker came to see us. He had just completed his first trip with Chapper on board the *Castle Wraith* and they had made good money. He told us all about the antics of Chapper and of Donny Mac Birney, the skipper of the fifty–foot *Quiet Waters*, as the two boats fished around Lundy Island for lobsters.

So that was that! Our Mouse had gone away and now he was different. The change was so very slight, but it was there in the way he looked and in the way he spoke. He was still the same old Cooker but now he was a fisherman.

Never in a Million

It was nearly mid–September and already the mornings were very dark. We still had two strings of French–style pots and three strings of wire lobster pots fishing. One afternoon we paused to check over our French pots. As the *Reaper* drifted with the tide, we payed out the backrope and, as the strain came on it, we dropped each pot overboard. In this way, we got a chance to briefly inspect each pot and to cull out any we thought not worth repairing. We simply cast those off, and out of the original 50, we ended up with 36. We shortened the backropes and made them up into two strings of 18 each.

The weather locally was fine but mid–Atlantic storms sent us frequent spells of heavy ground sea. Sometimes there were signs that down on the seafloor there was a lot of motion taking place. Then the sea fleas were very active and during the first haul of the day, we would notice that all the bait had vanished and only a few clean fish bones would be left hanging in the pots.

The French pots had almost stopped fishing. We believed that they were being rolled about whereas the wire pots, offering less resistance to the surge, sat firmly on the ground. The 1966 diary records, "We hauled the French pots twice and we hauled the wire pots three times. The French pots are a wash–out and only produced three lobsters for the day and the wire pots caught thirty three."

In fairness the French pots did catch a few crawfish during this period but obviously, had we been able to swap the French pots for wire ones, our catches of lobsters would have increased quite a bit.

Meanwhile Cooker seemed to fit in very well aboard the *Castle Wraith* and he went off on another trip to Lundy with her.

Although the summer was over and the evenings were drawing in, there seemed to be a sudden burst of energy and enthusiasm motivating the denizens of Newquay Harbour. New partnerships were formed, sometimes between even the most unlikely bedfellows. Guys talked of buying boats, of trading in what they had for something bigger, better and, of course, far more expensive. Money problems never seemed to enter into the stories going around the quays. Mike and I shook our heads and asked ourselves, 'What are we doing wrong?' We had just had a damned good season's lobster fishing and yet we didn't have money to splash out on a new boat!

"Never mind!" said Mike, "Even though the *Reaper* is thirty years old I wouldn't change her for anything!"

So we consoled ourselves and got on with the job.

The diary tells the story as follows:

Alfie Waters is selling the 44ft Seagull and he is looking for a 50ft Frenchman.

Bob Perrington was looking for a second–hand 25 footer but has decided to have a new boat built instead.

Bobby Broderick and Chris Moffat have teamed up together to go trawling in Bobby's boat, the Talisman. They are looking for a 40ft Looe lugger to go crabbing.

George Northey's Ripple is having engine trouble and after his many trips out with us in the Reaper, he has no liking for Stuart Turner petrol engines anymore. He is looking for a boat with diesel engines.

Malcolm Marr and Percy Bone have become partners. (Some wag has nicknamed them 'Marrowbone'.). They are going in for a spot of lobster fishing and have bought a load of French pots from Harvey's for £1.each. They are looking for a bigger boat.

Frank Dungey and Cyril Hubber are looking for a boat to go lobster fishing.

Rumour has it that the Burtie Boys are planning to give Mike Morris the push before he tells them to 'stuff it!'

On Thursday, 15 September, the wind was north west force 7–8. The *Reaper* stayed on the moorings. These were the biggest tides of the year so she stayed there the next day as well. I helped George to stow all his deck chairs away in the boathouse.

Several boats left the harbour and proceeded to their winter moorings up in the River Gannel. We went to sea the following day and, approaching harbour on our way home, we passed the *Talisman* with Bobby and Chris on board. They were struggling to get their trawl up which appeared to be fast solid on Listry. When Mike made fun of their plight, they insisted that they were not really fast on the rock at all!

We had light easterly winds all the next week and, with the tides getting weaker, our work was made easy for us. Pauline's dad, Charlie came out with us and it was a lovely day to be on the water. We caught 33 lobsters and 6 crawfish, which was about our average daily catch during this period. We were well pleased with that, and many boats would have loved to equal that kind of fishing.

One evening, on our way home, we came across the *Ripple*. George was working on the engine again so we gave him a tow home. On board, he had a load of pots baited and ready to shoot, so Mike kept an eye on our echo sounder. When he saw a good piece of ground rising up, we shouted to George to shoot away. We towed *Ripple* slowly and George threw his pots overboard so that they were nicely placed. A rather novel way of doing it!

At 6.45 am, on the 26 September, we left the harbour and, after hauling the gear once, we went into Crantock Bay and threw out the anchor. Bill and Ben in the *Evelyn Meyrick* came and joined us. We were nicely sheltered in there, but the south east wind increased and the ground sea started. With this new development, the two boats quickly hauled their anchors and headed for Newquay Harbour.

In the afternoon Pauline's parents, who were down on holiday, took us and the kids in their car to Newlyn. I was pleased that the ground sea had come and given me the afternoon off because it enabled me to attend this Very Important Meeting. Here, on this very day, Mr Edward Heath, Conservative MP, Leader of the Opposition in the House of Commons, was to meet with fishermen of the various Cornish Ports to discuss their problems and hear their views. It would have been an awful pity, in my view, to have missed the opportunity of telling the great man about our problems with the divers in Newquay, especially since Harold Wilson's Labour Government didn't seem to give a toss about the fishing industry.

So there I was, standing with about a dozen other fishermen on Newlyn pier, when Mr Heath, accompanied by Mr John Knott MP arrived. After cordial greetings and introductions, we were invited, one at a time, to step forward and say our piece. The chap ahead of me was Harry Barron from Mevagissey. One of the most experienced and respected fishermen in Cornwall, always soft–spoken and very polite.

He asked Mr Heath a question, "Why is it, that when you go into a grocer's shop, you can see thirteen brands of South African pilchards on display but there are only two brands of Cornish pilchards?"

Mr Heath seemed slightly rattled by this, as though the question was somehow a bit below the belt. "The answer is simple," he said, "We buy pilchards from South Africa and they buy cars from us."

Having dealt with that detail, Mr Heath looked expectantly at me for my contribution, but Harry Barron tried again.

"You see Mr Heath sir, pilchards are fetching three shillings and four pence a stone and this is the same price we were getting before the war."

Harry held out a photograph of Mevagissey Harbour. "See those seven drifters? As soon as the war ended, we were building boats, fine 50 footers and now we have to sell them off. There are only two major boats left fishing the pilchards from Mevagissey now."

Mr Heath glanced at the photo and handed it back saying, "Oh I could show you photos like that of Margate taken forty years ago. Those boats have all gone too."

Mr Heath fixed his gaze on me. There were a thousand things whirling around in my head that I suddenly wanted to say to this supercilious bastard. The treatment handed out to Harry Barron had enraged me but I kept my feelings under wraps and, keeping my voice down, I began a brief account of the effect the divers' activities were having on the Newquay fishermen's livelihoods. Before I had a chance to get really going, Mr Heath reminded me that the sea was free for everyone. I replied that indeed it was free for everyone, "with the exception of the fishermen of course," I added, with what I hoped sounded like heavy sarcasm. From then on things quickly went downhill and I was brushed aside like poor Harry. I had to content myself with going over to John Knott MP and savaging him instead.

I took solace from the fact that, having seen Edward Heath face–to–face, I just knew he would never make it to Prime Minister. Not in a million years!

The Wonder Pot

During the last days of September, the weather was kind and fishing was good. We were pleasantly surprised when, on 29 September, we caught ten crawfish in our French pots. On the following day, we caught twelve crawfish. We even had three in the one pot! We hadn't seen that kind of fishing in the French pots since 1964. It was quite remarkable because, by this time, we had only thirty–six crawfish pots in the water instead of one hundred and twenty five. It was a reminder of happier days, before the divers arrived.

During the summer, the wire pots did catch an occasional crawfish, perhaps one or two a week. The wire pot entrance was only six inches wide, so any crawfish that did manage to squeeze in had to be small: certainly not more than two pounds weight. This small six–inch entrance didn't deter a seven–pound lobster. However, crawfish ranging from two to seven pounds weight had no chance of getting in. Obviously, what was needed was a wire pot with an entrance of eleven inches. It appeared to us that, since a small crawfish would go into a small entrance in a wire pot, then a big crawfish would go into a big entrance in a wire pot.

I set about making the first wire crawfish pot in history. This was going to be tricky because simply making a larger entrance in the existing wire pot might allow a crawfish to go in, but it would also allow a lobster to flip out of it like a shot. A lot of thought needed to go into it. This job had to be kept quiet. Should it prove successful, we didn't want everyone on the coast copying it. At least we wanted to make a fortune with a fleet of our new wonder pots before the rest of the gang copped on. I spent every spare moment experimenting and soon I had my prototype wire crawfish pot completed. It sure looked the part and Mike and I were confident that it would do the business.

A couple of days later Mike and I went down the cliff path to George's boathouse. We walked in and we were amazed to see George putting the finishing touches to a wire crawfish pot. I don't know who got the biggest surprise, us or George on discovering that both he and I had produced identical pots, without the other's knowledge. The two pots were the same in every detail, down to the last half an inch! We all swore to keep the new wonder pots a secret.

We soon had our pot fishing. We simply attached it onto a string of pots which meant it got hauled a couple of times every day. It never did catch a crawfish. It caught crabs and spider crabs galore. It caught big, bull–headed murgy dogs and skinny little spotted dogs. It caught bream and pouting and wrasse and it caught conger eels as long as your leg. One day it came up with two fine lobsters in it. They sat there on the bottom of the pot facing each other with their powerful claws waving about in a menacing fashion. Mike snatched them out before they could crunch each other up and stowed them in the lobster box.

I exclaimed, "Those two are the first fish that damn pot has caught since we shot it!"

"Yes, those two kept each other in," said Mike. "They were squaring up to each other all night and if one 'em tried to escape the other would have grabbed him by the arse. Otherwise they would have flipped out like a shot."

I never did find out if George's wonder pot worked. After hauling ours a few more times, without it catching either a crawfish or a lobster, we cast it off and consigned it to the deep.

Some you win, some you lose.

Jimmy Treloar

It was a blowey day in October when I drove to the harbour to check up on the *Reaper*. I parked the motorbike at the top of the North Quay Hill, from where I would have a good view of the boats.

As I walked towards the railings, I saw Jimmy Treloar standing there, looking down on the harbour. It occurred to me that the years had been kind to Jimmy. I immediately scolded myself for entertaining such a stupid thought. It was true that Jimmy stood tall and straight and his shoulders were big and broad. However, there would have been very little kindness shown to either man or beast during most of his lifetime. Indeed Jimmy had been born in the reign of Queen Victoria and, dressed as he was, in his heavy black overcoat and black trilby hat, he certainly looked every inch a Victorian.

A bitter north easter swept across Newquay Bay as I greeted him.

"Hello Jimmy, a cold morning," I said, rubbing my hands vigorously to get some life back into my cold fingers.

"Ho! So you think it's cold eh?"

Jimmy reached into his breast pocket and pulled out an old photograph. "Take a look at that. Now that's what you call cold. What you're looking at there is the train snowed–up at St Columb Major."

I had seen it before because Jimmy always produced it when anyone mentioned cold weather. I took the sepia tinted, postcard–sized photo, which showed a steam locomotive standing at the platform, with snow up to the top of its big wheels. I peered at the photo admiringly and made all the right noises. It really was impressive anyway. From our vantage point at the railings, I could see that the *Reaper* was safe and I watched her tugging at her moorings as the wind drove steep breaking waves in through the quay gap. This was Jimmy's favourite spot. Sometimes I would meet him there, since it was quite close to our loft. I loved to listen to his stories and often when he spoke, he didn't look at me but stared out over the bay, as if he was watching scenes from the past.

"I drove a four–in–hand you know," he said in a matter of fact way. He extended his left hand, palm uppermost, "You held the reins like this," he went on, and he drew the imaginary reins towards himself and arranged them between his fingers. "Then you had the whip, you see."

Jimmy raised his right arm then, staring ahead of himself, he sent his arm forward in a graceful arc.

"Did you have to whip the horses to make them go?" I asked in all innocence.

"Oh no, you only controlled them with the whip," he explained patiently, lashing out again a couple more times. "You see, if a lead horse went off a bit to the right, I would crack the whip right beside his ear and that would bring him back into line."

Jimmy's arm went forward again and I swear I heard the crack of a whip! "I was an expert with the whip you know. My sister lived in a cottage out on the moor and any time I was passing that way, I would call in on her. One day, when I went up the path, I could see in through the open door and there was this flower, like a daisy, in a little jug on the mantelpiece. Well I stood outside on the path."

Here Jimmy altered his stance, spreading his feet apart as if to get his balance right. He raised his arm up and back and then forth again in one fluid movement. "I took that flower out as clean as a whistle, without the whip even touching the jug." He allowed himself a little smile.

"Jimmy it's freezing here in this wind. I must go to the loft and put the netting on a couple of pots."

Jimmy wasn't finished yet though. "I remember one time when I took the boss and his guests out and it was bitter cold that day. We drove here and there, all over the county but in the end, we stopped outside this tavern and in they all went. It came dark and the footman and me were both frozen stiff from waiting outside. We were starving hungry too because we hadn't eaten anything all day. We searched through our pockets and all we had between us was one ha'penny. All we could find to buy with it was some big Spanish onions, so that is what we ate."

I said, "Jimmy, that's a terrible story. I'm frozen stiff myself now."

I bid him goodbye and escaped to the cosy shelter the loft. Mike Lyne knew Jimmy Treloar well and he told me that Jack Trouson, a mine owner from Camborne, was Jimmy's boss. When Trouson replaced the coach and horses with a car, Jimmy became the chauffeur. The car was a 'Sleeve Valve' Daimler. No doubt it was an aristocrat in its day, as befitted a Cornish tin mine owner.

October was disappointing as far as the fishing went. The weather was too disturbed for lobster fishing but it still seemed like our best option. We just battled on and somehow managed to wring wages out of the job. When bad weather threatened, we had to respond quickly. At this time of year, things changed suddenly and the nights were long. One day we came back after a haul. We had five crawfish and nine lobsters and, since the wind was increasing, we decided to 'save water back' and we arrived back on our moorings, just a few minutes before our keel grounded on the sand.

I was enjoying my day–off when George arrived at the door. Mike had phoned him to say that the forecast was very bad. It was 6pm when we jumped into George's car and drove to the dock. Mike was already on board and the *Reaper* was just coming afloat. George and I went quickly down the steps to the punt and Harold Bullen elected to come along with us. As I sculled the punt across the dock, I heard *Reaper's* engines roar into life. The three of us clambered on board and *Reaper* sped off into the gathering gloom. Within twenty minutes, we were hauling a string of our wire pots aboard. George's pots were close by and we hauled those and kept them on board too. By the time we picked up the last dahn, the night was pitch black and we hauled the pots in darkness.

It was lucky we made the effort to save that gear because there was a mere ten fathoms of water there. Also, it was an area that was close to the headland with its hard spiky rocks and its powerful tides. The strong wind and the sea that came with it would have crunched those pots up for certain! Several boats lost gear during that spell. Anything laying in less than twenty fathoms, you could kiss goodbye.

Winter was coming, that was obvious but instead of winding down, Newquay Harbour was a hive of activity. We lobster men were much in evidence because every time severe weather threatened, we all brought in a couple of strings of pots, so as not to leave too much to the mercy of the elements. This was always a bit hectic, with boats jockeying for position as the skippers tried to get berthed alongside the centre jetty. It involved lots of yelling between the crewmen on the jetty, who were dragging the pots up and the skippers down in the boats, who were clearing tangled ropes and gear. (It is a fact of life that pots that shoot away clear out of the boat as smooth as silk, will usually try and come up on the pier in bunches!)

Of course, it followed that as soon as the weather showed any sign of moderating the race commenced to get the gear fishing again. If, as so often happened, the tide was falling while we loaded pots, then the excitement became more intense as the water got thinner. Nobody wanted to be stuck high and dry on the sand for six hours while the rest of the fleet went fishing, but that was your lot if your keel touched the harbour bottom. Happily, it never happened to the

Reaper. I am quite sure that Mike would have suffered a seizure if ever it had. Other boats did get caught on occasion of course.

News in Brief
Mike Morris and the *Bacchus* parted company.
Bob Perrington advertised in the newspaper for the kind of boat he wanted.
Jimmy Hoare bought the twenty–two foot Chennel.
George Northey bought the Star and renamed her *Sunrise*.
Keith Bray bought Dashers' boat from Padstow.
Mike Morris tried to bring *Trevose* out of the River Gannel but she was beneaped and didn't float at the top of the tide.
David Chapman's *Castle Wraith*, with 'Cooker' Mountford on board, was fishing locally and berthing at the north quay.
Some of the small boats headed for the River Gannel for the winter lay–up.

Two weeks Later
Mike Morris tried to bring *Trevose* out of the River Gannel, but again she didn't float.
Castle Wraith headed back to Padstow. She was parting ropes due to the heavy 'run' in the harbour and they had to clear out at 4 am.
Ronnie Harvey offered Mike Lyne the skipper's job on his French crabber. He declined but it was a great compliment to Mike anyway.
Mr Toad had an argument with Bill and Ben over their punt's moorings.
George Northey had his finger lanced as it was badly poisoned.
Chris Moffat and Dave Sleeman went and hauled the pots for him.

On the evening of 28 October, Mike Morris and his brothers brought the *Trevose* out of the River Gannel. Next day, *Castle Wraith* came in to Newquay again. Only 'Chapper' and Cooker on board because 'Pablo', John Brinham, went off to purchase a boat called *Star of the Scillies*.
John Pardoe, Liberal MP for North Cornwall came to Vyrn Cabin to meet us and discuss the problem of skin diving. Those present, Mike Lyne, Mike Morris, Kelvin Moller, Graham Moller and me. It was a good meeting.
Bacchus was visible working just to the westward of our gear. We heard that Jimmy Hoare and Mart Burt had shipped on.
October was a surprisingly busy month!

There is a Row Going On

1 November 1966 was savagely cold, a full gale from the north east hurled hail and rain upon those Newquay Fishermen brave enough to go down and check on their boats. The crew of the *Castle Wraith* had been awakened at half past four that morning as the boat began to pound heavily on the sand. They got quickly out of their bunks, dressed and pulled on their oilskins. Up on deck they struggled with extra ropes and fenders, trying to control the boat's violent surges and to prevent her from slamming against the quay wall.

As the weather worsened even some of their steel wire ropes parted. Chapper used both engines to help take some of the strain off. Nobody could ever accuse Chapper of having too delicate a touch; he was an all–or–nothing kind of a guy. In fact, as he went from full ahead to full astern repeatedly, the wash from *Castle Wraith*'s propellers sank Bobby Broderick's punt.

The row over the divers continued to simmer. Now and again, it boiled over. Percy Bone and Malcolm Marr were taking out divers using some other person's boat. Worst of all, Cavell was the diver they carried most often and we were all too familiar with his intentions!

Mike had words with Percy Bone about him taking divers out close to our pots. This passed off peacefully enough but when Mike tackled Malcolm on the same issue things went quite the other way. It was all fine and dandy until Malcolm stuck his nose in the air and said haughtily, "It has yet to be proved that Cavell has dived on any of your pots."

The effect was immediate! Mike's jacket came off and he flung it aside as he leapt at Malcolm and thrust his fist under his nose. Mike roared his words into Malcolm's face, "I was fishing here before you knew where Newquay Harbour was and you have the bloody cheek to bring those bastard parasites out onto our gear. You bring them out to the lobster ground! You only know where to go because our dahns are there."

Malcolm stood there, visibly shaken. The look on his face seemed to say, "Did I say something wrong?"

"And," Mike continued, "you wouldn't know a lobster if one jumped up and bit you on the fuckin' leg!"

There was more, much more, before Mike had finished letting off steam.

When Harvey's lorry arrived, I went up to Walter and said, "We are against divers' fish being landed here. Now, if you want our fish, then no divers' fish goes up on this lorry."

Walter wasn't too pleased and he said he was worried about what Ronnie Harvey would say. I knew that our position was weak because, especially at this time of year, we needed Harvey's much more than they needed us. However, I stuck to my guns and in the end, Walter agreed. The divers were caught unprepared by this. Usually they would wait until we had finished landing and had gone away to sea. They would then put their fish up. On this occasion, they watched us land from a distance and they were probably surprised to see the lorry pull away up the hill.

We got to sea on 3 November. This day was horrible for me because a wave came aboard and hit me, full force, in the back. It filled up my thigh–boots. I was very cold and that made a long day of it. Mike Morris's *Trevose* landed sixty–five stone of trawl–fish. This made sixty pounds, which was not bad money.

On 5 November, we went out to rescue some of our pots, which we had placed in fairly close. The forecast was very bad for the next day and George Northey came with us, as he also had some pots in close that he was anxious to shift into deeper water. Although the wind was light westerly, the seas were really enormous. Mike and I enjoyed George's surprise when an occasional extra big one came rolling towards us. George was used to fishing a small boat single–handed, so he wouldn't be out in these conditions normally. I reckoned George hadn't seen seas like these since he served in minesweepers during the war.

We loaded up both lots of pots and carried them off, leaving them in twenty fathoms and we were home nice and early. Since it was 'Guy Fawkes', Pauline and I built a bonfire in front of the cabin and made a guy. George, Nora and their kids came down to the cabin. We gathered around the bonfire and had drinks and sandwiches. We let off fireworks as soon as it got dark. The evening was a great success and everyone enjoyed it. The following day our baby Jenny stood up for the first time.

The weather eased off and we got out fishing for a few days. Meanwhile:

Marr and Cavell went away east for the day. They caught nothing, so it was said.

Bob Perrington bought a boat in St Ives.

Mike Morris and his brother Brian got themselves jobs ashore.

Bill and Ben's exhaust blew out.

The Bobby Broderick/Chris Moffat partnership broke up (again!).

The *Bacchus* sailed for France to have work done on the engine.

I received an encouraging letter from John Pardoe MP, concerning our problem with the divers.

It was rumoured that Alfie Waters had gone back in the Merchant Navy or else had gone to New Zealand.

We were at sea every day for the next week and, apart from one day when we caught twenty lobsters, fish were scarce. Bob Perrington's boat arrived in the harbour. Mike, Cooker and I went aboard to have a look at her and Bob gave us the conducted tour. She was a handy twenty–four foot, clinker–built boat with a forward open wheelhouse. The twin cylinder diesel engine lived in under the tiny foredeck. Only its gearbox was visible, sticking back through a hole in the bulkhead where it joined the propeller shaft. There, on the gearbox, actually cast in the steel in bold letters, were the words, "JOE'S GEAR BOX". I don't know why this was funny but it set the three of us giggling. Mike said, "Go on Bob, start her up."

Bob needed no more encouragement and, assuring us that she started very easily, he got down on all fours and squeezed his rather beefy frame through the tiny doorway into the forepeak. We peered in and were surprised to see him crouching in the tiny space beside the engine, flicking his cigarette lighter. Bob said, by way of explanation, "She'll need a bit 'o heat you see."

He aimed his lighter into a shallow biscuit–tin containing a diesel–soaked rag until it burst into flame. Bob waved the blazing tin up around the engine manifold and then, with his free hand he swung the starting handle. We lost sight of him, as he was soon enveloped by thick black smoke, which poured out to meet us. We listened to the sound of the engine turning over as Bob applied himself with vigour to the starting–handle. Faster and faster the cranking went, until it suddenly trickled to a halt, to be replaced by the sound of serious coughing. Bob's head appeared and pungent diesel smoke curled around his ears. He hauled himself out into the fresh air and stayed there, on hands and knees, coughing his heart out until the spasm passed. While Bob was thus occupied, we were killing ourselves laughing. This was rotten of us but we couldn't help it. Mike recovered his composure first and with a completely straight face he said, "I was certain she was going to start Bob. Give her another go."

I was surprised at the eagerness with which Bob turned and re–entered the forepeak. In beside the engine once more, he sloshed some oil into the biscuit tin and set light to it again. Again, we watched the smoke pour out and again we heard the engine turning over. The effort of cranking caused Bob to emit a grunt in time with each revolution. It sounded like, 'Grunt–ticketty–boo, grunt–ticketty–boo.' But just as the engine almost reached its starting–speed another bout of coughing interrupted things. Bob thrust himself halfway out of the doorway coughing violently. With his blackened face and reddened eyes, he somehow made me think of *The Hound of The Baskervilles*. As soon as the hacking cough subsided, Mike said, in a voice tinged with disappointment, "Aw Bob! You almost had her going that time. One more turn would have done it."

Bob hauled himself back into the forepeak and the whole process began again. This time however, just when failure seemed certain, the engine started. Bob emerged with his eyes streaming. He stood up and looked at Mike as if seeking some kind of approval. As the boat shuddered from stem–to–stern, to the regular thumping of the two cylinders, Mike looked Bob straight in the eye and said, "Well Old Man, that is one sweet little engine."

I turned my head away because my eyes were streaming too.

Mid–November passed and we were hit by westerly gales, which then veered northerly and increased to storm force. Conditions got very bad in the harbour and Bob's boat became a casualty. She broke adrift when the after samson post cracked off at deck level. Poor Bob was up all night, struggling to save her and she finished up against the cliff in the little cove under Pendrellen House. Bob was devastated of course. A couple of days later he got Sammy Malone with the tractor to haul his boat up the slip and onto the hard. During this operation, the keeliron got pulled off. Trouble begets trouble!

We continued fishing until the end of November, when severe weather set in again and it blew hard, right into the first week of December. George came down to Vyrn Cabin for a yarn. He said that he feared the worst and reckoned his pots would suffer a total smash–up this time.

Mike and I got to sea again on 5 December and steamed straight to where we had placed our pots in twenty fathoms, down off Perranporth. The dahns and the metal buoys had all survived the storm, which surprised us. Our strings of wire pots had remained stretched out straight, just as we had left them. We did have great difficulty hauling one string though, and nine of the pots were gone, twisted off their lanyards. The remainder were all perfect, so we considered ourselves very lucky indeed.

Bill and Ben only had one string of pots still in the water. They only salvaged half of it and proceeded up the Gannel to George Northey's quay. George himself lost thirty pots. His biggest loss though was seventy buoys.

Meanwhile

Everyone down quay was all worked up about the forthcoming public meeting to be held at the Cosy Nook Theatre. This was about the Newquay Urban District Council's proposed new powers that, said some, will turn Newquay into a police state.

We heard that *Trevose* would embark on a marathon trawling programme. She would stay at sea, only coming in to land fish. Two crews would work alternate twelve–hour shifts. Crews were already picked as follows: Crew A – Mike Morris and his three brothers, Crew B – Martin Brimble Burt, Frank Cox and George Northey. Following the 'Turf War' over the punts moorings, Mr Toad wrote complaining to the Newquay Council about Bill and Ben. Now Mr Smith of the Newquay Council had written to Bill and Ben, advising them that unless they mended their wicked ways they would be banned from the harbour. The public meeting called by the NUDC took place but the diary records no details except to comment, "The roof should have caved in."

On 14 December, Mike and I in *Reaper* and George Northey and Dave Sleeman in *Sunrise*, tried to get into the river Gannel. There was too much sea on the bar. We had our three–year–old, Martyn, on board with us and when we had to turn and face the incoming seas, he exclaimed, "The boats are going up like rockets."

We had to abandon that attempt and head back to Newquay. We tried on two more evenings when the tide was right, but the weather beat us each time.

On Christmas morning there was a social gathering at Fern Pit with friends and neighbours of the Northey's. At three o'clock that afternoon, I stood on Pentire Headland and watched *Reaper*, with Mike and Cooker on board and *Sunrise*, with George on his own, come safely up the Gannel to George's Quay at Fern Pit. Pauline and I saw the New Year in. We opened the cabin door and listened to the bells of Crantock Church. It was a fine night with a good moon.

Some Achieve Greatness

Reaper and *Sunrise* lay side–by–side at George's Quay. George hadn't liked his engine–box since the day he first acquired the boat so, at this first opportunity, he was tearing it to pieces with a hammer and crowbar. Mike was rearranging things in *Reaper's* engine room and wheelhouse, while I was busy hauling spare fishing gear out of the forepeak in preparation for our winter lay–up.

I was surprised to see Harold Bullen coming down the cliff path. Harold never usually came out that way; the harbour was his usual stamping ground when he wasn't actually digging graves. He stood on the little stone quay. He wore a fawn coloured raincoat, buttoned up to the neck and his motorcycle helmet, which at one time may have been white. He obviously felt the need to explain himself.

"The harbour is boring now, 'tis dead down there," he said.

He stepped aboard and chose his spot. Standing on our engine room deck and leaning against the wheelhouse, he commanded a position more or less equidistant between me, Mike and George. He undid the top button of his raincoat and let go the chinstraps of his helmet, so that they flapped around in the wind. From the lines on his weather–beaten face, it was plain that Harold was no longer young but he was lively, and his eyes and ears missed nothing. For the next hour, he entertained us with stories, rumours and gossip from around and about. I liked Harold.

The following day, we shifted out from George's Quay and moved up to Tregunnel, where Mike had placed our winter moorings. I returned to making pots while Mike worked on the boat. She was up near the high water mark and would only come afloat on the very tops of the tide.

One of the first jobs Mike attended to was renewing the two shackles connecting the steering chains to the head of the rudder. One of these proved to be seized up, so Mike set about cutting it off with a hacksaw. A steel splinter went into his right eye and he knew immediately that this was serious! He got into the car and drove to the eye hospital in Truro. The steel splinter was stuck firmly into the pupil and by the time he reached Truro, the splinter had lacerated the inside of the eyelid and blood was running down his face.

Mike sat waiting in the corridor until a doctor stopped by and asked him how long he had been sitting there. When told that it was half–an–hour he led Mike into his surgery. The doctor, apparently from India, sat him on a chair and told him to look at the ceiling then, using a powerful magnet, he removed the splinter. He explained that if the steel had remained in the pupil for too long then it would rust and cause permanent blindness. Applying some kind of soothing oil to Mike's eye, he then told him to give up driving for a fortnight and to keep the eye covered. Well, first there was about seventeen miles of a drive back to Newquay and, after that, Mike would hardly be moping around the house with his eye in a sling, would he now?

I liked Newquay in the winter because, when the emmetts had all gone home, the streets were empty; people could greet one another again and stop and talk, instead of being jostled and shoved off the pavement. It was really just a big village and you would always meet someone you knew. Like the time I had just stepped out of the barber's shop after Fernley had done his usual 'hatchet job' on me, commonly called a 'short–back–and–sides'. Ted, who was married to Alfie's sister, happened to be passing and stopped for a chat. We talked about all sorts of things, except the fishing that is. Whenever we drifted towards the subject, Ted seemed to steer us away from it. Eventually however, as my curiosity was killing me, I felt that I must chance ruining our friendship and broach the very thing that Ted was trying hard to avoid.

"Well, any news of Alfie?" I asked.

"Not one word since he left," he answered. Then he paused, as if struggling between the need to unburden himself and his loyalty to family. Then he said, "I suppose I shouldn't talk about him because he is, after all, me brother–in–law, but he lived with us all last winter and he never gave the Missus a ha'penny. One day he said that he would make the tea. Now me and Missus had reached the stage where we didn't argue because, when Alfie got an idea into his head, then he was going to do it, and that was that. Now then, I like an egg and bacon tart for me tea and Alfie said he would make them. Well I wasn't happy about it but he went ahead anyway. Missus went into the kitchen while he was making them and she saw him put ten eggs into his tart. He put a big letter 'A' on it, so no one else would get it. When it came out of the oven you could hardly lift it!"

"How many eggs did he put in yours Ted?" I asked, fearing the worst.

"Not one," he said, with some bitterness. "When I opened it up there was only a few potatoes and a little scrap of bacon in it. So I said to Alfie, 'Where's the eggs then?' He said. 'Oh! I forgot to put one in yours!' Well I was so mad I could have thrown it through the living room window, and like I say he never gave the Missus as much as a ha'penny."

Aiming to be sympathetic, I said, "Oh well, that's families isn't it?"

I had a sneaking feeling, as we parted, that my comment didn't help very much.

On 3 January 1967, I spent most of the day down at the harbour working on the punt. Then I went out to Tregunnel, where Mike was working on the *Reaper*. His eye was improving, he told me, but I was sure he was having a tough time with it.

Mike Morris brought *Trevose* up Gannel. There was not enough water and she got stuck on the footbridge at Trethellan. They said that Brian had to jump in and help to push her off and he was up to his neck in water. They got her clear and went back down river and secured at Fern Pit.

The next day as I worked on the punt, Chris Moffat saw some fish in Porth. He thought they might be bass. We made arrangements to meet at eight o'clock the following morning. As arranged, the usual crew assembled at Porth. A patch of colour was visible from Porth Island but we couldn't be sure that it was fish. Later on, the fish became visible but they were not in a position where we could shoot the net. We hung on, in the hope that the shoal would move away from the rocks and come in over the clean sand, but instead, as high water approached, they simply soaked away and we were left looking at the empty sea.

On the following morning, 6 January, several patches of colour were visible outside Butter Rock, so we brought the punt and net down to the water's edge. We waited patiently and at last, some fish were seen moving in towards the beach on the flood tide. I wouldn't have a clue myself but the experts among us reckoned that there was about a half ton in this small shoal. The problem facing us was, if we shot to this small lot we would startle the main shoal and they would vanish. Meanwhile, if we didn't act soon, we would miss this lot anyway.

Suddenly we were treated to a dose of heavy rain. The slight swell, which had been increasing since morning, seemed to be getting worse. When a couple of bigger seas broke across the beach, it decided things for us. It was a 'now or never' situation. We launched the punt and George manned the oars, while Chris Moffat payed out the net. It seemed at first that they would be beaten back, but thanks to George's great strength and his skill with the oars, the punt crashed its way out through the breakers. George and Chris did a wonderful job to get the net around the fish in those conditions. Most of the fish escaped, perhaps frightened by the unusually loud racket made by the punt on this occasion. There was only 24 stone of mullet, but they made a good price in Newlyn. The shares worked out to £4 each. Not a fortune but very welcome just the same.

Our crew was George Northey, Chris Moffat, Mike Lyne, Martin 'Brimble' Burt, Jimmy Hoare, Mike Morris, Kelvin Moller, Graham Moller and me. The weather was amazingly fine with frosty mornings, sunny days and light easterly winds. We walked the cliffs from Bedruthan to Pentire looking for fish, without success. We did see 'colour' off Towan Beach. We brought the punt down and shot to it; but whatever it was, small mullet or perhaps smelt, it passed through the meshes and all we got for our trouble was a good soaking.

On 17 January, the wind was north west five–to–seven, which heralded a spell of Atlantic weather. So that was the end of the beach seining. Our little holiday was over and we returned to our numerous chores in preparation for the lobster season. I went down to the harbour and finished the work on the punt. I decided then that I might as well repair the wheelbarrow, especially since my carpentry tools were all in Mike's shed.

This was no ordinary wheelbarrow. It had originally belonged to the boat builder, Joe Burt, who had sold the shed and its contents to Mike. It was a large, robust, wooden affair in the shape of a low sided, oblong box. It was big enough to carry ten stone of bait, two five–gallon cans of diesel, two crib bags (containing thermos flasks and pasties) and sundry other items. Although it belonged to Mike, other people used it to truck everything, from boats engines to anchors, about the place. In my view, this wheelbarrow had the status of a family heirloom. It should be used but at the same time, it should be minded. As I sanded down the finished repair work, I breathed a solemn curse on the philistine who had broken it.

I was disturbed in my reveries by two youngsters who breezed into the shed. We always had kids coming in; indeed, we welcomed them but these guys quickly got on the wrong side of me. The stroppiest one was called Wills. He was bragging that he had broken into the Cadoc Café and had great fun throwing eggs around. When I expressed my disapproval, he picked up my hammer off the bench. When I disarmed him and bundled him outside he said that he might burn the shed down! Wills was eight years old. Let me see, by now he must be forty–eight. After showing such early promise, our man Wills, if he is not being 'detained at Her Majesty's pleasure', must have achieved greatness. He could even be a local councillor.

Timing is Everything

Well, that was that. The pots were ashore, the boat was up Gannel, the beach seine had failed to produce a payday for us and now it was January. A hungry time lay ahead of us. It was time to visit the Snidey One. So there I was on that dreary Monday morning, heading into the Newquay Labour Exchange in Fore Street to sign on. The Snidey One's face lit up with pure joy as soon as he saw me and he greeted me with, "Oh hello and how is your little ping, ping, ping?"

This smart–assed greeting came from the time we fitted an echo sounder into Mike's previous boat, the *Twilight*. I had put on the claim form that the boat was 'Under repair'. I'd had to explain to him how we couldn't go to sea because we had bored a hole in the boat's bottom. Things had got complicated when I tried to describe how the transducer would fit neatly into the hole and what its function was. The fact that this short lay–up qualified me to a couple of days dole money was a blow to him. His confidence in the system that he loved had been severely dented. That was four years ago but he had never really got over it. Never mind, the Snidey One was not the worst of them, and it wasn't his fault that he thought our sounder made a pinging noise like you get in those 'war at sea' films. Echo sounders were quite new technology in small boats at that time.

On 13 January 1967, we brought *Reaper* down to Fern Pit and we berthed beside *Sunrise*. Our sudden departure from the winter berth seems to have caused a flap in some quarters. George was all grumpy and was moaning about my chickens trespassing and trampling down his lovely undergrowth. The poor chickens were getting the blame but the cause of George's annoyance was that he was too busy with his preparations for the holiday season to get his boat ready for the lobsters. With the chickens safely incarcerated in their new run, George was still grumpy; so to my way of thinking, that proved it.

Bill and Ben were caught napping by our move and, in an effort to catch–up, they were at Trethellan struggling with mooring chains in the black dark. They brought *Evelyn Meyrick* down river a short distance and moored there overnight to avoid being stranded by the tide. The following morning they shifted down and joined us at Fern Pit, so there were then three lobster boats lying alongside George's Quay.

The quay was not a safe place with too many boats berthed there, but it was so convenient and useful to us whenever we came to the River Gannel. Now ourselves, and Bill and Ben, waited for a fine day to get out over the bar and shift to Newquay. Meanwhile George's grumpiness had quickly evaporated; he was never a moody person anyway.

Dave Sleeman brought Mick Chegwidden out to Fern Pit. Mick had just recovered from an illness, which left him looking very tired. He was cheerful though and glad to be out and about again.

In town, I met Simon Drew, who told me that the boatmen had held a meeting the previous day. It was all about the Council's latest ruling, which made it compulsory for shark boats and angling boats to carry a crew of two. Simon said they were all shouting and hollering in the PSA but they moved out of there, because it wasn't big enough, so they all went into the Lifeboat House.

"The commotion continued in there," said Simon, "and they were looking for somewhere bigger to have yet another meeting."

On the morning of 8 February, Mike and I went to Newquay Harbour to launch our punt and put her on the moorings. We went down to Fern Pit then and waited for the incoming tide to float *Reaper*. George was hard at work on *Sunrise* and was clearly upset that we were ready to make such an early start.

"Humph! Where are all these lobsters going to come from, that's what I'd like to know?" he remarked.

Mike, of course, was quickly aware of what was tormenting George and he made things worse by talking cheerfully about the fine weather forecast. The more Mike went on about the high pressure and the big anticyclone in mid–Atlantic, the gloomier and the grumpier George became. To be honest, I had not heard anything of that forecast. However, Mike was the acknowledged master where weather was concerned, which made it all the more convincing.

"Harvey's lorry is coming tonight with bait for us," Mike shouted cheerfully to George from the wheelhouse as he steered us out into the channel. Because of the engine noise, I didn't quite catch George's response to Mike's parting shot.

It was wonderful weather for the trip to Newquay and I was glad I had brought Martyn along with us. We got in at four in the afternoon and we loaded a string of wire pots ready for morning. Bill and Ben were not far behind us and they brought *Evelyn Meyrick* into harbour an hour later. Mike drove Martyn and me home in the pickup.

On the 9 February, we shot our lobster pots and so did Bill and Ben. The weather was fine with calm seas and light easterly winds. We made a second trip to sea loaded up with pots in the afternoon. Mick Chegwidden and Eddie Hoare came out with us and Eddie was fascinated with the *Reaper's* echo sounder, never having seen one before. He watched the roll of paper as we steamed over rocks he had known all his life. As their profile was faithfully etched on the paper, he expressed his surprise at how different it all was from how he had imagined it.

The weather held good for a few days and ourselves, and Bill and Ben, were the first to sell lobsters to Harvey's that year. A shift of wind stopped our gallop. It went south east, a mere force 5 or 6 but it brought with it the ground sea and both boats hauled their gear for nothing. The next day it blew a screecher, with hills of sea rolling in against the wind. Mike and I went up on the headland to look at it and we saw ten large steel Belgian trawlers come into the bay, seeking shelter and drop their anchors. As they steamed in Mike said, "Oh boy, just look at the spray heaving back over them!"

He suddenly covered his left eye with his hand. Removing it again he said, "I thought as much, the right eye isn't as good as it was before I got the splinter in it."

I remember being quite shocked by this because I had always marvelled at Mike's superb long–distance vision and didn't like to think of anything spoiling it.

The wind went south west and we entered a really bad spell of gales. Most days we got force 8 and often it blew a hideous force 10. Well it was back to the Snidey One again to sign on. After all, I was a share fisherman. The form I filled in asked my reason for not fishing. It gave me three options: Repairs, Bad weather, or No fish. I wrote 'Bad weather' in the box provided.

Caution was required in one's dealings here, because the Snidey One was merely the shining public face of an inflexible, unfeeling bureaucracy. Somewhere in behind him were the Faceless Ones, who spent their working lives setting traps for geezers like me. If, for example, a pattern emerged, like perhaps I'd signed on stating Bad Weather for the winter months over the past couple of years and never bothered them during the summers, then they would cast me off without a shilling. This could happen despite the brutal fact, that we share fishermen had to pay a double 'stamp': twice as much as other workers!

The Snidey One perused the form and before stamping it, he went over to the window and peered up at the sky. This was rather pointless because even if he saw sea foam flying over the chimney pots, it wouldn't mean a thing to him. I hated drawing the dole but, since we paid so much for the privilege, I certainly didn't have pangs of conscience over it. The dole was a small amount but at least it did keep the bread on the table. During this period of enforced idleness, at least I got to see my kids. We behaved like a family should and, when weather was dry, we went for walks, with Jenny in the pushchair and with Martyn trailing along, wishing he was somewhere else.

One of our outings took us over the wooden footbridge in the Gannel and I saw the scars where the *Trevose* had struck it with her keel. Also very plain, were the marks made by her propeller blades. Mike Morris had told us that his quarter propeller was bent out of true afterwards. Sometimes we walked out to Lagonna. Once we passed beyond the King Mark public house. The countryside was beautiful whereas the Newquay side of it had been ruined by development!

One evening Mike called in and said that the forecast was for slack winds and he had been watching the sea. Already it had moderated and he reckoned that, by the time we got a couple of strings of pots on board, it would be fit for us to go. We wasted no time and indeed, by the time we had the fifty pots baited and stowed, we were able to beat our way out and shoot the gear on a favourite piece of ground a couple of miles off.

It wasn't nice at sea but then it wasn't terrible either. We were down aboard at first light the next day and there was almost no wind but what we did have was a tremendous sea. We had to wait for the flood tide. With four hours flood the seas could still be seen breaking on Nanny, a submerged rock away off. That was a fair indication that our pots were getting a hammering. It was a classic big ground sea with the occasional monster breaking across the quay gap in an avalanche of foam.

Mike picked his time and we charged out and got clear without mishap. As with most things in life, timing is everything! We hauled our fifty pots on board as the tide eased, in relative comfort, if you didn't mind great hills of blue water! *Reaper* rode the swells homeward like a surfboard, running straight and true. Then we came to the really tricky bit, entering the quay gap. We had completed our trip in good time and we were back before the ebb tide lowered the water level in the harbour entrance. That part was absolutely crucial. Mike reduced the engine revs and turned us to face the harbour. For a few moments we ran with the threatening seas on our beam, quaking at their crests as if they would surely break upon us then, with a burst of full power we were safely inside, with our precious cargo only slightly the worse for wear. Of course, there had been nothing at all in the pots when we hauled them, not even a watery crab had gone in; the ground sea had seen to that. When I signed on again I could honestly write 'No Fish' on the form. That should keep them happy.

Everyone was sick of the continuing bad weather. It just seemed to go on forever and small groups of fishermen gathered every day to look at the water and commiserate with one another, and to check their boats' mooring ropes and fenders.

Since we had completed making our new fleet of pots for that year, I made up some experimental lobster pots. Some were like the wooden American parlour pots and the others were like the Scottish creel. I made these at home and Mike collected them and took them to the loft in his pickup.

George saw Mike going up the cliff path carrying one in each hand. He missed his chance of a close–up view by a matter of seconds. Naturally, he was burning with curiosity. The next day I was down helping George to take the ballast out of *Sunrise* and he quizzed me relentlessly, looking for details. I would gladly share information with George, of all people, but found it more fun to string things out and fed him a crumb of information at a time. Besides, he was far too busy getting his boat ready to experiment with fancy pots.

Mike and I had misgivings about these pots. We thought that the Newquay ground might be unsuitable because of its teeming population of spider crabs. We reckoned these would most likely bung up the netted creel entrances before a lobster had a chance to get in.

View from top

View from side

Parlour

Entrance

Bait

Parlour

Entrance
(withy mouth)

Bait

Netting funnel

Concrete

Funnel

Parlour

Netting cover

Entrance

Parlour

Concrete

Funnel

Access to parlour

Lacing

Lanyard

Wooden base

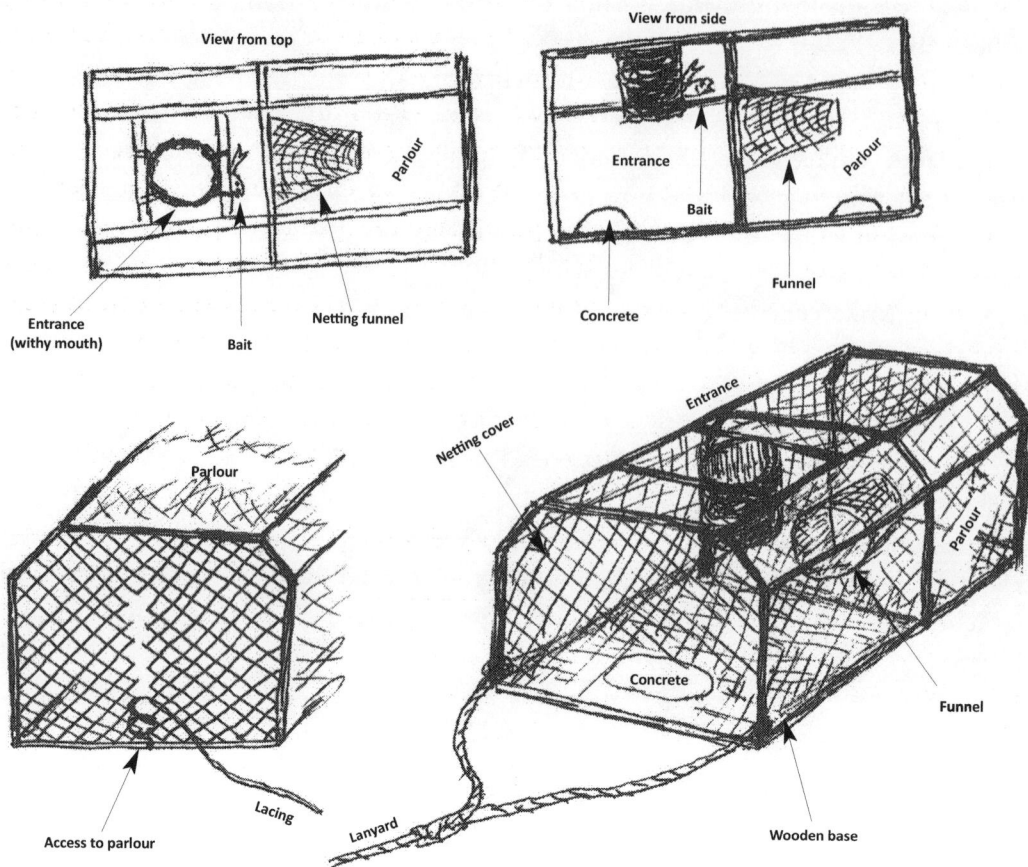

Our "American" Parlour Pot

Cooker told us that Chapper had damaged *Castle Wraith* in Padstow, when he rammed the quay after getting a rope in the propeller. On the same day, we heard Dave Sleeman had a crash and that his car was a write–off.

We were into the last week in February and I felt that if it didn't stop blowing soon and let us get fishing, I would become institutionalised and soon lose the will to live. Friday had become the most important day of the week. Monday was signing–on day but Friday was dole–day. As usual, the post office was crowded when I went in and joined the queue. Arriving at the counter I presented my driving licence to the cashier and expected, as usual, that he would hand me the dole money. To my surprise, he glanced at it and thrust it back across the counter to me. I just stood there feeling stupid for a moment. I asked him if something was wrong.

"Provisional licence is not acceptable. Only a full licence is acceptable as a means of verifying identification," he said, speaking each word loud and clear, as if he was proclaiming martial law or something.

"But last week …" I began, but the cashier was looking over my shoulder and inviting the person behind me with, "Next!"

"Hold on a minute," I said, standing my ground. I was aware of the people crowding the post office and hanging on to every word. "If my licence is no good then kindly tell me what is?"

"A letter addressed to you would suffice," he answered. I was boiling inside. The pompous bastard knew very well who I was and I wanted to reach in and grab him. However, first things first, besides I needed the money. I slunk out of there, went home and found a letter from my bank. When I presented this to the same cashier, he paid me without a murmur.

On Friday, 3 March, Mike arrived at the harbour without his car. On the way down Treninnick Hill that morning, a front wheel had come off and he was lucky to escape without injury. There was still too much wind for us to go to sea, so I made a dhan buoy and then went up to get my dole. As the morning was quite well advanced, there were plenty of customers in the post office and I took my place in the queue. As luck would have it, I arrived at the counter in the next berth to where my friendly cashier sat. I proffered my provisional driving licence and this other guy hardly glanced at it before shoving it back to me. I placed my hand on it and drew it towards me. I watched him counting out the pound notes, then the florins, a shilling and a sixpence. He placed the coins in a little stack on top of the notes and pushed the money towards me. I closed my fist loosely on it and held it there. He looked up from his cash drawer, obviously expecting to see his next customer but I stood my ground. The post office was suddenly quiet.

"What's this then?" I asked, "You are accepting provisional licences this week and yet last Friday, your mate here refused mine and sent me packing. How do you explain that?"

He made a grab at the money but I snatched it away saying, "Not so fast buddy."

He said, "Let me see that licence again!"

I said, "No! But I'll be in again next Friday and you can see it then."

I turned and strode out, knowing that with any luck, by next week we would be fishing. As with most things in life, timing is everything.

A Year of Surprises

It must have been sometime in late '66 when I read in *Fishing News* that the Republic of Ireland's government had outlawed the taking of shellfish by divers. I couldn't believe what I was seeing and I had to read the short article more than once. Indeed, it was true and it really did mean what it said: divers would be prosecuted for taking crawfish and lobsters in southern Ireland.

I was greatly surprised because as a regular reader of *Fishing News*. I would surely have read reports of disputes between divers and fishermen, or references to a campaign calling for a ban in Ireland, had there been any, but I couldn't recall having seen one word about it. How had the Irish fishermen achieved this? I asked myself. Perhaps a bunch of them went to their MP and complained that divers were raiding their pots and destroying their livelihood. Their MPs. must have been made of different stuff than our Scott Hopkins and Edward Heath, I thought. I imagined their bloke blowing his top when he heard the story. He would phone their Prime Minister on the red telephone who in turn would recall Parliament. Justice! That is what the Irish fishermen were getting, justice and fair play.

Meanwhile, we here in Cornwall were pleading with our politicians, government officials, scientists and others for these past couple of years and we had nothing at all to show for it. I was angry at the way these people were ignoring our genuine concerns for the crawfish stocks. I raced over to Mike and Joyce's house with the paper to show them the article. We discussed it at some length and decided we would look into the possibility of moving to southern Ireland.

Mike and I met down at the harbour each morning and watched the seas rolling up on Towan Beach. When there was no ground sea, it was because there was a gale of northerly wind blowing right in on us. We did odd jobs on the boat and gear but we were fed up with the weather and there seemed to be no end to these big depressions marching across the Atlantic to batter the coast. We discussed our situation and we both knew that we would have to catch an awful lot of fish in the forthcoming season to plug the gaps left by this hungry winter. More and more our thoughts turned towards Ireland. Pauline and I talked it over and, towards the end of February, she wrote to a Mr Brendan O'Kelly, Chairman of BIM, the Irish Sea Fisheries Board.

My motorbike started giving trouble. I managed to get it to Wayne Morris, the motorbike man and walked home. Mike called in the evening with some holiday brochures of southern Ireland. The news from Wayne was that my motorbike needed new main bearings, so I walked to town and tried to find a second–hand pushbike to buy. I had no luck until Dave Trebilcock heard I was stuck for wheels and gave me his old pushbike. I bought a few bits and pieces and fitted a new tyre, and then gave it a test run. I peddled like hell in the pissing rain and went from Fern Pit to the top of South Quay Hill and back in twelve–and–a–half minutes. 'Who needs a damn motorbike anyway?' I said to myself.

On Monday, 6 March 1967, a letter arrived from Mr James O'Connor, Secretary of BIM, in which he suggested that we visit him in Dublin. I took the letter to show Mike and we both thought that a good plan would be for me to take a quick trip over to Dublin in the very near future.

The yarn was that Mike Morris's *Trevose* was beneaped and some of our more knowledgeable Critics predicted she would not float again until the next equinox tides in September.

Keith Bray sold the boat he recently bought to go lobster fishing.

Young Johnny Morris was going lobster fishing with Bobby Broderick in the *Talisman*.

George's boat *Sunrise* was ready to fish, but gales all week kept him bottled up in Fern Pit. George was not very happy because he couldn't get his pots fishing. We ourselves were no better off of course, but we just had to grin and bear it. I went down to his boathouse and, after the usual pleasantries, I told George that the Association was in the red. I gave him a list of members who had bought boots, oilskins, paint and suchlike and who still hadn't paid up. George studied the list and the figures with a furrowed brow. The diary recorded his reaction merely as, "Humph!" I knew that George would seek out the debtors with ferret–like zeal.

Another week of gales passed and on Sunday, 12 March, the shipping forecast gave strong winds for all coastal areas with force twelve in sea areas Plymouth and Portland. Just in case George had missed the hurricane warning, I went up the cliff path to his house to let him know. We talked again about the Association's finances. He said that he had spoken to certain members and that they wanted to have a meeting to sort things out. I told him that there was nothing to sort out. All certain members had to do was to pay their debts to the association. When everybody's bill was paid, then the problem would go away and they could have a meeting whenever they liked. I'd paid my bill only the week before, but I didn't tell George that. I took some satisfaction from the anticipated furious reaction of certain members when George relayed my message to them.

A couple of days later Mike received a letter from the tax people demanding £360.00. As it was still blowing, we had plenty of time to discuss it, and we were in quite a sweat about it. It couldn't have come at a worse time!

Bill and Ben came into the shed, and we all moaned about the state of things. We were fed up we said, with the Newquay council's hostility towards us. We were sick of the Cornwall Sea Fisheries Committee, the Ministry of Agriculture Fisheries and Food, and the recently introduced Selective Employment Tax. This SET was the idea of Prime Minister Harold Wilson. It was designed to drive people out of fishing, farming and service industries and in to manufacturing industries. Wilson thought this would make Britain Great! What kind of a sick joke was that, we wondered?

I said, "Look, with fifty seven million people to choose from, the best leader they could find was Harold Wilson. It's a total disaster! He is a bloody economist for Christ's sake!"

I declared there and then that I would quit the country. Later, when we were alone, Mike and I talked things over and we decided that I would go to Ireland at the end of September and try to get myself a berth on a trawler. Mike would take *Reaper* to Padstow, get her overhauled and be ready to follow me in the spring.

Beware the Tides of March

We heard that *Bacchus* and the *Gillian Clare*, which were working somewhere to the westward of us, were very lucky to save their gear from the last spell of severe weather. The *Gillian Clare*, formerly the Burtie Boys' *Patsy Anne*, would founder on Hayle Bar a couple of years later, with the tragic loss of three men.

Simon Drew had been working on a toy fishing boat for Martyn. One day he walked into the shed and gave it to me. Simon was very skilful with boats and woodwork and it certainly showed in this toy. Every bit of its design had been thought through most carefully.

"You see," he said to me, "it's got a flat bottom so it will sit level on the floor, or else he can float it if he wants to. There is room back aft, in under the wheelhouse, to hold his shore crabs and there is room for'ard, for his bits of gear. I've made the truck of the mast like a big round button and painted it yellow because, you know, the very first thing a kid will do is bend down to get something out of the boat, forget the mast is there and bang his head on it."

When I looked closely at the boat, I realised that no amount of money could have bought a better toy. Martyn received it on the morning his fifth birthday and it proved a great success. Now, all of forty years later, he still has the boat at home, where it is on display in its happy retirement.

Half of March had slipped away with no sign of any fine spell coming. Some mornings, if it looked like staying dry, I would take Martyn with me to the harbour. We would walk along Pentire Road and then take a short cut across the golf links. While Mike and I worked on gear, Martyn would play on the beach or, if the tide was in, he would find plenty to keep him occupied amongst the fishing gear and around the boats up on the hard.

This should have been a pleasant time for Mike and me but we were not the least bit relaxed. We watched the weather and listened to forecasts and we grabbed any chance to carry our pots out and get them fishing. Then, after only a couple of days, we would be forced to bring the whole lot back in again, just ahead of the next series of gales.

Bill and Ben fared no better. Our two boats each made two hauls without either of us catching even one lobster. The ground sea had been increasing gradually all day and so we blamed that for the empty pots.

When we entered the harbour, we learned that George Northey had caught six lobsters. Jane, George's eldest daughter, imparted the glad tidings along with a triumphant, "Na–nah–nah–na–nah–nah". Ourselves and Bill and Ben were well used to the ups and downs of fishing and should have been able to laugh it off, but instead of that, as the diary puts it, "We were absolutely spitting."

On Tuesday, 21 March, we were all down there at the usual spot, watching the sea and the weather. We decided that though the wind had eased, there was still too much ground sea, so we left the boats on their moorings. It was very frustrating because, with shellfish at their current prices, even a small number of lobsters each week would have given us wages.

There had been some vandalism during the previous night. Bill and Ben's punt had been cast off and Mike Morris's store pots had been thrown off the quay into the dock. These mindless acts were on the increase and we were all heartily sick of it.

The next morning Mike and I loaded and baited fifty wire lobster pots. We did the same with another ten pots. These were experimental ones I had made: five parlour pots and five creels. Mike had rigged them up in pairs, two to a buoy rope. We went to sea as soon as the boat floated and, after placing the pots nicely off Newquay Headland, we steamed down to Perranporth to haul our old string of French pots. The first two pots came up intact but the remainder were smashed, even though they had been in twenty fathoms. We weren't too upset because those pots had paid for themselves many times over. We waited until the tide had turned and then hauled the fifty wire pots at Newquay Headland without seeing a living thing. We kept those two strings on board and brought them back into the harbour with us.

When we came ashore, everyone was talking about a big tanker, the *Torrie Canyon*, which had gone aground on the Scilly Isles. Apparently, the Council was asking us to spray detergent if any oil from the wreck approached Newquay.

We were surprised to see that Mike Morris had brought *Trevose* into the harbour. This suggested that the yarn that she was beneaped up the Gannel was somewhat exaggerated. On the other hand, I could imagine him using both propellers to plough his way down to open water, if he thought there was a bob to be earned. Anyway, there she was, alongside the quay ready for action, if required.

Personally, I doubted if there would be any action. The Scilly Isles lie about twenty–eight miles from Land's End. That placed the wreck of the *Torrie Canyon* about forty miles away from us in Newquay. I reckoned that with the disturbed weather we were getting, any oil slick would head away to Wales, Ireland or perhaps even Spain.

The next morning, Thursday 23rd, dawned bright and clear but the wind, being fresh and from a north westerly direction, prevented us from going to sea. At around midday, the wind eased and so we put fresh baits in the fifty wire pots, which we had on deck. As we prepared to leave, an elderly gentleman came and asked if he could come out with us.

"Yes you can, but mind you, it isn't very nice," said Mike.

I can remember thinking to myself that Mike's words might prove to be the understatement of the year. Never mind, it was warm and sunny and the wind had dropped away to almost nothing. With the pots stacked on deck, the only space for our guest was back aft. He took up his position there, chatting to Mike through the open wheelhouse doorway as we slipped out through the quay gap. As the first great lump of blue water flung *Reaper's* bow skyward, the old guy grabbed the mizzen mast. He wrapped both arms around the mast, hugging it tightly to himself as the boat climbed up and over the steep wobbly seas and slid down into deep troughs. Of course, although the wind had died, the further off we went into the guts of the tide the worse the dreadful northerly gulch became. There was nothing we could do to help him and he spent the entire trip like that, clinging on for dear life. All we could do was go about our business.

We shot the fifty wire pots on Carters Rock and then hauled the five pairs of pots near Newquay Headland. We caught one lobster in one of the parlour pots. It was the last pot to come aboard. Mike stood staring at it.

I asked, "What's up?"

"Well I'm Damned," said Mike, shaking his head, "He's in the parlour."

"Of course he's in the parlour," I said. "It's a bleedin' parlour pot ain't it?"

Privately I thought, "Wow! That's amazing!"

As soon as we'd finished with the pots, Mike steered for home. It was only a short trip and when we entered harbour, we put the old chap ashore. He seemed a bit unsteady on his legs and he went up the steps, repeating as if to himself, "The Cruel Sea, that's what I calls it, the Cruel Sea!"

At seven o'clock on Good Friday morning, we arrived at the harbour intending to go to sea, only to find we had a fairly big ground sea. This was a surprise, coming as it did, straight after the north wester. I was also surprised to see that George Northey had made a creel and put it on board his boat. I went straight home and made another parlour pot.

On the morning of Saturday 25th, the wind was south west force seven and increasing. The whole gang of us were down at the harbour and all the talk was about the oil from the *Torrie*

Canyon. Simon Drew had already been to Perranporth in his car and said he could smell the oil "real strong" down there. There was great excitement all round and everyone realised that if the wind stayed fresh westerly, the oil would be with us in a matter of hours.

Sammy Malone frightened the wits out of a couple of honeymooners. They had wandered blissfully, hand–in–hand, down across the harbour beach. On seeing them, Sammy raced down the sand roaring, "Clear the beaches. The oil is coming!"

He charged past the young couple and on down to the tide. There he swung around, his face red from exertion and, still roaring, he raced back up. Spreading his arms wide he scooped up the young couple and drove them ahead of him up the beach. Obviously shaken by the experience, the poor people scuttled away up the road, clinging tightly to one another. I like to think that their Newquay honeymoon resulted in a long and happy marriage, but then, I am an incurable romantic!

The harbour became a hive of activity, with people running around all over the place, though as a matter of fact, absolutely nothing was happening except for a lot of shouting and arm waving. Several councillors turned up and at least eight council workers accompanied them. Councillor Minns appeared to be in charge, while Harold Bullen seemed to have become his general factotum. No doubt, Harold's grave digging skills were going to prove invaluable in the impending struggle!

At two o'clock in the afternoon, the fishermen met with four councillors out on the south quay. The councillors stood shoulder–to–shoulder athwart the quay, as if to prevent any of us from escaping. They all looked very important and business–like in their suits. We, for our part, stood in a loose bunch, milling about and muttering and looking a mess. About three paces separated the two parties. The councillors had a plan and one of them set about explaining it to us.

"The situation is extremely serious," he announced. "Our Town, New–QUAY, is threatened with disaster. If this oil is allowed to reach New–QUAY's beaches our businesses will be ruined and the holidaymakers will not come back to New–QUAY anymore."

Mickey Burt was standing next to me. "Who the hell is this up–country bugger? He can't even say the town's name right," he said. (The locals called it NOOkee!)

I could appreciate Mickey's annoyance at the councillor's mispronunciation. Just hearing it once was enough to make me squirm and I wasn't even a native.

Their spokesman continued outlining the plan for us. "And well, we were thinking, that since most of you work on the buildings in the winter for three pounds per day, then the Council would be quite prepared to match that figure. That is of course, any day the boats are called out to spray detergent, we would pay each of you three pounds."

There was a stirring in the bunch of fishermen.

"Hang on a minute," we said, "you want us to spray detergent on the oil to save your hotels from ruin and, at the same time, we will be destroying our fishing grounds. All that for three pounds a head? Well thanks for nothing, let's forget about it!"

With that, some of us were about to walk off but the councillors were asking us to stay and to reconsider what was, as they said, a generous offer! After a bit more talk the fishermen withdrew to the Lifeboat House, to discuss things amongst themselves. Within a few minutes, we had decided what we needed. What we wanted was ten pounds per man and ten pounds for the boat. We would need to carry extra hands in most of the boats, at the individual skipper's discretion, of course.

We came out of the Lifeboat House and put our demands to the councillors. These were accepted without too much hassle. We also agreed to a payment of three pounds per head for any day when there was no spraying done and the boats were merely on 'standby' in the harbour.

This last piece of the arrangement was going to cause us some bother before long, but it was the best we could manage at the time.

Lorries, each carrying twenty tons of liquid detergent held in steel drums, began arriving on the quay. The lorries had been travelling down from Scotland throughout the night, with police escorts. Things began to move quickly then with boats pulling in alongside and loading drums.

Harold took charge of operations on the south quay and his voice rose clear and strong above the noise of engines. "Come away in easy," and then, "Go astern, go astern" and "Another touch ahead," then "Hold hard now and let this boat out first." He shouted to the crews as they jostled to get alongside to load detergent.

We took ten of the 45–gallon drums on board *Reaper* and tied them in place on deck. We also received two petrol driven pumps and we were pleasantly surprised at how steady *Reaper* was with all that weight above her waterline.

Before we moved the boat back onto her moorings, we noticed that Councillor Minns was using a walky–talky radio, identical to ours. This was very interesting, because we were all under constant threat of being prosecuted for using our sets!

Also, before the day ended, Harold had abandoned his post with Minns and shipped on with us. We can suppose the post with Minns was an honorary one, whereas being with us held the chance of earning money. To complete our crew, we shipped on Reg Trebilcock as well.

Things were really hotting up and the wind blew a steady half gale, from a point west of south west. Before we went home, we sniffed the air like bloodhounds and convinced ourselves that we could smell the oil, thick and plentiful and close at hand.

Black Gold

26 March was Easter Sunday. We were all down the harbour early that morning, but there was a whole gale of westerly wind and a big heaving sea. We hung around, waiting for news of oil and listening to rumours. More lorries carrying drums of detergent arrived and we unloaded them, displaying such willingness and such a generosity of spirit that it would really touch your heart.

John Pardoe, Liberal MP for North Cornwall arrived. I spent a useful few minutes talking with him about the oil situation and I naturally put in a few words about our problem with skin divers while I had him there. We all made the most of our opportunity to buttonhole the councillors regarding the skin divers as well. They had to listen to us and they nodded politely. This made us feel good, even though we guessed that nothing would come of it.

We were assembled at seven o'clock the next morning and the air was filled with the smell of crude oil. The wind had eased to a westerly force six and the sea was moderating. Things were looking quite promising, but then word was passed around that we were to stand down. Now this news didn't suit us one bit. We were all ready and willing to go and suddenly, for no good reason, we were being stopped.

Mike and I realised the seriousness of the situation, even if nobody else did. We went around trying to convince the councillors that the oil was here and we pointed out the folly of allowing the oil to come ashore instead of sending us out to deal with it at sea. Oh but what a stubborn bunch they were! They refused to budge for a long time, even though we used our utmost powers of persuasion on them. How much longer would they keep us idle while the deadly black tide raced towards us? We asked them, hinting that some serious questions would need to be answered if they didn't act quickly to avert the disaster. (Besides, if the wind went south east, it would blow the oil all the damn way to Ireland, wouldn't it?)

In the end, our persistence paid off and at ten o'clock, we got the word to go. *Reaper* was the first to leave and we ploughed through big lumpy seas until, within a few minutes, we could see the oil. A vast area of the sea, going away off into the distance, was calmed by the oil and it rolled towards us in low, sluggish swells. Mike closed down the two throttles and *Reaper* slipped quietly through a slick of transparent, thin oil, which stained the sea with pale rainbow colours. Suddenly we were in amongst the heavy stuff. It was dark brown, almost black and it looked solid enough to walk on. There was no way of knowing how thick this layer of crude oil might be, but its surface was marked with a tracery of cracks and the oily smell stuck in the back of our throats.

We tried to start the two petrol driven water pumps but they both resisted our most determined efforts to get them going. There was nothing else for it. Mike came out of the wheelhouse and the four of us humped the heavy detergent drum up onto the boat's gun'l. Then, with Mike back at the helm, we removed the bung and let the detergent flow out while our bow cut a swath through the heavy oil. The oil smelled bad but it was nothing compared to the strong smell given off by the detergent! It made our eyes sting and the awful stuff went everywhere.

Harold, Reg and I clung onto the drum and tried to keep it balanced on the gun'l, despite the boat's rolling and yawing about. The beastly drum teetered and slithered about, threatening to maim us. The detergent was like thin white custard and it was amazingly slippery. It was soon on the outside of the drum so that we couldn't get a firm grip on it. Detergent was all over the deck so that we slid and fell and collided with one another. Somehow, we managed to discharge all ten drums overboard without suffering the loss of a single limb. With great relief, we watched as drum number ten gave a last few convulsive glunks and emptied itself.

We headed for home and when we got alongside, we loaded another twelve drums, aided this time by a mobile crane. We put the two pumps ashore and we were given two new ones. Loading completed we all went off home for dinner.

Mike and the other skippers received letters from the Postmaster General, giving them permission to use the little walkie–talkie radios. At last some common sense! At last, a grateful nation had recognised our selfless devotion to duty in the hour of need. Now they were showing us their gratitude by cutting red tape and dumping the stupid rule that isolated us from each other and from the shore. I felt really good about that.

Off we went to sea again in the afternoon and this time we took Councillor Minns with us. The wind had slackened a bit more and the sun had come out. The new pumps worked fine and we steamed back and forth through the oil delivering a jet of detergent up into the air from either side of the boat so that, from the shore and to the dignitaries gathered on the headland, *Reaper* must have looked like a fire–fighting tug. Everything went like clockwork and Norman Minns was obviously impressed. We hoped that his buddies, up on the cliffs watching us with binoculars, were suitably impressed too.

Tuesday morning saw us all down there raring to go, except for Eddie Hoare and Reg Morris. They both would sooner keep their boats on the moorings and get the three pound fee for 'standby' than endure the hardships of spraying. This was the first sign of a split within our ranks. The split seemed to be between the two age groups. On one side, we had the old–timers, who were happy to sit drinking tea in the Rowing Club all day for three pounds and on the other side, we had the young tigers, who would go through hellfire to get their paws on the ten–pounds– per–man–and–ten–for–the–boat for spraying. From here on there would be a struggle between the two sides: 'Them who wanted to stay in' and 'them who wanted to go out.'

Chairman of the Council, John Kennedy took command and Sammy Malone seemed to have shipped on as his 'dog's body'. They seemed to prefer to keep us in harbour, despite our splendid performance of yesterday and so we were condemned to hang around all morning.

In the afternoon, someone reported oil in the bay. Eddie Hoare and Malcolm Marr were sent off to investigate and, in a very short time, Eddie came back. He reported seeing no oil but Malcolm searched further west and radioed back to say that there was a big concentration of oil off the Goose Rock and that he needed assistance. Still they wouldn't let us go! Sammy drove out to Pentire Headland in his car for a look, but reported back that he saw no oil. Next they sent *Trevose* out and before very long, Mike Morris was on the radio saying he was in amongst the oil. At long last, our doubting councillors were convinced and they gave us the order to go. When we got out there, we found plenty of oil, enough for everybody and tons to spare as well! There was a big awkward swell running and we had quite a struggle. Although we had tied the drums in place, they wouldn't stay quiet and they needed our constant attention to prevent them from breaking loose and causing damage.

On the Wednesday morning the wind was north, force four–to–five but the oil had mysteriously vanished. We in *Reaper* left the harbour at eight o'clock and searched while the rest were kept on their moorings. Although we covered a wide area, we saw no trace of oil anywhere. Was this the end of the lollipop? We wondered.

On Thursday morning, we assembled at seven o'clock. We hung around but none of us were asked to go searching. Reports reached the harbour that oil was visible from Newquay Headland and it was estimated to be three miles offshore. Even when the RAF reported seeing oil off Watergate Bay, we were still kept tied up. A whole gang of us went around talking to councillors and other people of influence who were to be found mooning around the quay during those days. We explained to them that the tide was falling and soon the boats would all be aground.

We said it was just crazy to have the boats sitting high and dry for six hours while we all sat helpless and watched the oil come ashore. Could they not see that the wind had hauled out a couple of points? We warned them that this would surely bring masses of oil in. While we were thus engaged, the other crowd, the 'let me stay in harbour and gimme the three pounds gang', were equally busy putting forth the opposite point of view.

It was six o'clock when the boats came afloat on the evening tide and the *Reaper* was ordered to proceed and search. Mike steered up to the eastward, hoping to find the slick that had been reported earlier by the R.A.F. We went across Watergate Bay without seeing anything and continued on until we were off Porthcothan. Reg Trebilcock and I were standing on the after deck, sheltered by the wheelhouse and Harold Bullen was wedged inside with Mike. Harold was in the middle of an interesting yarn about grave digging when Mike saw the oil. In truth, it was only a small slick and mostly the light paraffin stuff.

"This'll do, start the pumps," shouted Mike.

We jumped to it and started spraying. That's what I liked about working with Mike. No shilly-shallying but a quick assessment of the situation, followed by instant action. A couple of sweeps back and forth across the slick and we had it dealt with. We were about to stop the pumps but then Mike showed what I can only describe as inspired leadership.

"Keep spraying," he yelled, steering towards Newquay Headland at full speed. "I'm calling the rest out because there's tons of oil out here somewhere but we won't find it single-handed."

Then by way of explanation he said, "If they damn councillors are watching us through binoculars and see we aren't spraying they won't let the other boats come out."

Soon we were a mere two miles from the harbour and Mike spun the wheel to starboard and headed off out to sea. At the same time, he reduced engine speed to a tick over. I could hear him talking on the radio now that the engines were running quietly.

"Big concentration of oil here now," he was saying. "There's patches of the real thick stuff all over the place. You'd better get the boats out here while there's a bit o'daylight left."

Glancing around I couldn't see what Mike was describing but then I didn't have my glasses on, so I supposed that explained it.

Mike shoved his head out of the window. "Pull the suction hoses out of the drums and hang them over the side, there's no need to waste detergent," he said.

We did that and two beautiful jets of salt water arced away from us on either side.

The little radio blared out, "*Reaper, Reaper*, Calling *Reaper*."

I couldn't make out what the caller wanted but I heard Mike say, "If we don't get help here soon Towan and Great Western beaches will be buried in oil come the morning."

Within minutes, the boats came pouring out through the quay gap with Bill and Ben's *Evelyn Meyrick* in the lead. The boats headed off to sea and fanned out at full speed, for already the light was failing. Soon we could see that they were all spraying detergent. All, that is, except Bill and Ben, who headed straight toward us with no sign of any detergent pumping out from the *Evelyn Meyrick*.

The radio was squawking again. Kelvins voice sounded full of puzzled indignation. "*Reaper, Reaper*, this is the *Evelyn Meyrick*. Where is the oil Mike?"

They were almost on top of us by now. Mike answered, his voice calm and steady, "Keep her going the way she's heading now and you'll soon come across it."

Kelvin reduced speed and they passed slowly across our stern. The two lads were standing up, clinging to either side of the wheelhouse and peering eagerly ahead. Kelvin was on the air again, "*Reaper, Reaper*, we still can't see any oil Mike."

I thought Mike was about to have a seizure. His face went awful red and he shouted, "Aw my Gawd!"

A stream of curses flowed out of the wheelhouse window. This was serious because he wasn't really a cursing kind of chap, not like Brownie and some of the other old–timers. I could understand Mike's frustration. He had caused the fleet to put to sea and now they were all scattered about somewhere off the headland, spraying happily away and not a peep out of anyone.

Meanwhile we were here, under the very noses of the councillors, being a shining example to the rest, while Bill and Ben were up alongside us and bellowing over the airwaves that they couldn't see any oil!

Quickly Mike recovered his composure and spoke into his radio. "*Evelyn Meyrick*, steer towards us, we are just on the edge of it now."

As they drew closer Mike stepped out of the wheelhouse and yelled, "Start spraying."

The two lads were standing side–by–side now and they were staring at us. Perhaps they were looking at our suction hoses trailing in the water.

"What?" they yelled back in unison.

Mike tried again, "Start your pumps and get spraying."

The lads stood with their hands cupped to their ears, straining to hear over the noise of their air–cooled Lister.

"Eh? What?" they chorused.

Only a few feet separated the two boats. Mike was going into spasm again. He dropped down onto his knees on our little after deck and shook his clenched fist at Bill and Ben roaring, "If you two don't start spraying this very minute, I will come aboard and stuff them hoses up your fuckin' assholes!"

At last, the message got through and soon our two boats were spraying away merrily together.

Suddenly the radio was squawking again. Everyone was trying to talk at once. The boats were meeting masses of heavy oil approaching the headland from the west. We went off and joined them and, in the gathering gloom, we sprayed real detergent until it was too dark to see. Mike's hunch about the oil had paid off. The oil had come and we were there with enough boats to deal with it. In our own case, we, by careful conservation, even had enough detergent left to last us into the dark.

A Lethal Dose

On the morning of the 31 March, *Reaper* was sent out on reconnaissance and we headed down west towards the Madrips. Traces of oil were surprisingly scarce, considering that the wind was northerly. Even so, after a bit of persuasion on the radio from Mike, the *Trevose* was eventually allowed out to assist us, in what I would best describe as a spot of random spraying. After a while, the two boats slipped in to Tolbar and anchored in the cove. It was pleasantly calm and peaceful in the lee of the great rock. A successful kind of a day.

In the evening, I went to Truro, for a meeting of the Cornish Inshore Society. The main concern of all the delegates was the possible long–term effects of the detergent. Everyone expressed some level of pessimism. We were certainly in uncharted waters. The next day was Saturday, 1 April and by 7am, we were all steaming up east for Watergate, except for George Northey and Chris Moffat who had taken their boats up Gannel to George's Quay, perhaps believing that the party was over. We worked on a large area of heavy oil and after a few hours of concentrated spraying by all the boats, the oil was dispersed.

The day had started off fine enough, with a light wind from the south but this quickly turned into a rising gale. We could have returned to harbour (saved water back) because the sea became too rough for us to operate. The strengthening wind hauled out to the south west, but our masters insisted that we remain at sea. I suppose they wanted to make sure we earned our ten pounds per man.

We had to stay out over the low water and then wait for another three hours flood to get to our berths. It made a long day of it and I remember that it dropped bitterly cold and I had developed a very bad cough. Plenty of detergent had been blown into my eyes and this was giving me a lot of pain. I scooped seawater out of the bucket with my cupped hands and kept sloshing it into my eyes to give me some relief. Swinging to an anchor in enforced idleness for hours didn't help things either and I felt really rotten. It was 1 April, All Fools Day, so perhaps that had some bearing on it.

On Sunday, 2 April, we hung around the quay all day waiting for the wind to ease, but we had a half gale of south west wind and then came a big ground sea along with it. The weather showed no sign of settling and indeed, it had been so bad since the New Year that I'm sure none of the Newquay boats had made any money from their fishing. If running costs were subtracted from their earnings, then they would, almost certainly, all have shown a loss.

Fishermen are used to bad spells like this of course and they just have to get on with the job until things come right. General opinion had it that the Burtie Boys had lost out by trying to fish throughout this period of appalling weather, instead of joining the other big boats spraying in the Newlyn/Penzance area. Really big money was being paid by the local authorities down there, or so we heard anyway. As far as we could see, the *Torrie Canyon* disaster was our good fortune, at least in the short term. Because people like us had to keep the bread on the table every day, we couldn't afford to dwell too much on the possible consequences of the spraying.

The next morning, the wind was from the north west and the bay was filled with masses of thick oil. Pandemonium reigned as boats came and went, loading drums from the quay, steaming out at full speed and then commencing spraying as soon as they cleared the harbour. Up across Towan, Great Western and Tolcarne and beyond Porth and Watergate Bay they went, ploughing swathes through the great solid–looking rafts of crude oil, which drifted relentlessly towards the beaches.

We in *Reaper* made four trips in quick succession that morning, carrying twelve 45– gallon drums out with us each time. Upon their return to the harbour, the boats simply tossed the empty drums overboard, so that very soon there were hundreds of empties floating around in the dock and blowing ashore on the harbour beach. The mobile crane was working at full speed to keep the boats supplied with drums of detergent and, as Mike said, Newquay Harbour had never seen the likes of it.

The whole scene was remarkable by any standards but to me it seemed that the confusion and nonsense that we had endured since the news of the wreck first reached us had been swept away. It had been replaced by a speedy and efficient operation by a bunch of guys who were doing what they did best. They were responding to the situation at sea as they found it. There seemed to be no overseers, no councillors with walkie–talkie radios and, surprisingly, we saw no sign of their hangers–on.

The system of replenishing the boats was improved upon by the arrival on the quays of the bowser lorries. Instead of dumping the drums, we just went alongside the quay so that a lorry could come and let the hose down to us. This proved a much faster method of loading. It did prove a bit too fast in my case! When I took the hose in my hands to fill the first drum I was totally taken by surprise. I had expected the stuff to pour out nice and easy, but instead of that, it came out like a cannon shot the instant I pressed the trigger. The force of the delivery caused the nozzle to leap backwards out of the drum. The jet hit the top of the drum so that detergent was blasted up into my face. A great shot of it went into my eyes and more of it went down my throat. It flew all over the boat before I managed to stuff the nozzle back into the drums' bunghole. I coughed and spluttered and snorted and snotted, and pure detergent ran out of my nose as I continued filling drum after drum.

Mike was yelling at me from the wheelhouse. He was raving about detergent going down in the bilges and destroying something precious down there. I had other concerns of course, because I had just swallowed a fatal dose of poison. A fat lot my brute of a skipper cared! I thought, 'Just wait 'til he comes looking for me in the morning. I will be dead, and that will serve him bloody well right!'

The diary records that spraying operations continued during the dark and that the harbour was all hustle–and–bustle, awash with empty drums and ablaze with the auxiliary lighting. By the time we finished work, the tide had dropped so that the boats 'missed moorings' and so we all squeezed in alongside the north quay and tied up whatever way we could. Fortunately for us, there was no sign of any ground sea coming.

When we arrived next morning, we saw that the tide had not yet floated the boats. We could see Frank Dungey, Cyril Hubber and Bobby Broderick working in under the stern of the *Talisman*. They'd had the misfortune to get a chain and a rope together in the propeller and were seriously wrapped–up.

There was a dispute going on which started over practically nothing but somehow it grew until it involved everybody. It was really about young Dougy King, who had taken command of his dads' boat for the spraying. Now it so happened, that George King's boat was not only a brand new one, but it possessed a Parsons Porbeagle engine of 56hp. Big stuff indeed for the Newquay of those days and, of course, Dougy, like any youngster would if he got the chance, used every ounce of power he had.

It was not what he did at sea that bothered people but it was his handling of the boat within the harbour that caused all the resentment. He was rather small as a young teenager and when he stood up, back in the boat's stern, you couldn't see much of him peeping out over the gun'l. Despite this, he threw the boat around as though he'd been doing it for years. He went from full ahead to full astern, stopping the boat dead in its tracks. He was fond of going full ahead with the helm hard over and coming round in a tight circle. The wash from these manoeuvres caused other boats to dance wildly on their moorings and, as for Dougy's high–speed zig–zagging amongst the fleet at large, well that caused many a heart to miss a beat.

As if all that wasn't crime enough, and despite all the predictions from our most seasoned mariners, Dougy never once obliged us by colliding with another boat. If he had even rammed the centre jetty and cracked a plank or two in his old man's boat, maybe things would have simmered down but no, instead of that, he just got better at it and, not surprisingly, he got even bolder.

So it was that on Tuesday morning, 4 April, a meeting of boat owners was arranged. As a non–owner, I had no business being there, but George and a couple of the others asked me to take the chair. The meeting took place in the PSA and, after some argument; a proposal barring crew members below the age of seventeen from taking part in any spraying activities whatsoever, was agreed. This ruled out Dougy but also George's crew, young Johnny Bennets. Young Johnny, it has to be said, was totally innocent of any brat–style behaviour. 'Old Kinger' himself couldn't attend the meeting because he held a strong permanent job ashore.

In the afternoon, *Trevose* and *Reaper* were sent out to search for oil. After a wide search, we found none so we came back to the harbour and collected a large boom, which was made, it seemed, mostly of hessian. It formed a sausage, a foot thick and about twenty fathoms long. It had wire rope with lugs spliced into it at each end and our instructions were for us to tow the thing with the two boats to find out how it might be used against the oil slicks.

We each made fast, to one end of the boom and then, we payed out ten fathoms of rope from our sterns. The two boats, each using both their engines on full power, were able to tow the boom at a reasonable speed. We looked back at the boom following us, which had assumed a gentle half–moon shape. We wondered what we were supposed to do if we did trap a couple of tons of oil in it. Were we supposed to tow it away off and let it go in the hope that the oil wouldn't follow us home? How effective this rig would be in amongst the thousands of tons of crude oil would be another question altogether!

'Never mind,' we consoled ourselves, 'so what if it was a daft idea?'

Today was another tenner each for us all and we would tow the boom for as long as they wanted. After the experiment, we brought the boom back into the harbour and we tied it up as best as we could. It remained there, a major nuisance to all harbour users.

The wind had been a steady north west, force 2–4 during the past four days, but on the Wednesday, it was force 5 and increasing. Mike and I were down aboard at 6am with the engines running. We let go our moorings just before our keel would have touched the sand and we left with the falling tide. We went out, anchored and awaited developments. Mike Morris intended following us but *Trevose* got a rope in the propeller and she went aground on her moorings. Jimmy Hoare was the lucky one who stayed in bed in the warm while the rest of us spent a thoroughly miserable time out there, as the wind picked up and the temperature zoomed down. No boats were ordered to go searching so we all came in as soon as the tide was high enough.

It was about 2pm by the time we secured the boat and, of course, we only qualified for three pounds per head. Mike and I were disgusted, that the mean bastards who held the purse strings, hadn't sent all the boats out on a search. We wondered how we could somehow even the score again.

Throughout the night and the next day, we had a northerly wind, which gusted up to gale force. When we got down the harbour at 6.45am, we saw that Chris Moffat's *Morning Star* had parted her moorings and she had driven ahead up the beach. A gang of us got together and tried to shove the boat back; but although there appeared to be plenty of water around her, she was hard aground and wouldn't move.

Bob Perrington took me up to his loft to see the pots he was making. He also showed me some photos of Dingle taken while he was on holiday in Ireland, which I found very interesting. After that, Frank Cox took Bob and me into his loft and showed us his pots. Proudly he showed me two new parlour pots he'd made. I made admiring comments of course, but I was a bit annoyed to see that his parlour pots were almost identical to my own! I thought, 'How can you ever keep a secret in this place, is nothing sacred?'

That evening George Northey came down to Vyrn Cabin to tell me that oil had been seen coming ashore in several places.

The next day, Friday, 7 April, the wind had eased a bit but it was still from the north and still too fresh to put to sea. Councillors Minns and Millward met with the Fishermen at 10.30am. They told us that the Ministry was cutting down on detergent. It was a fact, they said, that the Ministry was having second thoughts about using detergent from boats anyway. What the Council wanted to know from us was, in the event of the boats being stood down, would we still be available to go spraying in the event of an emergency? We were not long finding an answer for them. Certainly, we would be available for spraying, we told them. However if another authority asked for our assistance in the meantime, then of course we would have to go to their aid.

We left the meeting with the understanding that we were all still on stand–by at the agreed £3 rate. On Saturday, the wind moderated and hauled more to the north east. We were all down at the harbour by eight o'clock and as the diary puts it, "We were all ghastly, even me."

The reason for this anger was that when the boat owners got home on Friday evening they had each found a letter from the council awaiting them. The letter was blunt and brief. It merely told them that their services were no longer required, that the skippers, their boats and their crews were therefore terminated. None of us had been expecting words of gratitude and the coldness of the letter didn't bother us one bit. What really did infuriate us was that these two councillors must have been aware that the letters were already well on their way when they asked to meet with us. Even as they applied the soft–soap and reminded us of where our loyalties were supposed to lie, they both had already been a party to dumping us!

"So that's it lads, spraying is over so let's get these drums ashore."

"Wait a minute! What's all the yelling and commotion about?"

"What d'you mean, there's a flap on?"

"Oh, there's more oil coming in. We have to load up again?"

"Ok lads, here we go again, only make haste because the tide is falling and there's not much water in alongside the quays."

Before most of the boats were loaded, they all went aground where they were, so that none of us could put to sea until the next tide floated us anyway.

That afternoon we held a meeting in the Sailing Club, in anticipation of the council cutting back on the number of boats required for spraying, which we thought might well be their next move. The meeting was to try and decide, in that event, which boats would be kept on and which would be let go. Things got heated pretty quickly. Those who relied purely on the fishing said that if there were to be any cutbacks, it should be borne by those with jobs ashore. Of course, the guys with the shore jobs didn't see why they should miss a trick either. I was in the chair. I think, upon reflection, that they had me as chairman for these meetings because they knew I was a softy and so each faction reckoned that they would get their own way.

They were really having a go at each other when Hughie Olde, the town surveyor walked in and announced that *Trevose* and *Reaper* were to go to sea at once and commence towing the boom. I immediately adjourned the meeting, and as is faithfully recorded, we got up and left them at it, all snapping and snarling!

We made our way quickly onto the boats, which were now coming afloat again. We got under way and steamed out through the quay gap, towing the boom out with us. Now this boom was a much bigger thing than the previous one and instead of being made of hessian, it was a brutish sausage–shaped affair made of unyielding grey plastic. Our two boats pulled the boom along nicely between them and Hughie was on board *Trevose*, just to monitor the operation and gauge its effectiveness. As Mike commented, "It was about as much use as pissing into the wind."

It didn't really matter because the rest of the boats were ordered out spraying anyway. So, another day, another tenner!

The new boom must have failed the test because we were not asked to tow it again. The following morning it was tied to the pier heads, effectively closing off the harbour entrance, presumably to guard the harbour against future oil spills. It seemed to us that very little thought had gone into this latest strategy. In fact, the boom was to remain across the entrance as a hazard to harbour users for several weeks after the oil was gone and forgotten.

The page in the diary for Sunday, 9 April is headed, in block capitals, "CONTRACT EXPIRED". Quite how this vital piece of news was conveyed to us on a Sunday I have no idea. It just went to show, as I'd long suspected, when the welfare of the town was at stake, the councillors and officials of the NUDC never slept!

Economics of the Job

On Monday, 10 April, the Fishermen were all down at the harbour at around 8am. We hung about all day in the vague hope that the council would find some spraying work for us, despite our having been officially terminated. A couple of the boatmen did show up in the morning but they soon went off about their own business.

George Northey passed the day chatting to this one and that. It was soon obvious that George was doing a little survey for himself, trying to discover who had made the most from this oil spill. Of course, since nobody down Newquay Harbour would ever divulge details of something as sensitive as money, George would have to rely mainly on his instinct and on his sharp, calculating brain. The figures that he eventually arrived at, you may be certain, would be a fairly accurate assessment of each boat's earnings. That was George, teasing out the pounds, shillings and pence was a kind of hobby of his. I wouldn't be any good at all that mental arithmetic stuff myself but I was convinced, beyond any doubt, that the *Reaper* was the top dog on this occasion. My skipper hadn't missed a trick, he had created opportunities for us and for the rest of the gang as well and all this, against a background of the council's most appalling mismanagement and the resulting general confusion. When I look back from this distance in time, I can only marvel at the fact that nobody was drowned or seriously injured. Whatever anyone might think of us, it was our experience and our seamanship that saved us. These, together with a large measure of good luck, of course.

On Tuesday morning, Mike Lyne and Mike Morris went to see Councillor Minns in an effort to persuade the Council to employ us. We believed that the fishing had been destroyed. We heard stories of extremely poor catches of lobsters and crawfish from the few boats still fishing up and down the coast. The Burtie Boys' *Bacchus* returned to Padstow, it was said, with only nine crawfish after five days fishing. We never heard how many lobsters they caught but the indications were that things were very bad all around the coast. Mike and I discussed the situation at some length and we were both pessimistic about our fishing prospects for the immediate future.

The following day, Wednesday, Basil 'Bayzil' Hepper, a scientist with the Ministry arrived and Mike showed him the dead creatures, which he had collected from a small area of sand around the boat while the tide was out. There were sand eels, blennies, lugs, ragworms, shrimps, various little crabs, dog whelks and things we didn't have a name for. They were all very dead and bleached pure white. When he saw them, Basil told us that holding shellfish anywhere near Newquay Harbour was simply out of the question.

Mike and Mike Morris went to see Councillor Minns again and they told him what the scientist had said. They explained that without being able to use our store pots and hold our catch, we were virtually out of business and they asked if the Council could employ us, at least until it was safe to store our lobsters again. The answer was that the Council would be prepared to employ us but the problem was the Ministry would not foot the bill.

Fishery Officer Tonkin went with Mike Lyne and Mike Morris to the Newquay Council Offices to try and move things along for us. He said afterwards that he thought there was a good chance of us being re–employed. Mike and I met again in the evening and we wondered how we would manage if we were heading into a bad lobster season, which now looked almost certain. It seemed to us that, unless we fell into some really big fishing soon, we would be forced to pack–up and go our separate ways. This was the harsh reality.

At home, I talked things over with Pauline and it was just awful to think of giving up everything we had worked so hard for. What of my partnership with Mike? I really valued that and hated the thought of splitting up. It had been so good for me and I found myself reflecting back to when we first teamed– up together.

I remembered telling Mike that someday I would leave him because ultimately, I wanted a boat of my own. Mike had said he understood that perfectly. The truth however was, as time went on I had become lazy and complacent. My dream of becoming a big fat skipper had faded and I was happy just working the deck. I had learned so much from Mike during these years and he still shared everything with me. I recounted to Pauline how Mike would hold his little transistor radio up to his ear when the *Shipping Forecast* came on. I would usually be cutting up bait while he repeated the wind speeds and the barometric readings to me from the open wheelhouse window. He would then make his decision and tell me about it. "I don't think much of that forecast. That low is a nasty one so we will start moving the gear off into twenty fathoms."

Another time he would say, "There's no real anger, only pissy–wet if you ask me. The tides are cutting all this week so we'll give that little patch to the west'ard another rattle!"

So that is how I gained a little knowledge about the weather. As I stood there splitting gurnards in front of the wheelhouse, weather–lore soaked into my brain as if by osmosis. Like I said, money couldn't buy that! Pauline and I both felt that the arrangement with Mike was too important to be thrown away. We must hang in there and somehow make it work.

On Friday morning, everyone, the fishermen and a few boatmen without shore jobs, were down at the harbour waiting to be paid for the spraying job. Eventually someone phoned the Council and they were told that they would be paid at 2pm. Nothing happened however, even though the lads waited all afternoon.

Mike called round in the evening. He'd had a message from Tonkin to say that we will not be re–employed because (you've guessed it) the Ministry would not foot the bill! Instead, they were going to build us lobster–holding tanks. Amazing! We decided to start fishing in the morning and try, if we got any lobsters, to figure out a way of storing them.

'Make Your Mind Up' Time

Saturday, 15 April, 7am. Mike and I began loading the fifty pots down off the jetty and into the boat. Mike grabbed each pot as I lowered it down to him and he fitted two baits in it. He stacked the pots three high, each one in its allotted place, flaking the backrope randomly along the deck as he did so, to ensure that all went clear during shooting.

We worked quickly, without any need for talking. We made easy work of any task we set ourselves these days. We left as soon as the gear was on board and I stood back aft by the wheelhouse, watching our bow lifting to the seas and listening to the sweet reassuring throb of the two engines. I could think of no better place to be.

As we passed the Old Dane rock, Mike eased the engine revs down a bit and turned to face me. He said, "I'm going ashore Trev."

"Oh yes," I answered casually, and I waited to hear the rest of it, for indeed the importance of this announcement had not quite filtered through to me.

Mike paused and adjusted *Reaper's* heading, giving the helm a spoke or two before turning back to me. "You see, I've always promised Joyce that one day she would have her own house."

Reaper nosed into a steeper sea and fine spray lashed against the wheelhouse windows.

Mike continued, "We have the offer of a place; it will just do us fine and, well, Joyce likes it anyway."

"Well that's really great Mike," I said.

He looked steadily at me before he spoke again. "It will mean me selling the boat and getting myself a job ashore," he said.

I snapped out of my daydream. Mike was telling me something really serious. In fact, it was something massive and when the full importance of it hit me, it sent me into a cold panic. I should have been prepared for it. We had often discussed the possibility of us having to split up but bloody hell! It was actually happening, here and now, Lord help us, and here I was, suddenly lost and not knowing which way to turn.

I simply said, "Oh, that's ok."

But at the same time, my mind was racing. What was I going to do now? I did own all the pots and the other gear, that was our arrangement but what now? Was I going to look for another partner who owned a boat? There weren't any available boats in the offing and certainly, there was nobody to take Mike's place.

As if I was watching a film, I saw myself carrying two buckets of cement mortar and tending a short–tempered bricklayer. The scene switched and I was a hundred feet up on the steel girders with a big spanner, tightening nuts and bolts as if my very life depended on it. It switched again and I was dressed in a crumpled charcoal–grey suit, standing on a doorstep and trying to flog some poor soul a life insurance policy. Scenes from my past flashed rapidly before me. I saw myself as a fireman, a pick–and–shovel man, a painter, a grill chef, a lifeguard and so on, each scene evoking worse memories than the one preceding it.

I realised, in that split second, that ever since leaving the Navy, I had always been masquerading as something–or–other. That's the way it had been with me until the day I'd shipped on with Mike. Now here I was, having finally discovered what I wanted to do with my life, and I was watching it all vanish like a puff of smoke. I knew that I desperately wanted to stay fishing, but I couldn't see how this would now be possible.

Mike continued, "I can sell the boat, several have expressed an interest. Bobby Broderick and Frank Dungey both want her and I know Dasher from Padstow would buy her in the morning."

I thought, "This is the end of it. This is horrible!"

Mike said, "If you want the *Reaper* Trev, she's yours and you can have her for the same money as I gave Ronnie for her."

If Mike's opening words had upset me, his last statement just blew me away. Ten seconds ago, everything was impossible. Now, suddenly I had a chance, a slim chance but the chance of a lifetime in fact. I knew that we were facing into an uncertain future. Perhaps spraying had poisoned the grounds and destroyed all the lobsters. Even supposing they had survived, but now they were full of oil and detergent. That could kill the market for Cornish shellfish for years to come. I also knew, without even having to think about it, that Mike was offering me the *Reaper* for about half of her actual value. He had fitted a brand new main engine with more than double the previous engine's HP and he had made many other improvements besides.

We were approaching the high place, the sheer cliff jutting up near the outer end of Newquay Headland. The seas were bigger now and each time our bow sliced into one, a heavy shot of spray hit the wheelhouse, so that the windows were whitened and we travelled blind for a second or two, until the water drained away. Mike was altering course, steering us clear of the most turbulent area.

Once steadied on the new course he said, "I've been about a job but I don't know when they'll want me. It might be they want me soon, but it could be a few months before they call me. If you do decide to have her, Trev, there is no rush. You can take the boat and fish her and I don't want any money until September."

God this was awful. As usual, Mike was doing his best for me. I felt a bit dizzy. This was not surprising really, because there were no business tycoons in our family tree and so I had not the training, nor was I genetically programmed, to handle this kind of stuff coming at me all of a rush.

"Oh thanks Mike," I said in a small voice, as if he had just handed me a Mars Bar.

The swells were longer here and less steep. *Reaper* rode over and through them at full speed without heaving much spray. Mike was peering at the echo sounder now so I made my way forward and picked up the dahn. I held it like a harpoon, ready for throwing. I watched our bow waves curling away from us and I felt our graceful motion as we forged ahead. There was never a more sea–kindly boat than the *Reaper*. Our bow was swinging to starboard and we turned one–hundred–and–eighty degrees. I waited for the shout from the wheelhouse.

"When you've a mind to," he yelled, and I hurled the dahn overboard, then I was shooting the pots, one after another, as we ran swiftly ahead of the tide at half–throttle.

The voice inside my head drove all other thoughts away. 'Keep your wits about you, reach forward and grab the next pot, throw it clear and grab the next one. Don't lose concentration, the backrope is snaking out at a rate of knots, keep clear of it, Quick now, out with the pot and go for the next one, and the next. Mind that rope, if you step into a bight of rope you'll be dragged out of her.'

It took us about five minutes to shoot the string of twenty–five pots. We had often timed ourselves back in the early days and that is how it averaged, twenty minutes to haul and five minutes to shoot. We shot the other string of pots and steamed off to haul our old gear, which we had left in twenty fathoms for safety. I was busy splitting gurnards. How normal and ordinary everything seemed, yet everything had changed. Changed forever!

We fished away for the next couple of days and busied ourselves getting more pots out. We encountered plenty of problems. Ronnie Harvey sent an urgent message telling us all to store the shellfish well clear of any polluted areas. They had found that some lobsters were heavily tainted with detergent. They'd boiled some and it stank the place out.

We therefore took our store pots off with us and tied them on the ends of our strings of lobster pots, which were away off in twenty fathoms. From that moment on, we were in trouble. Boarding the store pots along with the fishing gear generally proved to be one almighty struggle. The store pots were big and awkward and when we got one up alongside, we both hung over the boat's gun'l trying to prevent it from slamming against the boat's side and damaging our precious lobsters. We had our lifting tackle on the foremast and as soon as we hooked onto the store pot, we heaved it aboard. Usually, by the time we had accomplished this, the tide would have swept us over the gear so that the lobster pots often came fast in the ground.

Every haul involving an attached store pot was a nightmare and took us ages to complete. Shooting the damned thing was another story. We had previously kept our crab store pots out in the bay but, in the hope of avoiding any pollution, we had placed them further off outside the Gazzle. The first time we lifted them we found the crabs were heavily lagged with black oil and all we could do was release them back into the sea.

The wretched plastic boom remained tied across the quay gap and this had to be carefully negotiated each time we left or entered harbour. The state of the weather and the height of the tide dictated how we tackled it. Each time it was different and we almost got its heavy wire rope in our propeller or else we almost rammed the pier. Everyone had problems with the boom. It was said that, whilst trying to avoid the wire rope, Kelvin got all excited and banged the *Evelyn Meyrick* into the pier. Mike phoned Geoffrey Woolaston of the Ministry of Agriculture Fisheries and Food and explained our problem.

Geoffrey asked, "Why don't you go under the wire rope instead of over it?"

Mike said, "Because of our masts."

Geoffrey said, "Well why don't you take your masts out?"

The diary merely records that Mike was furious. If he had explained to Geoffrey that *Reaper*'s masts weighed hundredweights, and that they were mortised into her keelson, I suppose it would have made very little difference. Geoffrey was a real nice bloke but a bit daft where boats and fishing were concerned.

Pauline and I discussed Mike's proposal. In fact, we talked about very little else. We went to bed and talked it over until we fell asleep. Then we woke up and rehashed all the aspects of it yet again. I got up and paced the floor.

"No, we can't do it, it's a massive amount of money and anyway the bank won't lend it to me," I said.

Pauline got up and paced the floor. "Yes it is too big a debt to take on," she said. "Perhaps we should move to Plymouth and both work and save up until we can buy a nice little crabber."

"That makes so much sense," I said, with some relief. "It will only take us a couple of years. We'll get something small that I can fish single–handed, and we'll have no debts."

"That's agreed then?" she asked.

"Yes that's agreed," said I,

"In the morning I will tell Mike that it's beyond our reach, we just cannot buy the *Reaper*."

The kettle had boiled by then and we made coffee and climbed back into bed. When our cups were empty we settled down to sleep, but sleep would not come. We talked some more, round and round in circles we went, and as the dawn light slipped gradually in through our bedroom window, so common sense, (which only ever had a nodding acquaintance with us) slipped quietly away out under the bedroom door.

"We'll go for it," we said.

"Who better than us?" we asked each other.

"We owe it to ourselves," we said.

"That's agreed then?" she asked.

"Yes that's agreed," I said, "In the morning I will tell Mike that somehow, whatever it takes, we just have to buy the *Reaper*."

Don't Bank on It

The morning of Thursday, 20 April was bright and sunny with a north west wind that soon increased to a full gale. I was home from the harbour before lunchtime and, as I was feeling unwell, I stayed indoors and took things easy. I had caught a cold during our spraying operation and had been unable to shake it off. Along with it came a persistent and painful cough.

On Friday, I felt even worse and so I stayed in bed all day. The following morning Dr Collins called in to see me and she told me to stay in bed, because I had bronchitis. Mike came to visit in the afternoon and brought the latest news from the quay.

Frank Dungey had teamed up with Bobby Broderick in the *Talisman* and they had put out pots.

Bob Perrington recently had the engine overhauled but still had to resort to holding flames up to it and cranking like hell to get it started.

Cavell, the diver had teamed up with Malcolm Marr but all they caught was four crawfish. They also were putting pots out.

On Tuesday, I felt a bit better but I stayed in bed for most of the day. Bob Perrington was crewing with Mike whilst I was out sick, so I didn't feel too bad about being absent. George Northey came in for a chat. He said he was fed up because there were no fish and no one was catching anything. Despite having said that, he was in good humour and told me all about their recent family holiday in the Scillies.

It was Friday, 28 April when I left my bed–of–sickness. I pounced out like a new man and, having had ample time to form a plan of action, I got cleaned up, kicked my trusty BSA Bantam into life and rode off to see my new bank manager. I had rehearsed my lines well and I knew what to say. Perhaps even more importantly, I also knew what not to say! Well even a donkey learns, doesn't it? Anyway, our meeting was friendly and I exuded optimism. Things were looking good, at least on the surface. In truth, Pauline and I were in an awful state and sometimes, when reality struck, we simply freaked out and said, "Are we mad or what?"

It really was a mighty lump of a debt to take on, but then, being us, we would just shake ourselves and our courage would soon return to us. Sometimes we even spared a thought for Mike and Joyce, who were obviously going through something very similar to what we were experiencing. I knew that this was particularly tough on Mike, because his heart was really in the fishing. Leaving it all to go and work ashore must have been a painful decision for him. On top of that, Mike, who never did anything without carefully thinking things through, must have been wrestling with his problems for quite a while. Last of all, he must have wondered just how in hell's name he was going to break the news to me. It couldn't have been easy.

I was back fishing again for a couple of days and although I felt a bit weak at first I soon got over it. We had nine lobsters in one string of pots so that cheered us up a bit but then the dreaded 'May breeze' came and put a stop to things. A big ground sea started on the morning of 3 May and we had a southerly gale by evening. It blew force 8, 9.and even force 10 from the south and the south west and we didn't get to sea again until Tuesday, 9 May.

This break suited me fine and I visited my friendly bank manager a few more times. One day I would come out of the bank with my head in the air because everything was going to work out for us. The next day I would come out with my chin down by my knees, because it just wasn't going to happen. I'd rush home and tell Pauline and so our emotions went up and down like yo–yos. I reported the daily results to Mike, accompanied with, "Yes we can," or "No we can't have the boat."

"You needn't worry because I don't want any money until the end of the year," he said.

This sent my hopes soaring again of course. I got Mike to give me the fish sales dockets for the past four years and the manager leafed through them. I think he was impressed because he suddenly stood up and said, "Yes, we can lend you the whole amount."

We shook hands and I walked out of there, wobbling slightly and feeling a bit weird.

After the May Breeze

You would think that things would come right for us after all we had been through. The accursed divers had destroyed the crawfish so we had to fit out with lobster pots instead, with all the work and expense that entailed. You would think too, wouldn't you, that after the *Torrie Canyon* oil spill and the hardship and anxiety which that had inflicted upon us, we fishermen were due for a lucky break? We could also have been forgiven for expecting that, after the violence of the recent May breeze, we would be blessed with a spell of fine weather so that we could do some serious fishing.

It didn't happen like that. Instead, Neptune or Poseidon, or whatever you like to call him, dished out north west winds, which were right in on us and then the north easters, which made entering the harbour deadly dangerous due to the seas breaking across the quay gap. Then came the day when the wind dropped away to nothing. That was when we got this great heaving billow indicating a gale in the Irish Sea. The motion was so violent it threatened to roll the pots clean out of her. That meant a really uncomfortable day on the water. We got ten lobsters alright and the next day the wind pulled in off the land, south east force three. Beautiful it was, the dreadful billow was gone and we worked in comfort coming home with twenty–one lobsters.

We came down next morning to find the ground sea had started. "Atlantic depression approaching Fastnet," said the forecast.

We dashed out and hauled the three strings that were fairly close to shore and brought them back in the harbour for safety. Of course, the pots came up empty because the onset of the ground sea had stopped the shellfish from feeding. "Everything is clinging on for dear life down there," as Mike put it.

The ground sea had turned into a real big one by the next morning so we pulled the seventy–five pots up onto the jetty. It was always a pain in the arse to do this but we wouldn't chance the boat pounding on the sand over the low water with that weight of gear in her. Meanwhile, a few of our lads had lost pots in the May breeze, but it seems that the story was much worse further west.

Bob Perrington's engine packed up. John Julian checked it over and declared it dead.

Young Garry had been going to sea with *Talisman* and, it was said, they were all nearly washed out of her the day before!

Bill and Ben in the *Evelyn Meyrick* shipped a green sea, which came over the top of the wheelhouse and filled her aft. Chris Moffat reported a similar experience. These were not good times!

Thursday, 11 May

Mike was told his new job starts on Monday. We have arranged for Bob Perrington to come fishing with me. Bob declares himself delighted, perhaps because his engine has just snuffed it!

Meanwhile, the MAFF's response to our requests for some form of assistance in the aftermath of the oil spill, came in their offer to pay 75 per cent of the cost of putting lobster–holding tanks in Newquay Harbour. While this was a brilliant idea and could be an absolute blessing to fishermen sometime in the future, it did nothing to ease our pressing problems. However, as if to prove their good intentions, Geoffrey Woolaston and Basil Hepper came and walked around with us, looking at possible sites for the proposed tanks. Geoffrey suggested that I write a letter to the Newquay Urban District Council about a site. Basil assured us that they would shortly be meeting with the NUDC to press our case.

Bob Shipped On

On Friday, 12 May 1967 at 6am, the *Reaper* left her moorings and steamed swiftly out through the quay gap, just as she had done a thousand and more times. This time though, things were different. The real skipper was gone and instead of him, I was standing there in the wheelhouse. I was acutely aware of how little I knew about this part of the job and the sudden responsibility of it weighed heavily on me.

Now we were at sea everything, including our safety, depended upon me and the decisions I would make. I gripped the wheel firmly and peered ahead into the thick drizzle. There was no chance of seeing any landmarks in this stuff. There was not much wind, but there was an uncomfortable billow. I glanced at the new crewman, Bob, who stood where I used to be, at the bait board cutting up gurnards. He looked happy enough despite the grey, wet morning and the fact that we were being thrown about quite a bit.

As soon as we rounded the headland, I set a course on the compass and found the two strings that Mike and I had left, about three miles to the westward. We hauled the two strings for nine lobsters and then, without too much difficulty, we got them shot nicely within a short distance of one another. I was well pleased with our first little trip because everything had gone smoothly. I spun the wheel and headed for home. It was time to clear out anyway because the billow was getting steeper, a sure sign of wind not too far away from us. Worse still, the shipping forecast gave north east wind, force 7 to 8 for Sole and Shannon. It was all too close for my liking and I knew how bad entering the harbour would be with even a small increase in the wind from that quarter.

It was just after 10am when *Reaper* approached the harbour. The wind had increased a fair bit and the seas were already breaking across the quay gap. I knew what to do because I had seen Mike do it so many times. First, I headed well up to the east and then turned to face the quay gap. I opened the throttles and on full power, we ran ahead, with Towan Beach on our lee and the steep seas crashing against our starboard side. With my heart in my mouth, I steered straight for the south pierhead. This was seemingly against all logic because wind and waves were shoving us relentlessly towards it. At the very last moment, when we were only yards away from colliding with the stonework, the powerful current that drains out past the pier grabbed the boat and flung her bodily to starboard, so that we shot straight in through the middle of the harbour's entrance and into the calm water beyond. I was so relieved to be safely in and I was really chuffed with myself. I glanced at Bob; I suppose I was seeking approval or a bit of praise for a job well done. I said, "See, that's how you do it in a northerly."

However, he just stood behind the wheelhouse with a blank expression, kind of looking around, and said nothing.

When all was secured, I sat down and studied Mike's battered notebook. I slowly turned the water-stained pages and read the names of the landmarks, which Mike had recorded in his bold handwriting. I realised that this unique little book would guide me precisely onto so many fishing spots. These rocks and reefs had ancient names, most of which were known only to the few local fishermen. I realised the historical significance of it and the tradition behind it all. I felt awe and respect for those who named those rocks and who fished these wild waters under sail. I could now face the future with confidence. Armed with Mike's notebook and with the horn-rimmed specs clamped firmly on my nose, I would be deadly!

Mike came to visit me in the evening and I told him how our trip had gone.

A Learning Curve

At 6am on Saturday, 13 May, we left the harbour and went looking for Bob's gear, which comprised of about twenty–four wire lobster pots rigged in two short strings.

Unlike the previous day, the day was fine and apart from a slight haze, the visibility was good. Even so, we spent a long time steaming back–and–forth and searching around the marks that Bob had given to me before we found the pots. There was no sign of lobsters in them anyway, so we carried his gear off and shot it close to ours. We hauled our gear twice before heading home at 8pm with sixteen lobsters.

The following morning, at 6am, we left and hauled it all once. Bob's 24 pots caught three lobsters and our 75 pots caught three lobsters as well. Bob was obviously very down–in–the–mouth and it took a bit of gentle probing to discover why. Well of course, he was disappointed at our getting only six fish in the first haul. Privately I thought, 'You ain't seen nothing yet!'

Bob was asserting himself a little more each day. One morning he seemed very grumpy and I soon discovered he was upset because he was only being paid a one–third share. He wanted to know what happened to the other two thirds. I told him that cutting him in for one third of the boat's gross earnings was really over generous and, besides that, nothing was being stopped for diesel. I tried to explain a bit of simple fishing arithmetic to him but Bob wasn't wearing it. He reckoned he was worth more.

We ate our sandwiches in grumpy silence, me sitting back aft and him up for'ard. As soon as the tide turned, we went to work again. We hauled it all for the second time. We caught six lobsters but there were none at all in Bob's pots. This seemed to depress him even further. Bob, I noted, was not anyway 'Poker faced'. In fact, as I would often observe later, his whole body would slump when things didn't suit him. I got quite smart at reading these signals and even a glimpse of Bob's back was enough to tell me the state–of–play. Accordingly, I knew when to tread lightly and pussyfoot around him so as to keep the peace. Being a new skipper was a learning curve for me. Of course, I knew I would have to become a navigator and an engineer and stuff like that, but a psychologist as well? That bit came as a surprise.

After our first couple of day's fishing, Bob and I got our fish out of the store pots and into Bob's van, to take them, together with Bill and Ben's fish, down to Harvey's in Newlyn. Ronnie weighed our fish and paid me in cash and when Bob saw the money our fish made, he was thrilled.

The wind stayed somewhere between north east and north west for the next few days, which was very uncomfortable. Lobsters were scarce and we couldn't even shift the gear to improve things. Bob was most unhappy. So was I but the difference was that I was used to spells like this: of just working hard for small returns until the weather turned in our favour again.

One evening, after a somewhat gruelling day, we chugged smoothly into our berth and picked up the moorings. We secured fore and aft and I said to myself, 'Well, I'm glad that's over, now I can go home!'

At that precise moment, I saw Bob jump off the foredeck. There was a sharp crack as his boot broke one of the bottom boards. I stood by the wheelhouse saying nothing. Bob glanced down at the damage and then calmly climbed into our punt, cast off and made his way over to his own boat. He checked her fenders and her moorings, like you would, and pumped her out in a quite leisurely fashion. I suppose he felt he owed it to himself after the rigours of the day.

I waited until he clambered back on board and then I gave him the bollicking of a lifetime! I handed him the hammer and a few assorted nails (he was foreman carpenter in his last job) and waited patiently while he fixed the broken board. We put our empty diesel cans and bait basket into the punt and I sculled us in to the harbour steps. We travelled in frozen silence. Psychology is two–edged sword!

A Cracking Pace

On Saturday, 20 May, the wind was west south west force 8 with a big ground sea. On Sunday, the wind strengthened and backed southerly and the seas grew even bigger. No boats got out to fish until the following Saturday.

We were lucky in *Reaper* and found our gear had stayed out straight, though several of our older pots had been smashed. They were at the end of their time anyway, so that was no real loss. When I spoke to Ronnie Harvey on the phone, he said there was much damage done to pots all around the Cornish coast. Just to cheer us up, we had two days of continuous rain. The sea conditions weren't great but at least we were fishing. Our catches were erratic and no matter where we went or what we did, it remained like that.

The day we sorted out the smashed pots, we caught 14 lobsters. The next day we had 27 and the day after that we came in with six, and so on. Bob's emotions were in tune with our fishing and his moods went up and down like a yo–yo.

Mike was often on the quay waiting for us in the evening after his day's work. He would suggest spots to try and did his best to sort out my problems. He gave me encouragement when I needed it most. He gave practical help too, like getting down in the bilges and changing the oil in the reductions. That was handy for me because I'd never even watched him do it before. The way our partnership had evolved, Mike minded the machinery while I maintained our fishing gear. Oh boy did I have to learn fast!

The weather fined away and Bob and I were working well. It was 10am on a calm, bright morning and we had just completed the first haul. We got 12 lobsters and I was satisfied that now we had every pot nicely placed. Things were looking good.

"This is it now," I told Bob, "All we have to do is keep going and the job will come right."

It was then that I noticed the Ford's ammeter needle had dropped to zero. I stopped the Ford and noticed that it seemed hotter than usual. I started the Petter engine but we'd only steamed a short distance when the revs dropped down to a tick over. I discovered the throttle cable had parted. Well, that was no big deal was it. Bob steered the boat while I squeezed myself down between the two engines and held the throttle open with my fingers.

The air–cooled Petter quickly heated up and soon I was being toasted front–and–back, as I lay on my side on the hard deck. The noise in the tiny engine space was deafening. When we reached the first of our gear again, we hauled two strings of pots by hand (Why not? The tide was slack and it killed time while I waited for the Ford to cool down.) I added fresh water to the Ford's heat exchanger and we were able to keep it at low revs and use our winch to haul the rest of the gear.

I kept a constant watch on the Ford throughout the hauling–and shooting operation. I stopped it again and we steamed home slowly on our faithful little Petter. It was late when we got in the dock. In fact, it was after 10pm by the time I arrived at Mike's house and Joyce opened the door to me.

Poor Mike was in bed, because most likely he had spent the last several hours behind the wheel of a heavy lorry. He got up and stood there in his pyjamas and dressing gown listening to my sad story. Instead of throwing me out on my ear he just asked me one or two simple questions, like for example, "Did the green light come on?"

"You mean that little one on the panel that goes off when you start the engine?" I asked. Mike nodded slowly, as if he knew he was dealing with a half–wit.

"Well yes, now you mention it, I guess it did," I said in a small voice.

"So that means the alternator was not charging."

He paused giving me a chance to cop on. I felt the penny was about to drop but kept my mouth shut.

"Which means," he said, looking at me hard, "the water cooling pump wasn't working either, which means," and he paused again, "the belt is either slack or it's busted."

"Oh yes, of course, I should have thought of it, how stupid of me," I gushed, backtracking towards the door. "Anyway thanks a million and goodnight."

Mike suppressed a yawn and said, "I will get John Julian to check the engine and see if there is any damage" and he toddled off towards his bed.

John checked the Ford the next morning and fitted a new belt. To my great relief there was no damage. Bob and I went back to work and we were improving all the time. Most days we managed to haul our gear twice and haul perhaps one or two strings of pots for a third time. As the number of pots hauled increased, so our catches improved; also I was gaining in confidence and knowhow. Of course, we never achieved the levels of efficiency that Mike and I had done and I should have been expecting that that was how it would be.

It slowly dawned on me that Mike and I had arrived at a point where we hauled gear at a cracking pace in total silence. Our movements were so synchronised that even on the worst rolly days, we worked together in the small deck space without tramping on each other's toes, or colliding with each other, or getting an elbow in the ribs. What we did was surprisingly athletic. Bob was a big strong lad, no doubt about that, but athletic he was not. Did I expect too much from him? Yes I did! Bob for his part was into something called 'time–and–motion'. I tried to tell him that it doesn't work in the fishing. If you double your fishing effort, you don't always double your income, because there are other things are going on. However, if time–and–motion was what he was used to, why not let him get on with it?

At the end of each day's fishing Bob would consult his notes. He would present himself at the wheelhouse window. "Do you know that today we pulled three hundred and ten pots and we caught 16 lobsters and one crawfish?"

"Really, well fancy that," I would say, pretending surprise.

By the end of the week, the numbers of pots hauled amounted to something impressive. I didn't want to know and I told Bob that all we were interested in was what weight of lobsters, craws and crabs we sent away on Harvey's lorry. Bob was not happy. He said he thought twenty–five pounds was not much to be carrying home for a week's work.

As the workload increased, so tiredness became a big factor. I was pushing us harder all the time. Had I been a little bit more experienced, I would have realised our limitations and maybe eased up a bit. If I was bombed out with tiredness, and I was used to all the hard going, then it was obvious that someone new to it would feel absolutely wrecked. Was I being a sensible, reasonable Mister Nice Guy? No I wasn't!

Bob wanted to know why we were not shifting further east, and the next day why we didn't work west or go deeper or closer in. It seemed like he wanted to be all over the ocean but not too far from home. Simply by chance, I found the main source of Bob's discontent. One sunny evening we came ashore and the place was swarming with emmetts. I stopped to secure the punt's bow rope and then followed Bob as he threaded his way through the crowd. There, outside the PSA stood a tight little knot of The Critics chatting amongst themselves. When Bob arrived they seemed almost to have been waiting to greet him, such was the welcome they gave him.

"Well Bob, how d'ye get on today then?"

I hung back in the crowd and watched as Bob obligingly produced his notes. "Well we pulled two hundred and seventy–five pots; that was two hauls and one string a third time. We got 13 lobsters then we hauled my …"

But another cut across him, "My God that's terrible. Tell us, where are you fishing?"

"Oh, we've got two strings of French pots on Pells ..."

"Pells?" screeched another. "Whatever is 'ee thinkin' of? Burtie Boys are up off Trevose and they landed a load of craws and lobsters last week. You want to tell 'im, the season'l be over afore you know it."

I suddenly asked myself, 'Does Bob expect too much from me?' The answer was, Yes he did! In fact, he expected me to fish the arse off everybody on the coast including, even, the 50 footers.

I threaded my way through the teeming emmetts, thinking black thoughts. I cranked up my little BSA Bantam and zoomed recklessly past the PSA scattering Critics and emmetts alike as I headed for home.

Truth Will Out

It was now June and the weather was still unsettled. Our lobster catches were down. I spoke to Ronnie Harvey on the phone and he told me that it was the same story all around the Cornish coast. When discussing the situation amongst ourselves down harbour, we tended to blame the *Torrie Canyon* oil spill and the detergent spraying. That whole fiasco sure didn't help the lobster stocks one bit. Of course, we knew who to blame for the fact that the crawfish were almost extinct. The rubber–suited vandals had already wiped them out before the tanker disaster happened!

On Saturday, 3 June, the wind was light westerly. At 4am, Bob and I cast off *Reaper's* moorings and we headed out to sea. I steered towards our nearest string of pots. This happened to be a string of 20 of our own French–style crawfish pots, which were close at hand. We had loaded them aboard on the previous evening, steamed off a short distance and shot them, really just to give the timber in them a chance to soak.

We weren't expecting to catch anything, because the pots were dry and too floaty. We had just dumped them off in the kind of place where a decent lobster wouldn't be seen dead anyway. True, we did place one bait in each pot because, well, you never know, do you?

We soon reached the dahn and Bob quickly had the buoy rope on the drum of the capstan. I boarded the first pot and there was a fine lobster in it. Up came the next pot with another lobster.

"There's a bit of luck for us," I said.

The next couple of pots came up empty, just as we'd shot them, even the baits were untouched. I changed the baits, as was usual practice, and fitted two nice split gurnards in the mouth of each pot. Turning to board the next one I said, "These pots are going to fish like hell now they are soaked–up," then, "Wow, there's three in it!"

I reached in and snatched them out before they could chop each other to pieces. Some excitement now; the next pot came up to the rail and I dealt with it, and the next, and the next. I was dragging out crabs, spider crabs and dogfish and flinging them wide. Was it my imagination, or was Bob hauling at twice his normal speed?

Another lobster and another! The lobster box was full because, in haste, I'd chucked lobsters into it any way at all and I'd also run out of sacking to cover them with. Open claws waved about menacingly, seeking a victim. The last pot was boarded, cleared, baited and stowed in fast time.

"Leave the buoy rope out," I shouted to Bob as I pounced into the wheelhouse.

Every second counted now, or the tide would sweep us away. *Reaper* rounded the dahn under full power and with her helm hard over. At my shout, Bob threw the first pot overboard. I put the helm amidships and eased the throttle back. Everything went smoothly and, as far as I could judge, we had shot the gear exactly where we had hauled it from. Or, as Mike would have said, "Zackly near enough."

The echo sounder showed the ground to be flat and featureless, not as much as a molehill of a rise on it. The next most urgent job was to sort out the lobsters. We picked them out of the lobster box and repacked them, layered with wet sacking. We collected the few strays, one was in the bait box and one was sitting in the bucket. Two more were on the foredeck covered by my donkey jacket. We'd caught 17 lobsters in 20 pots, where even one lobster would have been considered a bonus. A bit of good luck indeed!

No time to admire the scenery, down throttle and away for the rest of our pots a couple of miles away. We had reasonable fishing throughout the gear and raced back. We carried one string back in with us and ran it out next to the lucky one as a marker. We hauled that first string for the second time and there were eight nice lobsters in it.

"Nothing wrong with that," I said to Bob and he agreed wholeheartedly.

Shooting precisely back was made easy because now I had the two dahns of the newly placed string to guide me. Job done, we charged off deep again to commence the third haul. Did somebody mention stopping for crib? Forget it! We hauled everything three times and our lucky string caught another six on its third go. That brought the total number up to 50 lobsters for the day.

Bob was thrilled of course; ecstatic would not be too strong a word for it! I could see by the look of him that he was busting to get in and give The Critics the hot news. In the few minutes before we reached harbour I explained to Bob why he mustn't mention the 50 lobsters to a soul. I told him, "Our problem is that we are so close to the harbour that we are in full view and everyone can see us hauling. Lobsters are so scarce and if you even quote half that number then every Tom, Dick and Harry will be out here shooting pots down on top of us. There is only a tiny patch with fish on it. I don't mind who shoots here once we've finished with it. When you get in there, you tell them we got 15 lobsters today."

Poor Bob looked quite crestfallen but said he knew that what I was saying made a lot of sense. Anyway, our luck at that spot soon dried up and we shifted the two strings off deep. Bob worried then because, come landing day, people would see all these lobsters and know that he'd been telling 'porkies'.

The following evening, as we were steaming home I asked, "How many lobsters have we caught today Bob?"

"Sixteen," he answered. "Ok," says I, "now when we get ashore you can tell them we caught 50 today. That should help The Critics keep their arithmetic right!"

Short Tempers

If it was just a question of going to sea and hauling pots then life would be so simple, but we operated in a tough element. The pressure on men, machinery, boats and gear was relentless. We fished every hour God gave us, so now, with the longer days, we were fairly worn out. Too many mornings of setting the alarm for 3am and too many evenings struggling with the spanners until dark was certainly taking its toll. I was aware of being very short–tempered myself and it seemed to me that I was not alone in this. Everyone in fishing seemed to be on a short fuse.

Thinking back on those days, and looking at the diary, I can see that we had good reason to be touchy. The weather was bad, fish were scarce, prices were down and bait was scarce and expensive. We all had debts (don't remind me!) and families to feed. We were all hoping that things would change and come right for us.

The Harbour Master, Jack Carne, asked me one evening if I would go out and rescue some geezer who'd got himself cut off by the tide, between Towan and Great Western beaches. Now, I had no business taking *Reaper* in behind the Bothwicks Rocks, but Jack was a good old boy and I could have been nice about it. Unfortunately, I had just spent a tough day on the water and I yelled back at him, "Not bloody likely, it's only an hour to high water. Three hours from now and the silly bugger can walk home dry footed."

Bob and I were hauling the last string on one of those awful days, which are best forgotten.

He said, "I'm leaving on next landing day."

I said, "Bloody good job too."

On another day, Bobby Broderick told me he was going to take divers out because, he explained, he wanted to learn diving.

"Well get stuffed then," I said, marching off in fury.

One morning, when *Evelyn Meyrick*'s pots and *Talisman*'s pots were wrapped together, the two crews engaged in a severe shouting match. Of course Bill and Ben were at a disadvantage here, because they didn't ever use swearwords, only 'floppin' this' and 'flippin' that.' It was no contest! Bobby and Frank had a whole arsenal of serious cuss words ready at hand. Anyway, never mind the rights and wrongs of all that, it just shows how uptight everyone was.

The Ford's exhaust was leaking again, even though Dave Sleeman had done his best to effect a temporary cure. The fumes were making me feel really ill sometimes. There was no question of stopping fishing and getting a proper job done on it. That kind of wisdom was going to take me years to acquire. The only good thing was that I was out on deck working in the fresh air for most of the time we spent at sea. Even so, the time I did spend in the wheelhouse left my throat and nose sore and my eyes would be streaming.

It was the middle of June and no matter where we fished, catches remained low. I realised that Bob had several latent medical conditions. It was a peculiar kind of hypochondria that was linked specifically to *Reaper*'s catch rate. Days when we were steaming home with 23 lobsters Bob was as fit as a flea but on other days, when the pots were coming up empty he would go into a rapid decline. He would complain about his rheumatism, his sea boils, his blistered hands and so on.

One morning, we hauled three strings for nothing, well almost nothing! We actually hauled 74 pots without seeing a fish. The end pot came up to the surface and I yelled, "Yes there's three in it!"

As I boarded the pot, we could see plainly that the lobsters had been fighting, the two big ones had murdered each other and the smaller one had cast both of its claws. I thought Bob was going to pass out. He suffered acutely all day and, even though we did finish up with 12 lobsters, it didn't seem to bring him any relief.

Longest Day

Thursday, 22 June was the summer solstice, the longest day! June had been disappointing up to then, with unsettled weather and slack fishing. Looking at the landings, we were averaging the same as the rest of the boats. So far, we hadn't missed a landing day. Sometimes we were the top boat but there was no joy in that for me, because we were all struggling to make wages in what should have been our peak earning period.

The diary stated in small print, at the top of the page, that it was a full moon. That means big tides of course. I had written just below it, that the wind was south west force 3 to 5 and that we also had a ground sea.

As far as we on the *Reaper* were concerned, it certainly was one of the longest days ever. Most of our gear was down off St Agnes in twenty fathoms. We had placed it there for safety because the ground sea had been with us for a couple of days. Well big tides combined with a real big ground sea are not good for pot fishing. However, I was not expecting to haul the damn lot without seeing even one lobster. Being off there in the guts of the tide didn't help things either; and that ground was low and very patchy. We found the western ends of some strings of the wire pots had shifted, in spite of the hefty bunches of chain next to each end pot. As for the wooden French pots, they came up in lumps of three or four!

Bob and I were just about knackered after struggling to get that lot in over the rail and cleared again for shooting. One hundred and forty pots without a lobster made a long day of it. As Bob threw the last dahn overboard, I squared away for home. He came back aft and I handed him his crib bag. He grabbed it with a certain eagerness, because nothing would have passed his lips since leaving harbour that morning. I was probably looking for excuses for the day's dismal results, and shifting the blame away myself, when I said, "That bait we used the other day wasn't the best, was it?"

Bob paused in his chewing. He seemed to be in trouble for a moment and I did worry about him, but he gulped a couple of times and then blurted out, "It was terrible! It nearly made me spew."

"I know," I said soothingly, "It came from the bottom of that old barrel in the shed. It might even have been some of last years."

I concentrated on steering the boat, aware that bait was a subject best left alone.

We entered harbour and Bill and Ben were still aboard *Evelyn Meyrick*, so I went alongside. It was a big mistake! I told them our sad story. Was I looking for sympathy or what?

Graham said, "Oh, we got 19" and he permitted himself a little smile. Kelvin positively sniggered. (Were they winding me up?) No, I knew very well that they weren't, because the rotten little bastards were too honest for their own good!

Miserably I thought to myself, 'Just wait 'til The Critics get hold of Bob. They will eat him alive!'

The next day, we left in fog but after an hour's steaming, we were right on target and hit the first dahn 'zackly'. We hauled everything twice and got 17 lobsters. The day after was foggy, though it was not really thick. We loaded three strings of wire pots and I decided to carry them in close and give the shore a try.

Of course, I had the throttle wide open as we raced in towards the land. I was startled by a loud bang, followed by an eerie silence. Our main engine had stopped dead! *Reaper* was still slipping gently along and I glanced over our stern to see a great mass of green trawl netting trailing along in our wake. I had ploughed into it and the Ford's propeller was well wrapped. Bob hung over the stern trying to pick the net up with the gaff. The gaff got buried in the net and the pair of us hung head–down over the stern, trying to free it for what seemed like ages. We eventually dragged all the yarn up over the stern and lashed it tight around the base of the mizzen mast. It seemed to me like the whole belly of a big trawler's net. It had obviously been in the water a long time because it was covered in the tiny shells of tubeworms and barnacles. I started the small Petter engine and we steamed slowly home.

Late that night, when the tide dropped back, I went down and hacked the net from around the propeller. I gave the net to Bobby Broderick, who told me later that it was enough to cover forty pots.

The bait situation remained critical, though Harvey's did their best to keep us all supplied. Bob and I jigged for mackerel at every possible opportunity. This meant no break times or lunch times at all. The best we could hope for was a sandwich in one hand and mackerel line in the other, in between pot hauls. We who were lobster fishing were used to these periods of bait scarcity and we just managed them the best way we could. The bait came first; Mike and I wouldn't care if we didn't get to our crib bags until we were homeward bound and passing the High Place. However, Bob's poor tummy was used to a more structured life, with regular feeding times and he suffered terrible hunger pangs. It was only natural that he would bemoan his unhappy lot at such times.

He told me he had only earned fifteen pounds a week since he'd started with me. As if that wasn't bad enough, Bob reckoned we were working harder than the other lads. I made sympathetic noises and explained that we needed to catch seventy mackerel to do one haul, allowing half a mackerel per pot. Also, I pointed out that *Reaper* had kept hauling every day, whereas other boats had to take days out to go fishing for bait. I told Bob that that wasn't a bundle of laughs either. Some had been down as far as Madrips the other day, and only got a couple of baskets for their trouble. While they were gone, mackerel were seen, boiling on the surface a mere hundred yards off the harbour wall.

"That's mackerel for you," I said with a laugh, but even that failed to lift his spirits.

July came in, bringing better weather. Harvey's lorry brought bait and, at last, the fishing was improving. We still worked the feathers and caught sometimes 50 or 100 mackerel, but the urgency about getting bait had gone. A couple of days with twenty or thirty lobsters cheered us up too.

The weather held good until the third week in July, when we were kept in by a strong southerly and a big ground sea. I was glad of the break because I had things to do ashore. Mike came down and checked the machinery for me. I went to Hawkey's Garage and bought some flexible steel pipe so that Dave Sleeman could have another go at fixing the Ford's exhaust.

I went to see the bank manager and this time he authorised the money.

That evening Mike came to the house to tell me something about the boat's insurance. It was just a wonderful moment when I gave him the cheque to purchase the *Reaper*. It took him a moment to get over the surprise but then he too was thrilled that I was having the *Reaper*. We got yarning then and we talked about the good times we'd had. Later that night, Pauline and I went out and had a drink or two to celebrate.

The Share System

By Tuesday the big ground sea, which had been with us for the past three days, was falling away. I went down to the boat and over the low water, I painted creosote over as much of the boat's bottom as I could reach, hoping to slow down the growth of weed. When she floated at noon, we put to sea and hauled our gear. We got 14 good–sized lobsters.

"Not bad for one haul," I said to Bob.

He seemed preoccupied but after a moment he said that he didn't think twenty–five pounds was much to carry home for a week's work.

Up until then Mike and I hadn't told anyone about our transaction but I decided to bring Bob up to date with things. I told him that I'd bought *Reaper* from Mike and there would be a few changes. I explained that the proper share system worked as follows: there would be one share for the boat, one share for the gear and one share for each man. Since I now owned both the boat and the gear, I was entitled to a share for each. This meant four shares, which meant Bob would receive one fourth of the boat's earning instead of one third of the boat's gross earnings, as he had been doing. I also said we wouldn't change things until August. Therefore, if he decided to leave, it would give him plenty of time to make other arrangements. I said if he went back to fishing his own boat, he was welcome to share the shed with me. I think Bob was taken by surprise. He said he wouldn't fish his own boat because it had let him down and so he had no confidence in it.

It came to the last week in July and we had a good day. We threw back 12 undersized lobsters but still we had 28 nice big ones. I told Bob that we could expect better lobster fishing from now on. Next morning the ground sea started and, just to make a liar of me, we hauled one hundred pots for one lobster. We headed for home. I was glad we had to be back in harbour. It was landing day and Harvey's lorry was due, so I had the perfect excuse to get the hell in out of it!

We didn't do much good from then on because, although we fished every day, the weather was bad. The ground sea remained with us, falling away sometimes but then coming on strong again. George 'Gingey' Northey brought all his pots ashore so that he could look after his other business, running the Gannel Ferry.

Graham 'Cooker' Mountford had just left the fifty–foot Padstow crabber, *Castle Wraith* and I asked him to come and fish with me. He couldn't because he was going back to the family business at The Fort restaurant, which overlooked the harbour. I was disappointed of course. A waste of a damn good fisherman was how I saw it.

Frank Dungey said he would like to come with me but he was committed to stay with *Talisman* for a while yet. Frank would have suited me fine because we had worked together in the past and we had been friends for a long time.

Harold Bullen offered to help me by coming out hauling pots in the evenings when he finished work. I thought that was a nice gesture. As things turned out, Guy, another friend of ours suggested a young man called Martin, who might like to come with me. He was a student at the London School of Economics and he was keen to try his hand at fishing.

Meanwhile Norman 'Cap'n Bones' Harris agreed to come with me during his holidays from work. I looked forward to having him aboard very much. Cap'n Bones had spent years as a merchant seaman and he had been fishing. These days, he had a punt and took his kids, of which he seemed to have several, out fishing with him in the evenings.

At the end of the month, Bob and I went out and loaded the two strings with Bob's pots attached. We brought them in and hauled them up onto the jetty. That was the parting of the ways for me and Bob.

Looking back on our rather rocky relationship, I think things had been very tough for Bob. *Reaper* was really hard work with her wheelhouse aft and her capstan for'ard. Of course, back then Mike and I thought she was lovely, which indeed she was, but you couldn't compare her rig with what came later. Hydraulic sheave haulers and a modern deck layout with everything handy took away a lot of the hard work. In our situation, being just two–hands on a 35 footer put a heavy workload on both skipper and crewman. It was especially so when those same two men were aiming to haul 140 pots three times per day.

Also, *Reaper* was Bob's first ever berth on a fishing boat He would have been better off had he gone with one of the three–handed 40 footers for his first ship. Having an experienced fisherman working on deck beside him would have given him a chance to get into the swing of things and learn as he went along. Instead, he was thrown in at the deep end and the pressure was on from day one.

On top of all that, it was just a rotten bad season. Having me, a first–time learner skipper, didn't help his case either! As it turned out however, Bob survived the experience and went on to fish as a skipper/ owner for many years after.

The next day young Gary Eglinton came up on the jetty and helped me to cast off Bob's thirty–five pots and bend on some of my own to replace them.

The Wind of Change

I telephoned Ronnie Harvey and told him I was fed up with the poor results we were all suffering in the Newquay area and that I thought I might do better by fishing *Reaper* from Hayle. I said that we could safely carry 75 pots on board and I asked Ronnie if one of his lorries could transport the remainder, another 50 pots, to Hayle for me. He said he thought my idea of moving west was a good one and he would move the pots whenever I needed them.

On the last morning of July, Cap'n Bones shipped on. As soon as we cleared the harbour, I asked him to take the helm while I arranged things on deck and prepared the bait. It soon became plain that Cap'n Bones could be trusted and it was such a relief to have an experienced man at the helm, so that I could relax and just get on with the job in hand.

We made one haul and got a dozen lobsters. My new shipmate fitted in nicely and we worked well together. I toyed with the idea of kidnapping him but I realised that I wouldn't get away with it. After all, he did have a horde of kids and it followed that he had a wee wife somewhere who would not be too pleased. Never mind, Cap'n Bones would do just fine for the next two weeks.

I spent the rest of the day working in the engine room and preparing for the trip to Hayle. In the evening, Pauline and I went aboard and made coffee and discussed what alterations were needed in the little forepeak cabin to make life easier.

I really enjoyed the next two weeks. Cap'n wasn't used to our system, but he very quickly adapted himself to it. I didn't have to tell him anything, he just saw what was needed and he did it without any fuss. He told me about the ships and schooners he'd sailed on and I loved his stories. We had a few laughs as well.

On Saturday, 5 August, we took young Gary Eglinton to sea with us. We slipped our moorings and left on a falling tide, just before our keel would have touched the sand. We cleared the harbour and it was then that Cap'n realised he'd come without his boots He had left them in Mike's shed! There was panic at first. Of course, we couldn't get back in again and it looked like being a long day's crabbing for Cap'n, with him being wet from the knees down to his soggy shoes and socks. However, help was at hand, as Jock Bleakley was leaving harbour too. His boat was smaller and drew much less water than *Reaper*. Jock took Gary back in to the harbour steps. Gary ran to the shed, grabbed the boots and young 'Bilcock (David Trebilcock) brought Gary and the boots back out to us in the punt. It was really a community effort.

We went away and hauled it all twice in comfort and Cap'n remained dry footed. His last trip with me was on 12 August. The diary records the wind as "NW 5 increasing to 7" and adds that there was a "big steep billow."

It goes on to say:

> Bones and I stowed everything nice and neat and cut up bait before we left. We went away quietly and crept out to the gear. *Reaper* handled wonderfully, in what was, really awful conditions. We pulled one string of pots and shot it away again. We dodged away off for the next string but the wind freshened even more, due to a big shower outside to the north of us. That was enough to make up my mind for me, and we headed for home.

Mike came down aboard in the evening and showed me how to change the oil filter in the Ford's sump.

We couldn't go to sea for the next two days because of a gale from the SW. Meanwhile Guy brought my new crewman out to meet us, young Martin Doyle, a fine chap with dark wavy hair and an easy smile. On his first trip, the sea was billowy and the movement of the boat was very lively. Martin had trouble finding his sea legs. Once he fell back and sat in the crab box (a trick not to be recommended). A couple of times he went sprawling on his belly and once he stepped into a bight of rope while shooting (the crabbers nightmare).

Considering the conditions and Martin's inexperience, he did very well. We hauled it all twice and caught 11 lobsters. The diary states, "Apart from all that he did a damn good job and only spewed once."

Despite his punishing first day on the water, Martin seemed keen to stay with me. I had already told him of the planned move to Hayle and he was looking forward to that. I had also said that sometime in the future, I would think about moving to Ireland.

Martin's response to that was, "Oh great! I've got an uncle in Cork who owns a yacht."

Things Conspire Sometimes

I don't think I am any more paranoid than the next fellow, but sometimes, just sometimes, things really do get to me. When things seem to conspire against me in rapid succession, then I am inclined to turn, albeit briefly, into some kind of a monster.

Like that day when my new crewman, Martin and I were out there hauling pots. We were at the back of Carters Rock and it was one of those sloppy days with steep wobbly seas coming at us from all angles. Sometimes an extra big one towered over our rail, threatening to break in on us. *Reaper* slid down into deep troughs, only to be flung skywards again. There wasn't enough wind to fill the mizzen sail and so, as we hauled away, our bow swung this way and that. One minute the pots were coming up under our keel and next, the backrope was away to starboard and stretched like a harp string. Martin was coping well and I showed him how to keep an even strain on the backrope and how to work with two or even three turns on the capstan.

My guts were sore from dragging up pots that would sometimes stubbornly hang under our bilge and I was glad we were nearing the end of the day's fishing. It was time to head for home anyway, because the tide was flooding. In another hour, it would be in full spate. That awful westerly gulch would get much worse.

I boarded the last pot and went into the wheelhouse. I had noticed that our dahn seemed to be getting a bit too close to our stern as Martin hauled in the buoy rope. 'Starboard wheel and a quick shot ahead should do the trick,' I said to myself.

I put the engine in gear and gave it a burst on the throttle. "Oh Fuckin' lovely!" I yelled.

Martin looked up in surprise.

"It's ok," I said soothingly, "I've just managed to put our buoy rope into the prop and now we're wrapped up."

I had done it all by myself and that didn't make things any better. I couldn't even turn around and savage poor Martin. He spent the next half–hour hanging over the stern along with me while we struggled to free the propeller. In truth, things were not as bad as I had thought and the buoy rope was only looped around the propeller blades.

The problem was finally overcome by lifting the engine room floorboards, getting down on my knees and turning the propeller shaft by hand, back–and–forth, while Martin pulled on the rope. Pity about the weather though, kneeling with my head down and gripping the greasy shaft with both hands was, in these conditions, somewhat trying! It was very hot down there! Black oily stinking bilge water, carrying the odd crab's leg and some fragments of decomposing bait swirled up over my wrists repeatedly, while I lost all sense of what was up and what was down. Meanwhile *Reaper* yawed about and gyrated like crazy and the strengthening tide swept us a couple of miles to the eastward.

At last, we were free and so we shot the pots and steamed for home. We moored up, climbed into the punt and I sculled us across the harbour to put away our lobsters and crabs.

Even before we reached the carves, I could see the sand piled up on them. Some horrible little snots of children had been making sand castles on top of the carves, whilst they were aground over the low water. Of course, the padlock was full of sand and I could not get the key into the keyhole. Leaning out of the punt, which obligingly listed over until she was nearly gun'ls under, I tried to force the key into the keyhole. I wouldn't have minded but this wasn't a crappy rusty old lock; no indeed, it was a shiny new one, bought only the last week in Westlake & Biscombe, hardware purveyors of repute.

By the time I got the lock to work, I was pretty steamed up. I wanted a law preventing people from bringing children on holiday, or at least to keep them corralled over the low waters. That didn't seem unreasonable, did it?

Nicking the crabs is always slightly dangerous and, of course, this bunch of crabs seemed to be absolutely manic. Each one of them fought me to the bitter end, so that it was sometimes a toss–up as to who nicked who! I had to keep telling myself, 'Cool down, don't get mad with them.'

I suddenly saw a picture of myself, crab in one hand, knife in the other, dying in the bottom of the punt with blood gushing from a severed wrist. That image had a calming effect. Job done, all we had to do now was tie up the punt and go ashore. Naturally, being the kind of day it was, all the punt's stern moorings were wrapped around each other. We had hell's own job sorting them out.

'Why me?' I howled. 'Am I the only responsible punt owner in this harbour?'

My inner voice told me, 'Cool it, just moor the bloody punt and go home.'

Well that made sense but I promised myself that if anyone said a wrong word to me they would get a knuckle sandwich. Up on the quay awaited the faithful old wheelbarrow. We threw in the empty diesel cans, bait basket and crib bags. I grabbed the shafts and marched ahead, cutting a swathe through the teeming emmets.

Suddenly, there was Councillor Norman Minns coming to meet me. Now I must confess that I actually liked Norman. After a cordial greeting, he asked me what I thought of the proposal to open a skin divers school in the harbour, because the divers had applied for a licence.

I started to tell him but he wouldn't wait. He said, "Ok, Ok, that's all I need to know."

And with that, he beetled off. Annoying really! I could have told him so much more.

We progressed a little further and young Gary came rushing up to tell me that there was someone on board the *Reaper*. That did it! I ran down the slip and across the short strip of sand to the water's edge. There, larking about on the boat as if they were in a playground, were two twelve–year old boys. I roared at them, telling them to get the hell off it before I came and threw them off. They immediately jumped off into three feet of water even though they were fully dressed.

'Simmer down,' said the Inner Voice. 'If you don't stop grinding your teeth you will have only the stumps left.'

I walked back across the sand, taking long deep breaths, making myself relax as I pushed the wheelbarrow across the car park towards the shed. There were several parked cars but plenty of spaces too. It was only when I got close to the shed that I saw my way was blocked by a large blue van. Well, if I couldn't get around the front of it, then I would surely get around the back. I found a problem there too though, because a car was parked just a wee bit too close to the blue van for the wheelbarrow to pass through.

I thought, 'That's alright; I will just empty the wheelbarrow and carry it bodily around to its proper berth at the side of the shed.'

It was a heavy brute to manhandle but I managed it without scratching the car or the blue van. That was when I found out there was not enough room to pass around the back of the van either. I flung the wheelbarrow down in frustration and cursed the stupid headed bastard of a van owner. Then I went and peered in through the dusty windows of the van.

What I saw sent my temperature soaring. Amongst the pile of gear was air bottles, flippers and suchlike, it was obviously a bloody skin diver's van! I went to the front doors and found them both locked. I tried the back doors and they were locked. I tried again but this time I gripped the handle with both hands and wrenched it with every ounce of strength in my tender little body. Amazingly, the handle came away in my hands and the doors flew open.

I was seeing red now. I scrambled over the diving gear and let go the handbrake. I jumped out the back and shoved the van forward with all my might until it stopped with a satisfying crunch from somewhere up front. Now we had ample room to get to the shed.

Sometimes, you know, just sometimes things really do get to me!

A Sudden Notion

We got in a couple of days fishing but the weather was awful and the lobsters scarce. We struggled to haul our gear and shoot it without any mishap. In preparation for our move to Hayle, I shot the three strings of wire pots out in a straight line so that their dahns were close to each other. This would make loading the seventy–five pots easy. Next, we boarded the two strings of French pots and brought them in the harbour. We cast the pots off the ropes and stacked them alongside the shed, where Harvey's lorry could collect them. We then stowed the carefully coiled backropes down below in *Reaper's* fishroom. Now we were all set to move our operation to the west.

On the morning of 17 August, we had a rising gale from the south west with heavy rain. I stopped the motorbike at the top of the South Quay Hill, just as the daylight was coming in. I went and sat alone in the green–painted wooden shelter, Rose Cellars, looking down on the harbour. I gazed through curtains of rain at the boats surging and dragging at their chains.

I sat there quietly for a while, just trying to work things out. I wanted to shift to Hayle in the hope of increasing our earnings. It was a mere four hours steaming time away but the damned weather was against it. I needed at least two fine days together to relocate our one hundred and twenty–five pots and I needed to be able to see where we were. Also, I needed the weather clear enough for me to pick out some useful landmarks ashore.

I asked myself, What difference would it make? I knew that there was more fishy ground to the westward of us, but there would almost certainly be stronger tides off there too. It would all be strange territory to me. I had to consider my own lack of skipper experience and also think about young Martin, my new crewman. He was doing the job but he was still only a kid with no experience.

Hayle, like Newquay was also a tidal harbour, with all the problems that that entailed. It suddenly struck me that sitting weather–bound in Hayle would not be one bit better than me sitting here suffering in Newquay's Rose Cellars. As a tiny trickle of rainwater crept under my collar and made its way down my back, I wondered, where was the advantage?

Suddenly it hit me! Why was I wasting my day? I must get up off my arse and go to Dublin. It was time to talk to the people in Ireland and find out what was needed for me to go and live and fish over there.

In a matter of seconds, I was on the bike and zooming through the wet empty streets heading home to Fern Pit. I parked the bike by George's shed and bounded down the cliff path. I was bursting to tell Pauline my latest thoughts. She listened carefully to my ranting while the kettle boiled and then, as she filled the teapot, said, "Well yes, that sounds like a good idea to me."

I don't know if I drank the tea but I do remember jumping up and yelling, "I must get hold of Dave Sleeman."

With that, I dashed out and away up the steep winding cliff path. I really don't know what happened next. Did I ring Dave from a phone box or did I charge over there on the motorbike and beat on his door? The diary is not giving away very much. It merely records, "Saw Sleeman, who got his car out and we drove to Fishguard and caught the ferry to Rosslare."

Just like that! In reality of course, there must have been much frantic comings and goings. I must have contacted BIM (the Irish Sea Fisheries Board) and arranged a meeting with them. We must also have found out the sailing times of the ferries and the train times in Ireland too. Anyway, off we went at a fair speed in Dave's 500cc Fiat, all the way up to Bristol and then west again through Wales, to the ferry port, Fishguard.

The whole thing began to feel like an adventure, as we boarded the ferry as foot–passengers, and we were as excited as a couple of teenagers. It was fine that we were having fun, especially in Dave's case because he surely wasn't in it for the money. If I remember rightly, we shared the cost of everything on this trip, including fares, grub, pints and even petrol. That is how it had to be, due to my usual state of penury!

Once we were under way, Dave and I gave the ship a thorough inspection and we poked into all the nooks and crannies we could get at. We peered down an engine room grating, fascinated by the sound of the machinery. We asked an officer type if we could go down and have a look. He hesitated for a moment before refusing us, saying that, unfortunately all machinery spaces were out of bounds to passengers. He was quite nice about it and I think that if we had been wearing suits and ties he would have given us the OK. It was disappointing really. I mean, we weren't stinking of last week's bait or anything. We were nice and clean but we were wearing blue denim smocks and pants and donkey jackets, just as we usually did down harbour. To him I suppose we did look a wee bit dodgy.

After a pleasant crossing of the Irish Sea, which took about three hours, we disembarked at Rosslare. We hardly noticed going through Customs and all that stuff and nobody seemed to take a second glance at us. We walked the long pier to the railway station and boarded the morning train for Dublin. We were then treated to a scenic rail trip northwards, along Ireland's east coast. Every so often, we got splendid views of the sea as the tracks ran close to the foreshore. We could see dahns marking fishing gear; lobster pots perhaps? We saw hills and mountains and forests and farmland, which was very pleasing to look at as we travelled towards the big city.

I can't remember us arriving in Dublin, or how we made our way to Hume House, but we got there anyway. Up on the second floor we were ushered in to a large, rather smart office and introduced to two men. They were Jim O'Connor and Sean Moriarty. We were made to feel very welcome, as though all other business was put on 'hold' while the two men attended to us.

I realised quite quickly that we were in the very nerve centre of BIM and that 'Jim' was in fact Mr James O'Connor, Secretary of BIM, the person who had answered our letters. We had a good old chat. Dave explained that he was not at the fishing himself but was just there as my friend, so that cleared the decks for us. I told them a lot about myself and they told us about the fishing scene in Ireland. From the conversation, I reckoned that Sean was from the more technical side of the fishing industry.

Jim leaned back in his chair. "We were thinking," he said, "considering the type of boat you have and the kind of fishing you are engaged in, we do have a place which might suit you very well."

Sean took me over to a large chart on the wall. He placed his finger on a spot on the south west of the coast.

"This is the village of Goleen," he said, "A Fr Murphy is there; he's trying to get the fishing going and he's having an uphill struggle so far, so we thought that if you went there, it might give them a bit of encouragement."

Suddenly, to realise that these two, obviously important, office holders had even discussed my case amazed me! Was I dreaming or what? I was thrilled to bits of course but I tried not to lose my composure.

After a bit more talk, I suggested that I'd bring my boat to Goleen at the end of September, so that was agreed. I asked what formalities would be required for me to make this transition. Jim explained that a reciprocal agreement existed between Great Britain and Ireland. This allowed members of each state to work within the other state's area. In fact, all that would be required was for me to re–register *Reaper* as an Irish vessel.

That was it, the interview was over and Jim offered to give us a lift back to the railway station. I thought this was very kind of him and he even went off course a bit, to show us some of Dublin's most famous buildings. He seemed very proud of the city and as we cruised around in his big posh car, I was indeed impressed by what he showed us. He was particularly fond of a new building called Liberty Hall, a kind of mini–skyscraper. I thought the thing was a monstrosity that really smote the eye. I thought it totally out of keeping with the look of the city, but hey, what the hell did I know about it?

So Dave and I headed for home. First the train, then the ferry and then Dave's brilliant rally style driving through Wales, Somerset, Devon and Cornwall and back to Newquay. I am forever in his debt!

When I got home, I told Pauline all about our great adventure and then, when I'd been fed and watered and was ready for bed, I reached for my faithful diary and in the space underneath the date, 19 August (Saturday), I wrote, "Evening, arrived home."

That was all! I really must stop blaming this diary for its shortcomings. It is just me I guess. I'm just not dedicated to filling all the pages up. Anyway, we do have the bones of our story so here we go.

I spent the next day, Sunday the 20th, down aboard *Reaper*, frantically preparing the boat for our move to Hayle because, at long last, the weather seemed to be improving. Sometime that evening Mike arrived on the quay. He said, "If you are thinking of going to Ireland Trev, now is your chance. They're giving a fine forecast with light southerly winds over the whole of the British Isles."

This stopped me in my tracks. Then, just like old times, we put our heads together and discussed the problems and, just like old times, Mike had most of the details worked out already. His suggestion was for me to head east up the coast as far as Lundy Island and then steer north west, until I reached the Welsh coast. Once there I could find my way into Milford Haven. From there a westerly course would bring me to Ireland. As he said, this would be better than heading straight for Ireland, a journey of about one hundred and forty miles. Taking the longer, roundabout route meant that I would remain in sight of land except for a few hours on each leg of the trip.

That sounded like good sense to me and so the plan was put in motion. Mike went away to get me some extra five–gallon diesel cans and Dave Sleeman, who was probably just out taking the air and minding his own business, got press–ganged into service yet again. Off he went in his car to get a few more of the things I needed.

It was midnight when I finally staggered down the cliff path and went indoors. It had been a long day but, as things turned out, it wasn't over yet! Awaiting me were our friends, Guy and Denis. They were both students and we had been friends for a long time. During my time as Newquay's head lifeguard, Guy had been a lifeguard on one of the town's beaches. Denis was Guy's buddy at college, which is how I came to have Denis's younger brother Martin on board as my crewman.

Well, so far so good, but after our cordial greetings the purpose of this late night visit revealed itself. Guy wanted to join me on this trip to Ireland. He put up a very strong case for including him, so strong in fact that it set alarm bells ringing in my head. I liked Guy but I would never carry him as crew because he was a very determined character. He was the leader of his little group of college friends, the Alpha Male you could call him. He was used to always getting his own way and I just didn't need two skippers on board. I knew that what I was about to attempt was fraught with danger. I had enough sea time under my belt to know how things can go badly wrong. I would have to be the one to deal with whatever problems confronted us.

Denis fully supported Guy and he behaved almost a though he was Guy's legal representative. Playing for time, I said, "Well, I will have to think about it."

At this, Guy became very annoyed, but I still managed to keep my temper. I was glad of that for old time's sake but privately, I just wished they would go away so that I could share my thoughts with Pauline and get myself to bed.

It was 2am before they left and I needed to be on the water before dawn.

Monday morning, 21 August at 4.30am, saw *Reaper* creeping up to the first dahn. It was a fine morning but very dark and I'd gone down on my hands and knees in order to see our dahns, silhouetted against the first streaks of light in the eastern sky. Martin was soon hauling away with a couple of turns on the capstan like he was born to the job.

Time really mattered so I gave the engine a few extra revs and the pots came up at a quite respectable speed. I boarded, cleared and stacked the pots three and four high so that the deck from the wheelhouse to the foredeck was full. We tied the gear down securely, anticipating any change in the weather. I dreaded most of all, meeting strong headwinds for, although she carried the three strings of pots and the additional gear beautifully, *Reaper* was, after all, only an open boat. Shipping heavy spray could overwhelm us if things got really bad.

My other dread was the fog. The thought of being hopelessly lost haunted me. In fog, there was the very real risk of being run down by a ship. I didn't like to think about that too much.

Well never mind all that; by now, the daylight was properly in and the morning was fine and clear. I put both engines to 'Ahead' and opened the throttles, setting a course that would carry us clear of Trevose Head and the Quies Rocks and so onward towards Lundy Island. Actually, I had never steamed east of Trevose before so we were already breaking new ground.

All of a sudden, I found myself with nothing to do. I wasn't at all used to this condition. I was used to long bursts of activity, punctuated by short breaks. Now I just had to stand in the wheelhouse, with one hand resting on a spoke of the helm while *Reaper* virtually steered herself. This unusual condition allowed thoughts to come flooding into my head. I was leaving Newquay; in fact, I was tearing us out it. I loved living in Newquay; I had been there for eight years, which was longer than I'd lived anywhere. It was where I met Pauline, where we made our home and where our babies were born. We were leaving so many good friends. The feeling of loss was almost too much to bear. It put a great lump in my throat. We were leaving lovely Fern Pit and the Cabin and George and Nora and their kids and Auntie Molly and Harold. All of this mattered enormously and I had to get tough with myself and fight to control my emotions. It was as though I was being tried and tested.

Next question to pop up was, suppose I made a hash of things and we got drowned? I struggled with this and reasoned that Martyn would be ok. He was five and would remember his daddy, but what about my little fat Jenny? She was only a year–and–half old! That hit me hard. At last I got a grip, I cursed like blazes and then put these things behind me. There was no turning back now.

After an hour's steaming, we could see a French vessel ahead of us. As we got nearer, it proved to be the *Bacchus*, the 50ft crabber now owned by the Burtie Boys, John, David and Mickey. Also, Rodney 'Courty' Lyon had shipped on with them. We passed about half a mile from them and I could see the lads working on deck as they hauled their pots. Truly, this was my last link with Newquay! I glanced back at the bay and the headland and I had another bad few moments.

We passed Trevose Head at 9am. There was a slight haze but I felt sure that the sun would soon burn it off, so I wasn't a bit worried about it. However, the further east we travelled, the thicker the haze became until, within the next hour the visibility had reduced to about one mile and I lost sight of the Cornish coast. From then on I steered by the boat's compass. Lundy Island would still be some twenty miles distant and it was essential that I didn't steam right past it.

The haze, instead of thinning out became a typical low–lying sea fog, with the sun above us looking like a pale white disc. The visibility reduced even further so I became really worried. Martin sat on the deck facing aft. He was slumped against the back of the wheelhouse and I reckoned he was fast asleep; and why not? He wasn't used to leaping out of the bunk at such an early hour. I could have done with a kip myself but I had to keep a sharp look out and pay close attention to the compass. This was certainly not the time for me to doze off.

After what seemed like ages, I saw dark cliffs looming out of the fog. The pocket watch fixed above the compass told me that the time was 12 noon. I just hoped that this was Lundy and turned to port with the engines at half speed. I followed the coast and the compass told me that our heading was mainly northerly. Martin and I were both staring ahead now, fearful of half–submerged rocks or some other hazard. The tops of the cliffs and the land above it were hidden in the fog, making it very hard to judge our distance off the shore. At last, we saw a lighthouse up on the cliff. I decided that this must be Lundy's north light and accordingly, I set a course for the Welsh coast.

I increased our speed again and Lundy was swallowed up in the fog. We ploughed on and at least the sea was calm, just a bit of a southerly swell coming up on our stern. As the afternoon wore on the fog got thicker and the danger of a collision worried me. Martin made his way to the forepeak and made us tea and sandwiches.

At 7pm, the fog suddenly thinned out ahead of us. The first thing I saw in the distance was what appeared to be a ship and, thankfully, the dark smudge of land beyond it. As we got nearer, I saw that it was marked *St. Gowan's Lightship*. I steered up alongside her and two men appeared at the ship's rail looking down at us. They seemed surprised.

"Long time since we seen a Cornish crabber here boy," said one of them.

He had the most beautiful Welsh accent, which I took to be confirmation that we were right on target. Daft really, because his accent proved nothing! I mean, suppose he'd greeted us in a brummy accent?

I asked them, "Where is Milford Haven?"

"Keep going until you see the four stacks," they shouted, waving us onward.

I thanked them and we waved them goodbye. *Reaper's* engines were full ahead and we needed every ounce of power we had. The sun was well down and I needed to find my way into Milford before dark. As we steamed along, I kept looking in towards the land and wondering what the *Lightship* men meant by 'the four stacks'. Would that be four chimneys on the land, or four sea stacks, like rock pinnacles standing out from the cliffs? In the failing light, would I be able to see them?

At last, I saw tall chimneys peeping out over the land and gradually they revealed themselves as tall stacks, as you might see on a power station. The darkness closed in, but soon I could see the channel buoys winking and before long, we were inside this enormous harbour. The vastness of it amazed me. Powerful lights blazed all around us and I couldn't tell which was water and which was land.

A coaster passed us, she was all lit up and looking as big as an ocean liner. I tagged on behind, which worked out very well but he was going too fast and soon left us behind. Well never mind, there up ahead of us all floodlit in a blaze of glory was a big steel jetty. It carried a BP sign with letters about twenty feet high and it was conveniently vacant. Naturally, we went and tied up there. Such a relief!

At last, the propellers had stopped turning. I had been standing in the wheelhouse peering at the fog for far too long and just being able to relax and to bend and stretch a bit was great. Suddenly we were blinded by a powerful searchlight. A voice boomed over a megaphone demanding to know who we were and where were we bound.

My Navy training clicked in. When faced with authority, never be caught without an answer. Shading my eyes with my hands, I yelled, "Cornish crabber short of fuel. I need to buy diesel."

In truth we had cans of the stuff, enough to take us to Madeira but my answer made them pause for thought anyway. They seemed to be studying us and then the searchlight went out. The megaphone boomed again and commanded, "Follow me."

Obediently we followed in the wake of this big black–hulled launch until we reached another quay with a variety of small and medium–sized craft berthed alongside. The megaphone told us to tie up to a harbour tug called the *Scuter*.

I half expected us to be boarded by marines in full combat gear but instead a nice man came and took our ropes. This happened to be the skipper of the Tug. I decided to stick to my claim of needing diesel. Our new friend told us that we would find the oil man in the pub, and he would be happy to take us there. It was only a short distance along the quay.

We went inside and soon met up with the oil man. I bought pints for the four of us and then I used the pub's payphone to ring Aunty Molly. My message for Pauline was that everything was fine. We were safe and sound in Milford Haven and we would be staying in harbour overnight. That was a lie of course, I was going to clear out smartly and head for Ireland in case the fog returned. I knew Pauline wouldn't sleep a wink if she thought I was still steaming through the night.

We had another round of pints and then we walked back to the boats, where the oil man sold me four drums (20 gallons) of diesel. The tug skipper invited Martin and me into his wheelhouse and he told us about fishing around Ireland on trawlers in his younger days. He gave me directions for getting clear of the harbour but, unfortunately, I am not much good at absorbing that kind of thing. With me, it is usually a case of 'in one ear and out of the other' and long before he reached the end of his instructions, I had forgotten the first bit. Never mind, he wasn't to know that.

Next, he used his radio to call 'the Office' and asked for the courses that would take us clear of the offshore islands.

'The Office' wanted to know whether we possessed a giro compass or a magnetic one.

The skipper answered, "Magnetic."

After a short pause, the radio squawked out a series of compass courses and the skipper copied them down on the back of a cigarette packet. This was great, compass courses I can handle anytime.

The skipper explained which points of land had red or green lights and their flashing sequences, and which places carried no lights. All this he noted down on the fag packet, which he then handed to me. Listed were names like St. Anne's Head, Skokholm, Skomer and Grassholm. I couldn't believe my good luck. This was going to make our departure so easy. The last entry gave the course to steer to bring us to the Irish south coast. I thanked our host but before we said goodbye, I gave him the seven lobsters we had caught that morning. They were all good and lively and he was obviously pleased with them.

We set off and I was confident that once we were out of the harbour, it would all be plain sailing. The only problem was that within a few minutes I was completely lost again. Damn Milford and its stupid clusters of blazing lights! It was dangerous too and I eased the engine revs right back to a steady tick over and cruised along, peering all around and trying to get my bearings.

It was almost midnight and thankfully, the night was brilliantly clear. I hated wasting precious time, but if I had to cruise around like this all night, until I could see my way out in the morning, then I would do it.

Suddenly a large hull loomed out of the darkness. I spun the wheel to starboard and thrust the throttle levers forward. *Reaper* leapt ahead and I saw that we were passing across the bows of a grey ship. In almost the same instant, I saw the chain. I snatched the throttle levers back and knocked the engines into neutral. I held my breath, waiting for the crash. Nothing happened, we shot past the chain and half slid over it. As it went close by our port side, I saw that it was a studded link mooring chain. It was only then, while the engines were out of gear that I realised the power of the tide.

We were being swept quickly past some small warships, which were moored in line ahead. From what little I could make out, I took them to be minesweepers, all without lights or any other sign of life. The realisation that I had blundered in amongst the Royal Navy Reserve fleet didn't do my palpitations any good at all. The old saying, 'up shit creek' came to mind and I wondered how the hell I was going to get us out of this mess.

We continued on at low revs and after a while, a ship appeared in the distance. Well, where that ship could go then we could go too, and so I followed on. We were soon left behind but the ship had shown me the way out. Then, to my great relief, I saw the channel buoys and steered by them. I studied the cigarette packet and quickly identified the first light listed on it. From here on it would be a piece of cake, I assured Martin.

So it should have been, except that the compass course given did not bring us any way close to the next point on our fag packet. I could see the light I was looking for, blinking at us in the near distance. Something was wrong. It dawned on me then, that when the tug skipper asked 'The Office' for the compass courses, some bloody clown in there had given him giro instead of magnetic! Blast them!

There is about ten degrees of a difference between giro (true) north and compass (magnetic) north. However, whilst knowing what had gone wrong was very nice, it was of no actual use to me and I just muddled through somehow. Without warning, the fog came and instantly blotted out everything. I tossed the packet out and chose a bearing that I hoped would take us to Ireland. We needed to get lucky!

Changing from the giro course to the magnetic course was hard for me to figure, because I was steering the boat and watching the compass at the same time. Anyway, 'navigation and chart work' was not my pet subject, even supposing I had a chart! I thought that if we pressed on, we might get lucky and if the fog lifted in a couple of hours, then we should be in sight of the Irish coast.

The risk of collision haunted my every moment. I had no idea how many ships passed up and down the Irish Sea but I knew only too well that we were crossing their paths.

Suddenly the smooth surface of the sea changed and we were in amongst white horses. My reaction was to quickly reduce speed, thinking there were rocks ahead. We were still slipping ahead in neutral when this enormous white tower appeared right in front of our bow. I steered away from it and the tide carried us clear. We had almost rammed a lighthouse!

It was lost in the fog as we increased speed again. The broken water seemed to be just a tide race kicking up and we were soon out of it and the sea ahead was smooth again. We continued on without incident, visibility was about one hundred yards. A smooth oily swell rolled up on our beam. It was quite harmless but it caused the steering to need constant adjustment. *Reaper* yawed gently off to port or starboard as each successive swell slid under us. The swinging motion was sending me to sleep.

The sun was climbing higher and, being filtered through fog, it made a terrible glare. Our air–cooled Petter Engine was pumping out warm air, which was adding to the heat in the wheelhouse. As the hours passed, the two engines did something strange. Their distinctly different sounds merged and I heard a higher pitched two–tone hum. I was alarmed at first and thought we had developed engine trouble, but we ploughed steadily on.

The weird sound was relentless and after a while, it was really getting to me. I wondered if it was only in my head. I thought of asking Martin, who was asleep behind the wheelhouse, if he could hear it too. Then it occurred to me that if he couldn't hear it then he might think I was cracking up. So instead, I woke him and asked him to make coffee.

He made his way unsteadily forward, but if I had expected instant coffee, I sure didn't get it. He was gone for so long that I was certain he'd fallen asleep while the kettle boiled dry. Eventually he emerged from the forepeak hatch and picked his way around the pots and back to the wheelhouse. After handing me the mug, he slid smoothly down onto the afterdeck and instantly fell asleep. The mug had lost half of its contents in transit and the coffee was almost cold, but it tasted wonderful and it lifted my spirits.

By midday, it was uncomfortably hot in the wheelhouse. I needed to lie down and take the weight off my legs. I was desperately in need of sleep; my eyes hurt and my throat was sore. It was seven hours since we cleared Milford Haven and, had there been no fog, we would surely have sighted the land.

As time passed, I grew more anxious. *Reaper* was making about eight knots and, by 2pm, we had been steaming for nine hours. That added up to seventy–two nautical miles; so where the hell was Ireland?

A voice in my head kept telling me to alter course. 'Just give the wheel a couple of spokes to starboard and you'll pick up the land,' it said. The urge to do that was very strong and I fought against it. When I thought I had it beaten, the voice would come back, stronger and more insistent than ever. I knew I had to win this battle within myself and not alter course, even by one degree. I even thought, at one stage, that our compass had gone haywire and it was leading us miles astray.

More time passed and I wondered if we were going up the Irish Sea, or were we heading out into the Atlantic. I worried about the rocks, sand banks, islands and other hazards that might lie ahead of us. More vigilance was needed now, not less, and here was I feeling close to collapse.

It was fortunate that I was in the habit of glancing down at the engines every few minutes. It was always the same, except this time the Ford's green light was on and the ammeter needle had dropped back to zero. I knew straight away that the alternator belt had broken. This belt also drove the cooling water pump, so if left to run, even for a matter of minutes, the Ford would overheat and that would be a disaster. I stopped the Ford and Martin steered while I squeezed myself in between the two very hot engines and fitted a new link–belt.

The heat in the engine room was awful and adjusting the tension on the belt seemed to take me ages. I could tell that Martin was having trouble steering because I felt the boat rolling one moment and pitching the next. It wasn't his fault: the Petter could only drive us along at about three knots and at that low speed in that swell, any boat would wander all over the place. Martin would never have experienced anything like this before.

At last, I got the Ford going again on full power, and I took over the helm once more. It was time to get tough with myself and cut the crap. I convinced myself that we were definitely travelling westward along the south coast of Ireland and therefore, we would soon make a landfall. I promised myself I would not allow any more negative thoughts to creep in.

I had been struggling with the question of whether to switch on the echo sounder or not. My problem was that if the echo sounder showed the depth increasing, how would I cope with that? Suppose it just kept showing deeper and deeper? Just thinking about that had been doing my head in!

I devised a routine, which I hoped would keep me awake and also help to keep us out of trouble. I would switch the echo sounder on every five minutes, and then I'd stoop down and look at the engines. With some trepidation I switched the sounder on and off again. The mark on the sounder paper showed 29 fathoms. That was ok and I glanced down at the engines. All was ok down there and the ammeter needle was steady, which told me that the new alternator belt was working.

The pocket watch in front of me told me when five minutes was up and I switched the sounder on and off again. A second dot appeared on the paper, half an inch from the first dot. This also recorded a depth of 29 fathoms. I liked this routine and it meant that I only took my eyes off the compass and the way ahead for a couple of seconds every five minutes.

The fog remained as thick as ever. The next few marks on the sounder paper showed very little variation in the depth and I was pleased about that. It let me relax so much that I actually fell asleep standing up, and then I nearly missed the five minute check–up. The next time, when I looked at the sounder, it showed 30 fathoms and next time 32 and then 33 and then 35 fathoms. That drove the sleep right out of me and I was worried sick! I wondered where the hell we were going. The next mark showed 36 bloody fathoms! I was cursing myself for putting the sounder on at all and I was willing the seabed to shoal up.

Gradually it did shoal up. Bit by bit, at five–minute intervals, I watched the seabed rising up until there was a steady 20 fathoms under us. The sun was lower now and the glare had gone. The fog was a dirty grey colour but it was becoming patchy. Sometimes I could see quite a distance in one direction but only a boat's length in another. The swell seemed to have eased a bit too. I kept to my 'five minute routine'. First look at the sounder, then peep down below. But wait, this time I saw something that shouldn't be there. A football, which was rolling around in the engine room! I watched it, fascinated, as it rolled around in time with the motion of the boat. It bounced off the Ford's gear lever and vanished somewhere back under the stern. I shook my head in disbelief. But it was definitely a football, a leather one. I knew that because I had seen the lacing on it.

I looked at the compass and then, lifted my gaze to look ahead and was shocked to see a strange face looking straight back at me from up for'ard. I shouted, "What are you doing on board my boat?"

The face immediately drew back behind the stacked lobster pots. Another face appeared nearby and I yelled at it, "Fuck off you bastard!"

This face withdrew slowly, as if it resented being challenged. I saw that it was evil looking with heavy features. I turned around and reaching through the wheelhouse doorway. I grabbed Martin by the shoulder and shook him awake.

"Get up quick and get us some food. I'm fucking hallucinating here!"

Poor Martin scrambled to his feet and stumbled his way forward. He paused for a moment and steadied himself against the roll of the boat but I roared at him, "Get moving, I'm serious, I'm going mental; off my fucking head! I'm seeing things for Christ's sake!"

Martin disappeared down the forepeak hatch. The faces came back to taunt me. Now they were more like extreme Neanderthals, but I didn't care about them anymore. I knew them for what they were, simply the result of hunger, (we hadn't eaten since yesterday), thirst and tiredness.

The sun peeped through and the sea on our port side became sheets of shiny corrugated iron, undulating in the swells. I looked to starboard. That side was still shrouded in grey fog and the swells had become long dark hedges. 'Bloody hell! Get a grip,' I told myself.

Martin made his way aft and in his hands, he was balancing a soup plate. He managed to reach me and in the plate was tinned stew with a thick slice of bread on top of it. I grabbed the spoon wolfed the food down in a matter of seconds. It was only barely warm but it tasted wonderful.

Fortified by the food I soon felt much better. Of course, I still felt overwhelmingly tired and the air passages in my nose and my throat felt on fire. That and the prickly pain in my eyes drove any other aches and pains into the background. The funny gargoyle faces and other things just vanished.

Best of all, the echo sounder showed we were getting into shallower waters. At five minute intervals, it showed 17 fathoms, 15 fathoms, 12 fathoms.

The fog was coming and going. We steamed into patches of it, brown–grey and solid looking, then we emerged briefly into clear sunlit areas.

A couple of times I thought I saw land ahead, but it was only banks of fog, looking darker now as the sun declined.

The sounder showed 10 fathoms. I glanced below and all was well. I straightened up and saw the land. My heart pounded and I yanked the throttle levers back but in a split second, I was looking at another bank of fog.

Martin heard the engine revs drop and was getting to his feet.

I said, "Martin I think I saw land but my eyes are just about done in."

He looked past me. "Yes you can see land," he said. He sounded excited and then he said, "I can see a lighthouse."

"Well thank God for that," I said, relief flooding through me.

"I can see two lighthouses," said Martin.

I said, "That's brilliant." Privately I thought, 'Great! He is looking at two pier–heads, or perhaps two leading–lights.'

Martin then announced, "I can see three lighthouses."

I grabbed him by the lapel. "Listen you idiot," I yelled, "Nowhere, but nowhere, is there three shaggin' lighthouses."

Privately I thought. He's lost his bloody marbles! Of course, I wasn't to know that Newtown Head in Co. Waterford has three huge white towers on it, was I?

"I can see three," Martin protested. "I can see houses and things."

He was really excited and pointed ahead. I looked and as I did so, the fog rolled away and I could see a town with a church steeple. Now it was my turn to be excited. It was 6pm and we had reached Ireland. I was absolutely delighted!

Reaper slipped quietly along at a tick over, while we studied the land. Both of us were enjoying the moment. I turned us to starboard and we saw a beach, with children and people paddling and swimming. I looked down through crystal clear water and I could see ripples in the sand, which was only a fathom or so beneath our keel. I steered us off into deeper water. Fog swallowed up the land again but I didn't care. It looked like being a fine night and, if we had to, we could throw out the anchor here and I could sleep. I would be able to find the land easily in the morning and then follow along the shore heading westward.

Meanwhile this town looked important enough to possess a harbour and I set about finding it. We had not gone far when we came across two men in a punt, jigging with handlines. They would have been listening to our engines for some time and would have been keeping their fingers crossed. They must have been relieved when *Reaper* appeared and stopped alongside them. They'd stopped jigging and their lines hung from their hands as they stared at us. They were obviously wondering who and what they were looking at. They would almost certainly never have seen a typical Cornish crabber before. The rake of her masts, her rigging and the stacked Cornish–style pots were bad enough, but when they heard my accent that would have confused them even more.

I greeted them and asked them where we were.

They had trouble understanding me. Then they both said, "Tramore, Tramore" but because of their accents, I had trouble understanding them and they repeated it for me.

They explained that Tramore's harbour was small and we would be better off in Dunmore East, which, they said, was only about one hour distant. At last, here was something familiar. I had been reading about Dunmore East and the 'Herring War', as reported in the *Fishing News* newspaper during the previous winter.

My next question had them confused. "Is there anything to fetch us up?" I asked.

By their blank looks, I soon realised my mistake and re–phrased the question. "What I mean is, are there any half–tide rocks we might hit on the way?"

"Yes there's Fyleskirt, you'll want to watch out for Fyleskirt."

They waved us away to the eastward. "You'll see it alright," they said reassuringly.

I didn't share their confidence in me seeing this rock, but I was very grateful for their help.

We steamed for an hour without seeing anything and then I reduced speed. The fog had closed in again and the visibility was the same in all directions, down to about one hundred yards. After a few minutes travelling at low revs, we came across a small varnished yacht with a little family on board. I gave our engines a kick astern and we stopped alongside her.

"Where is Dunmore East?" I asked.

The man at the yacht's tiller pointed across our foredeck. "Head away in there, past the lighthouse," he said.

I put the engines slowly ahead. We had only moved a short distance when I saw this rather elegant lighthouse above us. We passed along the breakwater, which was constructed of black rocks and then turned in through the harbour entrance.

It was just after 7pm on 22 August 1967.

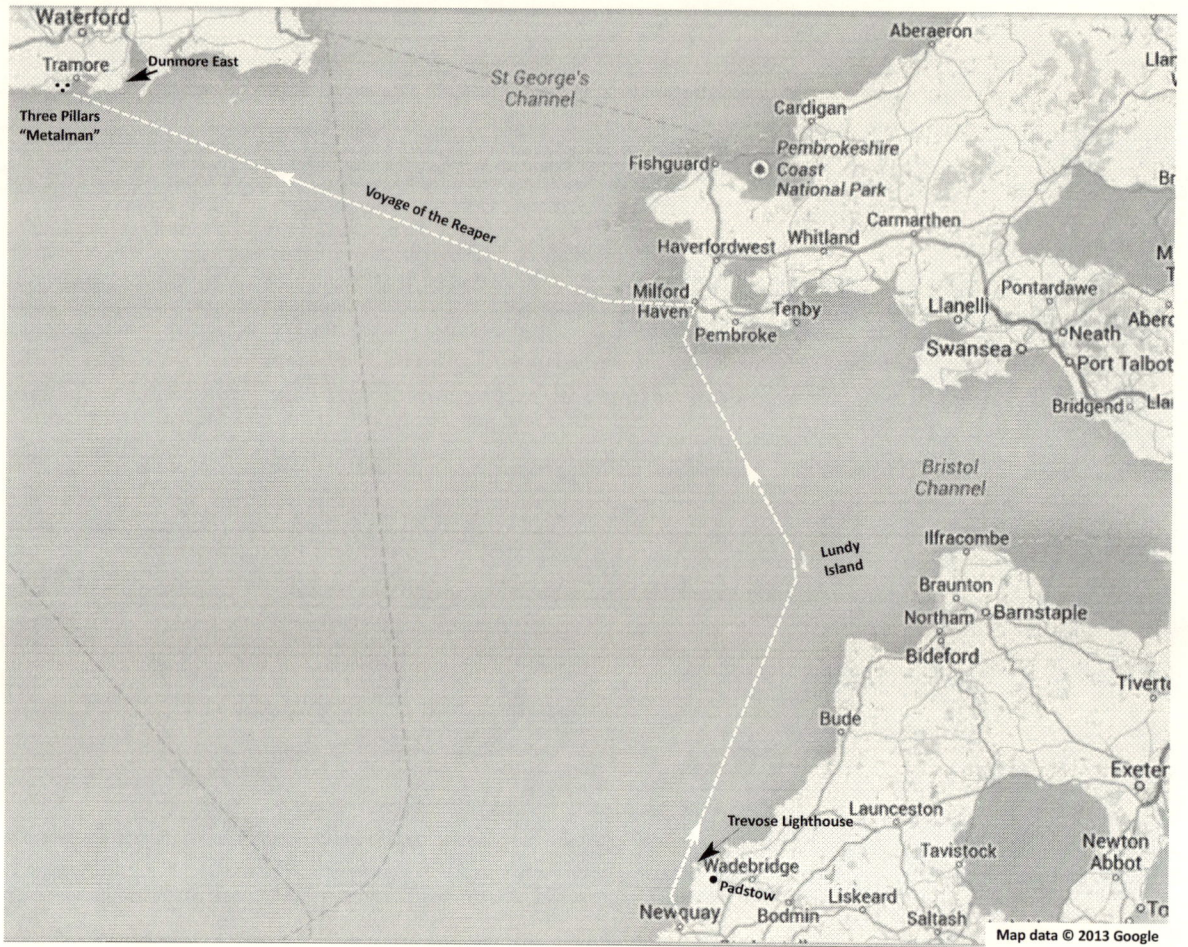

Waterford
Tramore
Dunmore East
Three Pillars
"Metalman"

St George's
Channel

Aberaeron
Llar

Cardigan

Fishguard

Pembrokeshire
Coast
National Park

Carmarthen

Voyage of the Reaper

Haverfordwest
Whitland

Milford
Haven
Tenby
Pembroke
Llanelli
Pontardawe

Swansea
Neath
Aber

Port Talbot

Bridgend
Llar

Bristol
Channel

Ilfracombe

Lundy
Island

Braunton

Northam
Barnstaple

Bideford
Tivert

Bude

Exeter

Launceston

Newton
Abbot

Trevose Lighthouse
Wadebridge
Padstow
Tavistock

Newquay
Bodmin
Liskeard
Saltash
To

Map data © 2013 Google

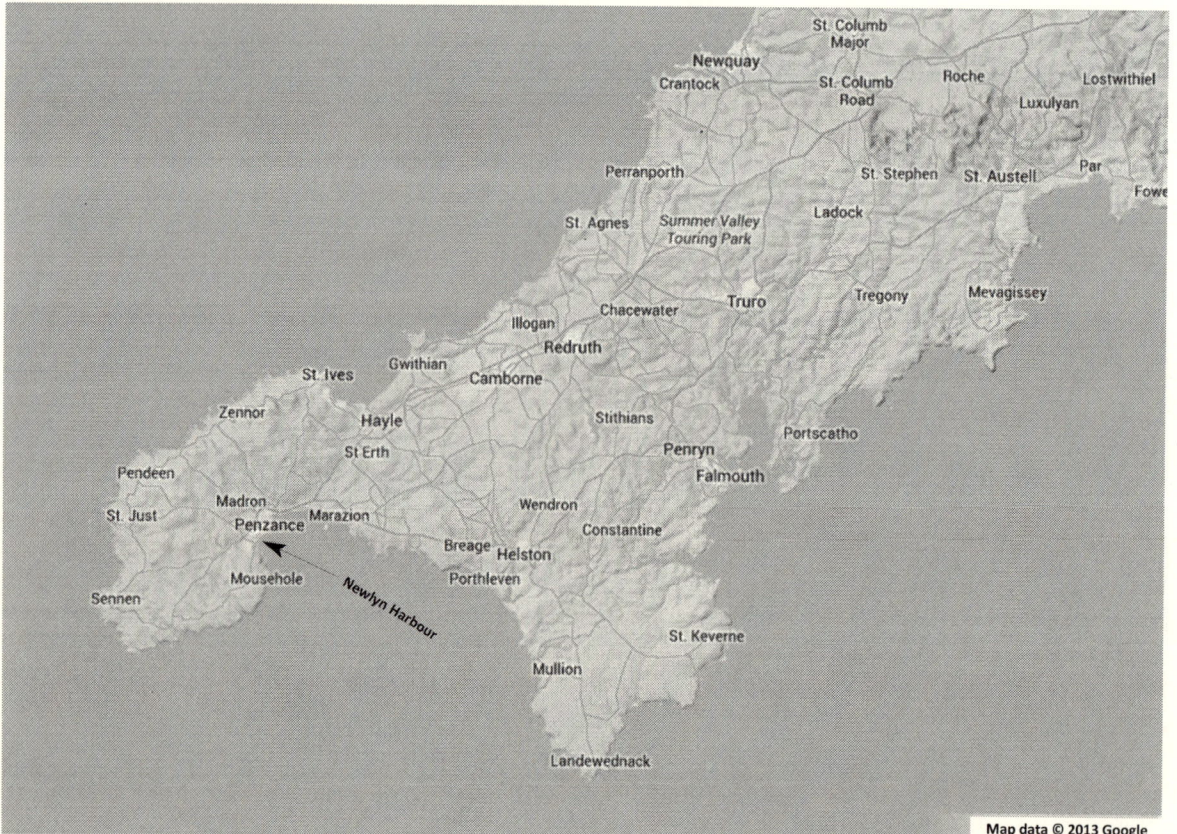

St. Columb
Major

Newquay
Crantock

St. Columb
Road

Roche

Lostwithiel

Luxulyan

Perranporth

St. Stephen
St. Austell
Par

Fowe

St. Agnes
Summer Valley
Touring Park

Ladock

Tregony

Mevagissey

St. Ives

Chacewater
Truro

Gwithian

Illogan
Redruth

Zennor

Hayle
Camborne

Stithians

Portscatho

Pendeen

St Erth

Penryn

Falmouth

St. Just

Madron
Marazion
Wendron

Constantine

Penzance

Breage
Helston

Mousehole
Porthleven

Sennen
Newlyn Harbour

St. Keverne

Mullion

Landewednack

Map data © 2013 Google

Glossary of Nautical and Fishing Terms.

Afterdeck — Decked area at the stern (back) of the boat.
Alternator — Electricity generator, driven by boats' engine.
Alternator belt — Driving alternator and cooling water pump.
Ammeter needle on — Gauge indicating charging of batteries.
Astern — "Going astern" i.e. going backwards.
Back aft — At the back of the boat.
Backrope — Main rope, with pots attached at intervals.
Baffle — Strong blast of wind rebounding off cliffs.
Ballast — Concrete, stone or metal weights.
Bar — Sand or gravel piled up by tides and waves.
Beam — Widest part of boat.
Beneaped — Due to the fortnightly tidal cycle, a boat stranded at high water "springs" will not float during neap tides; it must wait for the next high water "spring tides". Growing tides are referred to as "making tides". Weakening tides as "cutting".
Berth — Boats' regular mooring place in a harbour.
Billow — Steep tumbling waves.
Bilge — Boats' bottom.
Bilge water — Water that that collects in the bilges.
Blackjacks — Black Pollock or Coley.
Blennies — Small rockfish of the shore and rock pools.
Boat hook — Pole with a blunt hook at the end.
Boom — Can either refer to the pole securing lower edge of sail or a floating barrier.
Bowsprit — Strong pole on bow of sailing vessel carrying fore sails and fore stay etc.
Breakers — Breaking waves.
Broken water — Sea surface covered in breaking waves.
BSA Bantam — Motorbike with a 1.75cc. two stroke engine.
Bulkhead — Wall or partition in a boat.
Brit — Type of marine engine that started on petrol but ran using paraffin.
Bunt — Deepest part, centre section of beach seine net.
Carvel–built — Planks fitted edge–on–edge and nail fastened to sawn frames. Heavy boat construction.
Cats–paw — Swirl on surface of a smooth sea. A first sign of wind on the way.
Capstan — A winch, shaft driven from the engine, often adapted from a car back axel.
Carves — Store pots.
CSFC — Cornish Sea Fisheries Committee
Clinker–built — Planks overlapping and fastened to steamed timbers with copper rivets. Light construction.
Clove hitch — Type of knot.

Crawfish	Large crustacean, also called crayfish.
Crabber	Boat engaging in pot fishing for crab, lobster and crawfish
Crib bag	Lunch bag.
Crib time	Lunch break.
Cuckoo wrasse	Brightly coloured fish of the wrasse family.
Dahn	Buoy with a pole and flag, attached to the end of a string of pots.
Ebb tide	Tide going out; sea level dropping for six hours approximately.
Echo sounder	Depth recorder using sound waves which leaves a profile of the seabed on paper.
Emmetts	Cornish term for tourists (from an old–English word for ants)
Ex–WD	Ex–War Department kit was sold off after W.W.2. Army gas mask bags made handy crib bags.
Ex–MTB	Ex–Motor Torpedo Boat. The Royal Navy sold off their old stock too.
Fathom	One fathom equals six feet.
Fenders	Usually disused motor car or lorry tyres.
Fender lanyards	Short lengths of rope tying fenders to the boat.
Flood Tide	Tide coming in, sea levels rising for 6hrs approx.
Francis Barnet	Makers' name of motorbike.
Full spate	Tide running at its hardest.
Gaff	Pole with sharp hook used for boarding large fish. The gaff is also often used as a boat hook.
Galleon	Medieval sailing ship.
Gardner	Type of Marine diesel engine.
Gazzle	Bay at east shore of Towen Head, Newquay.
Gig	St. Ives Gig. General purpose fishing vessel built for the North Coast of Cornwall.
GPS	Global Position System.
Gun'l or Gunwale	Side "wall" of a boat, also called The Rail.
Gun'ls under	A sailing term. Boat lists until her gun'l dips and water comes aboard.
Green sea	A big wave just before it breaks.
Ground sea	Waves originating in storms and disturbances in the distant ocean. The waves approach the shore in groups of six or seven, followed by a brief calm before the next group arrives. Ground sea is what gives North Cornwall its, often spectacular, surf.
Gurnards	Spiny bottom dwelling fish.
Half–hitch	Type of knot.
Half–tide	Midway between high–tide and low–tide.
Halyards	Ropes for hoisting sails, yards, flags etc.
Handlines	Light line wound on a frame with pollock or mackerel lures and with a 3 lb lead weight.
Harbour tug	Small powerful ship used to assist in berthing big vessels within the harbour.
The hard	Concrete area of harbour for parking and servicing boats.

Headwind	Wind meeting the boat bow–on.
Helm	Spoked steering wheel, or a tiller.
Hessian	Sacking.
High water mark	The highest level before the ebb starts.
Highwater springs	Highest tides of the fortnightly tidal cycle.
Huer	Man on the cliffs who directs the seine–net fishing operation from his vantage point.
Hydraulic haulers	Development of a variety of sheaves and rubber coated hauling heads, driven by hydraulics, has taken much hard work out hauling pots and nets.
Jigging	Short up–and–down movement applied to handlines when fishing with lures, e.g. mackerel feathers.
Keel	A boats' spine or backbone.
Keelson	Internal section of boats' keel.
Leading lights	Two lights, usually mounted on towers on the land, which are visible from the sea. Vessels approaching can, by keeping the two leading lights in line, navigate safely into harbour.
Lee	In the lee of the land. i.e. in the shelter of the land.
Lee side (of the boat)	The sheltered side.
Lanyards	Short lengths of rope connecting lobster pots to the back rope.
Longlines	Heavy line fitted with several hundred hooks. Used for catching spur–dogs, ray and other large fish.
Lister	Manufacturer of marine diesel engines.
Looe lugger	Traditional 40–50 Ft fishing boat of the South Coast of Cornwall. Originally a sailing Vessel with Lug–and–mizzen rig.
Lugger	Traditional small sailing vessel with lug sails, commonly used for fishing off the coasts of Britain and France.
MAFF	Ministry of Agriculture Fisheries and Food.
Magnetic compass	Used for navigating small vessels. It is comprised of a card marked in degrees and cardinal points and a magnetised needle. The needle always points to the Magnetic North Pole. Larger vessels use a Giro Compass, which is driven by a Giro motor (at twenty thousand rpm). This compass always points to the True North Pole. The difference between True North and Magnetic North is called "Variation" and can be around 10 degrees.
Maelstrom	Area of wild confused sea.
Moorings	A boat is "on moorings" when she is "moored off" as opposed to being "tied up" to the quay.
Mooring chains	Chains secured at bow and stern when the boat is on her moorings.
Mooring ropes	Addition to mooring chains.
Murgy dogs	Spotted dogfish, type of small shark.
NUDC	Newquay Urban District Council
Parsons	Name of manufacturer of diesel engines.
Petter	Manufacturer of marine diesel engines.

Pintals and gudgeons	Rudder fittings.
Pitching and rolling	Motion of boat.
Pollock feathers	Lures, feathers mounted on hooks.
PSA	Refers to a rest–room facility for fishermen in Newquay Harbour, 'Pleasant Sunday Afternoon'.
Punt	Small boat, 15–20 Ft long propelled by oars or an outboard engine.
Quay gap	Harbour entrance.
Radio buoy	A buoy fitted with radio transmitter.
Rake (of masts etc.)	Angle from the perpendicular.
RIB	Rigid Inflatable Boat (as Inshore Lifeboat).
Round turn and two half–hitches	Type of knot.
Samson post	Strong post for securing mooring ropes or chains or anchor cable.
Save water back	Returning the boat to her moorings before the falling tide prevents access.
Schooner	Topsail Schooners. 200 tons with two or three masts. Bringing cargoes of coal to Newquay and exporting Iron ore and China clay up until the 1940s.
Scottish creel	Type of lobster/crab pot used in Scotland.
Scull	Using a single oar over the stern to propel a punt forward.
Sea fleas	Tiny scavenging crustaceans dwelling on the seabed.
Shifting gear	Moving pots, usually into deeper water for safety when stormy weather threatens.
Shoaling up	Water getting shallower.
Shore crabs	Small crabs, green/ brown in colour, found near the shore in shallow water.
Slip	Concrete ramp within the harbour where boats can be launched or taken up from the water.
Snoods	Short lengths of twine attached to the longline, each length having a hook at its end.
Sou'wester	Broad–brimmed oilskin hat.
Spider crabs	Large crabs with long legs and pinchers. In those days, there was no market for them in the UK so they were thrown overboard.
Spotted Dogfish	Several kinds of dogfish came up in the pots but there was no sale for them and they made poor bait for lobsters so they were dumped.
Stuart Turner	Manufacturers of small marine petrol engines.
Starboard	Right–hand side of the boat, looking forward.
Steering chains	Chains connecting the Wheel with the head of the rudder.
Stuka	German World War 2 Dive Bomber.
Swim bladders	Most fish, apart from bottom dwellers, have a swim bladder in their stomach cavities.
Tackle (pronounced *tay–kul*)	Usually with a double and a single pulley block suspended from the mast for hoisting heavy weights aboard.
T–handle	T–shaped handle on hand bilge–pump.

Tick–over	Engine running at low speed.
Tide race	Disturbed area of sea, usually near headlands or islands where the tides meet.
Time–and–motion	A study of the most efficient use of a workers' time. As per Factories etc.
Topsail	Trading schooners carried a square topsail on their foremast.
Transom	A square stern.
Trammel	A net set on the seabed designed to entangle Fish.
Transducer	The echo sounder transmits supersonic sound waves and receives echoes from the seabed via the transducer, which is located in the boats' bottom.
Trawling	Towing a net (bottom trawl) over the seabed.
Turned turtle	turned upside– down.
V (Vulcan) Bomber	RAF bomber.
Walkie–talkie radios	Small transmitter/receivers. These sets were illegal, being outside the specifications to qualify for a radio licence. Radio licensing rules were rigorously applied and the Postmaster General promised dire consequences for anyone caught using a Walkie–talkie.
Warps	Ropes for hauling nets.
Western end	Of a string of pots. Pots were normally shot with the tide, i.e. in the same direction as the tide was running. This would be approximately from east to west on a flooding tide and from west to east on the ebbing tide. Therefore, dahns were identified as marking either the western end or the eastern end of the string.
White horses	White breaking waves.
Wire pots	Lobster pots built mainly by weaving fence wire.
Withy pots	Built by weaving withies (willow wands).

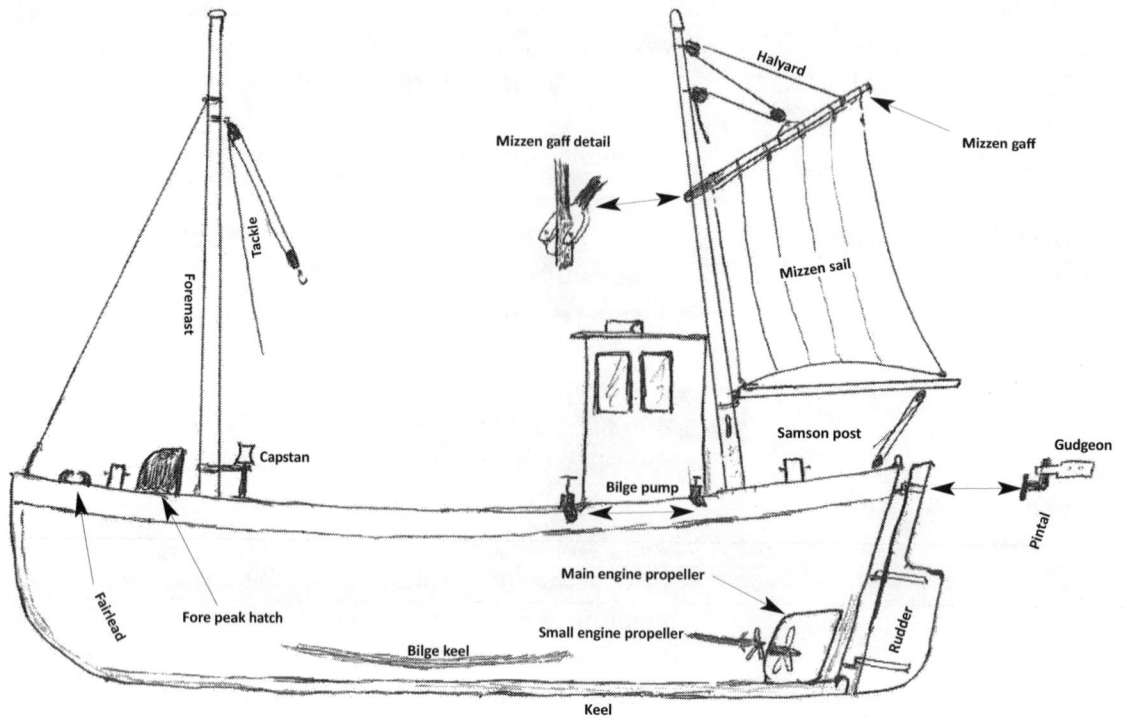

Halyard

Mizzen gaff detail

Mizzen gaff

Mizzen sail

Tackle

Foremast

Samson post

Gudgeon

Capstan

Bilge pump

Pintal

Main engine propeller

Fairlead

Fore peak hatch

Small engine propeller

Rudder

Bilge keel

Keel

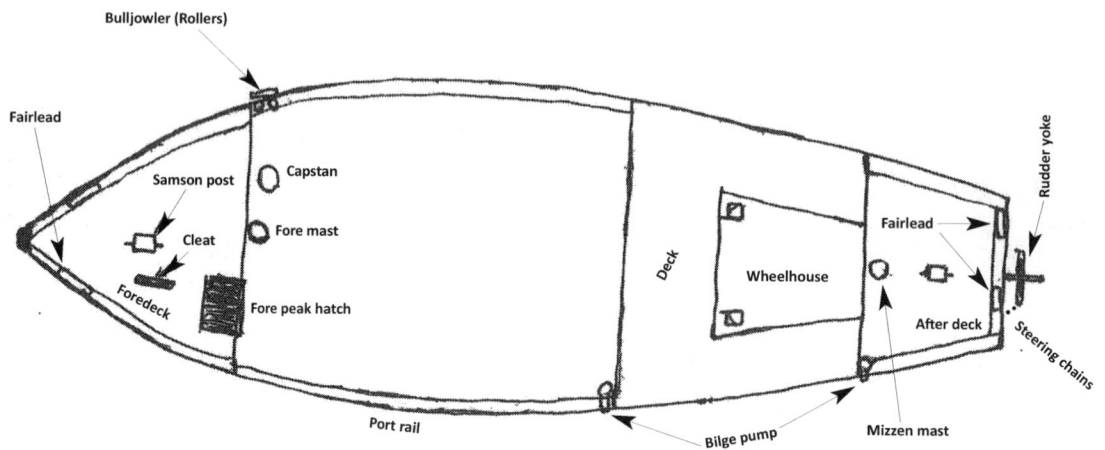

Bulljowler (Rollers)

Fairlead

Rudder yoke

Samson post

Capstan

Fairlead

Cleat

Fore mast

Deck

Wheelhouse

Foredeck

After deck

Steering chains

Fore peak hatch

Port rail

Bilge pump

Mizzen mast

Made in the USA
Charleston, SC
09 May 2014